VITAMINS AND MINERALS: HELP OR HARM?

About the Author

Charles W. Marshall earned B.S. and M.S. degrees in chemistry at the University of Chicago shortly before World War II. During the war, he won two U.S. government citations for research into the detection and identification of poison gases as part of our country's program to defend against possible enemy use of chemical warfare. After the war, he did research on hormone structure for three years while completing his doctoral training in biochemistry at the University of Chicago. In 1949, he was a post-doctoral fellow at the Worcester Foundation for Biological Research, Shrewsbury, Massachusetts. He continued his work in investigative biochemistry for 19 more years with the pharmaceutical firm of G. D. Searle and Company.

Dr. Marshall is the author of more than a dozen scientific publications. He began his intensive study of vitamin and mineral nutrition in 1975.

About the Editor

Stephen Barrett, M.D., a practicing psychiatrist and consumer advocate, is author/editor of 11 books, including *The Health Robbers* (a comprehensive expose of quackery), *Vitamins and "Health" Foods—The Great American Hustle, The Tooth Robbers: A Pro-Fluoridation Handbook, Shopping for Health Care,* and the college textbook *Consumer Health—A Guide to Intelligent Decisions.* An expert in medical communications, he is medical consultant to WFMZ-TV, Allentown, Pa.; Consumer Health Editor of *Nautilus Magazine*; Consumer Health Editor of *Our Age* (the newspaper of the National Alliance of Senior Citizens); and Contributing Editor of *Environmental Nutrition Newsletter.* He is also a scientific advisor to the American Council on Science and Health and serves as Consulting Editor of its bimonthly newsletter.

VITAMINS
AND
MINERALS:
HELP OR HARM?

Charles W. Marshall, Ph.D.

A People's Health Library Book
Edited by
Stephen Barrett, M.D.

George F. Stickley Company   210 W. Washington Square
Philadelphia, PA 19106

Printed and Manufactured in the United States and published by the George F. Stickley Company, 210 West Washington Square, Phila., Pa. 19106.

Contents

This book is dedicated to:

Charles Glen King, Ph.D.
Emeritus Professor of Chemistry
Columbia College of Physicians and Surgeons

and

Thomas H. Jukes, Ph.D.
Professor of Medical Physics
and Lecturer in Nutrition
University of California (Berkeley)

Dr. King, co-discoverer of vitamin C, helped to organize Columbia University's Institute of Human Nutrition and was a founding Scientific Director and later President of the Nutrition Foundation.

Dr. Jukes, another pioneer vitamin researcher, contributed to the understanding of several B-vitamins, particularly pantothenic acid, and has crusaded relentlessly against dangerous vitamin misinformation and other forms of nutrition quackery.

Acknowledgments

In researching and writing this book, I leaned heavily on the generous assistance of many, many persons. Despite the risk of omitting someone who helped, I wish to express my gratitude to the following:

Dr. Thomas F. Gallagher, Professor of Biochemistry, who long ago taught me the scientific method.

Dr. Victor Herbert, whose indignation against health quackery inspired me in January of 1975 to start the research for this book.

Dr. Stephen Barrett, my trusty editor, whose expert guidance helped transform an overly long manuscript into a readable, reliable book.

Mrs. Jeanne Hartenstein, Chief Librarian, Health Sciences Library, Bronson Methodist Hospital, Kalamazoo, Michigan, who scoured libraries nationwide to obtain copies of references difficult to find.

Mrs. Louise Lasworth, Librarian in the Science Library of G. D. Searle & Co., Skokie, Illinois.

The Upjohn Company of Kalamazoo for granting me guest privileges in its medical-science library; and also its librarians, Mrs. Lyga Greenfield and Mrs. Herberta Carver.

Mrs. Frances McAfee, who helped type the original manuscript under difficult circumstances.

Mrs. Shirlee Cummins, who typed the entire second draft manuscript under rush request.

Mrs. Kathleen Onofrio, Chief Librarian, South Haven (Michigan) Memorial Library, who read much of the original manuscript and offered comments based on her estimate of the general public's interest in vitamins.

A very special appreciation goes to the following scientists who read one or more selected chapters of the first and/or the final draft of my manuscript and offered constructive criticism and encouragement.

Roslyn Alfin-Slater, Ph.D., Professor and Chairman, Department of Environmental and Nutritional Sciences, School of Public Health, University of California, Los Angeles.

Terence Anderson, M.D., Head, Department of Health Care and Epidemiology, University of British Columbia.

Jay Arena, M.D., Past-President of the American Academy of Pediatrics and Professor of Pediatrics, Duke Medical Center.

Ernest Beutler, M.D., Chairman, Basic and Clinical Research, Scripps Clinical Research Foundation, La Jolla, California.

John Bieri, Ph.D., National Institutes of Health (now retired).

George Briggs, Ph.D., Professor and Past-Chairman of the Department of Nutritional Sciences, University of California, Berkeley.

Charles Butterworth, M.D., Professor of Medicine and Nutrition, University of Alabama.

William J. Darby, M.D., Ph.D., Emeritus Professor of Medicine, Vanderbilt University School of Medicine.

Hector DeLuca, Ph.D., Professor and Chairman of the Department of Biochemistry, University of Wisconsin.

Alfred Harper, Ph.D., Professor of Biochemistry, University of Wisconsin.

Victor Herbert, M.D., J.D., Chief of Hematology and Nutrition, V.A. Medical Center, Bronx, New York.

Thomas Jukes, Ph.D., Professor of Medical Physics and Lecturer in Nutrition, University of California, Berkeley.

David Kritchevsky, Ph.D., Associate Director, Wistar Institute of Anatomy and Biology, Philadelphia.

Morris A. Lipton, M.D., Professor of Psychiatry and Director, Biological Sciences Research Center of the Child Development Research Institute, University of North Carolina, Chapel Hill.

George V. Mann, M.D., Professor of Medicine, Vanderbilt University.

Jacob Nevyas, Ph.D., Sc.D., Emeritus Professor of Chemistry, Philadelphia College of Optometry.

Irwin Rosenberg, M.D., Professor of Medicine, Director of the Clinical Nutrition Research Center, University of Chicago.

Howerde E. Sauberlich, Ph.D., Professor and Director, Division of Experimental Nutrition, Department of Nutritional Sciences, University of Alabama.

William Sebrell, Ph.D., retired Director of the Institute of Human Nutrition, Columbia College of Physicians & Surgeons.

Noel W. Solomons, M.D., Professor of Nutrition and Food Science, Massachusetts Institute of Technology.

Fredrick J. Stare, M.D., Ph.D., Emeritus Professor of Nutrition, Harvard University School of Public Health.

Philip White, Sc.D., Director, American Medical Association Division of Personal and Public Health Policy.

Hilda S. White, Ph.D., Associate Professor of Home Economics, Northwestern University.

Myron Winick, M.D., Professor of Pediatrics and Nutrition and Director, Institute of Human Nutrition, Columbia College of Physicians & Surgeons.

George Wolf, Ph.D., Professor, Department of Nutrition & Food Science, Massachusetts Institute of Technology.

Vernon Young, Ph.D., Professor of Nutritional Biochemistry, Massachusetts Institute of Technology.

Foreword

Millions of Americans now dose themselves frequently with vitamins and minerals they don't need. Some do this out of fear that they won't get enough from their food; while others hope that extra large quantities of nutrients can prevent or cure a wide range of diseases. Although thousands of books encourage self-medication with nutrients, only a few warn of the dangers involved. Yet the scientific evidence is clear: all substances, even vitamins, are toxic in sufficient excess—and legitimate medical uses of large amounts (megadoses) are quite rare.

How did vitamins become so popular? Dr. Marshall explains that although the word "vitamin"—like "vital" and "vitality"—suggests great importance to health, there is no simple way for individuals to measure how much they need. These facts, combined with a large army of Pied Pipers and the persuasive power of the mass media, have produced a $3 billion/year industry. During many years as a nutrition educator, I have painfully observed the growth of this problem.

Vitamins and Minerals: Help or Harm? is a much-needed book, useful to laypersons and health professionals alike. It answers basic questions like: What are vitamins and minerals? What do they do for you? How much of them do you need? Who is at risk for deficiency? Which foods contain which nutrients? How can you tell if you are getting enough? How much is too much? What happens if you ingest more than you need? When can vitamins and minerals be used legitimately in the prevention and treatment of disease? In this book you will find documented facts that completely counter the myths of Pied Pipers.

While there is little scientific controversy about vitamins, there is genuine controversy about the role of diet in producing heart diseases and cancer. This book examines these issues and provides practical advice for healthy eating.

Adelle Davis, a major promoter of nutrition misinformation, dominated the talk-show circuit until her death in 1974. Her books sold millions of copies and still are popular. Did you know that much of her advice was irresponsible? Or that her book *Let's Have Healthy Children* was quietly recalled from the market after the death of a child whose mother followed the book's advice? You will find the details in Dr. Marshall's book. Linus Pauling's zealous advocacy has also played a big role in the current vitamin boom. This book examines his speculations and the evidence against them—perhaps more thoroughly than any other book published.

The authors of the recent book, *Life Extension,* claim that hundreds of research studies support their unorthodox ideas that extensive nutrient supplementation may prolong life. *Vitamins and Minerals: Help or Harm?* contains facts that refute these claims.

Dr. Marshall deserves our thanks for consolidating and interpreting an enormous amount of information published in scientific journals and elsewhere—a process that has obviously taken countless hours of effort. He deserves further appreciation for the care he has taken to seek expert review of his work to assure its soundness.

This is a book you can trust!

William J. Darby, M.D., Ph.D.

Dr. Darby is Professor Emeritus of Biochemistry (Nutrition) at Vanderbilt University School of Medicine and is a member of the American Society of Clinical Nutrition and the National Academy of Sciences. He was President of the Nutrition Foundation from 1971 to 1982 and has been President of the American Institute of Nutrition. He has served on the editorial boards of three scientific journals: *Nutrition Reviews,* the *Journal of Nutrition,* and the *Journal of Clinical Investigation.* He has written approximately 200 scientific articles and two books: *Food: The Gift of Osiris* and *Nutrition and Diet in Health and Disease.*

Introduction

Even nectar is a poison if taken in excess.
—Old Hindu Proverb

The purpose of this book is to discourage you from taking extra vitamins and minerals—especially large doses—if you don't need them. It is based on years of intensive study of the scientific literature and correspondence with many of the nation's top nutrition experts. I wrote it because I became angry about the dangerously misleading advice the public has been getting from popular "nutrition" and vitamin books and from talk show interviews with phony "experts."

The discovery of vitamins is one of mankind's greatest achievements. Yet it has also led to widespread hucksterism. There is no shortage of so-called "experts" to tell you to supplement your diet, to diagnose your every symptom as a "deficiency disease," and to treat yourself with one nutrient or another. *But what about risks?* Although the dangers of unnecessary vitamins have been reported in scientific journals, they are seldom brought to public attention. This I determined to do soon after I retired from 25 years of active research in the field of biochemistry.

This book tells how nutrients can harm as well as help, how self-appointed "experts" can lead you astray, and how to tell the difference between a real expert and a phony. It may also shock you with real stories based on medical reports of vitamin and mineral poisoning of adults and children.

Charles W. Marshall, Ph.D.

1

How Supplements
Are Promoted

"A great deal of intelligence can be invested
in ignorance when the need for illusion is deep."
—Saul Bellow[1]

A visitor from outer space might get the impression that Americans are now in great danger of vitamin and mineral deficiency. One hundred years ago, such a visitor would have seen pioneer settlers of America's West able to toil 14 hours a day on a daily intake of only 15-30 mg of vitamin C,[2] and able to beget many children on a daily intake of not more than 15 IU of vitamin E.

Today, to the horror of nutrition scientists, enormous quantities of vitamins and minerals are being sold in doses up to 30 times this high in pharmacies, supermarkets, department stores and "health food" stores. They are being sold by mail. They are also being sold person-to-person by huge numbers of individuals who have become "distributors" for giant companies like Shaklee and Amway. Total sales are close to $3 *billion* a year.

Millions of Americans are now on the vitamin bandwagon of daily, and often too potent, vitamin and mineral supplements. They are being lured to the "vitality with vitamins" parade by a strange band of Pied Pipers—untrained, pseudoscientific, self-styled "nutritionists," supported by a small, well-educated but often irrational group of Ph.D. and M.D. scientists. (Just because someone has earned a doctoral degree in the biological or medical sciences doesn't mean that he or she is immune to faulty scientific judgment!)

The main sales pitch of these vitamin salesmen is "Make sure you get enough!" They don't usually tell you how much is enough. And *they rarely tell you how much is too much.*

2

An Innocent Victim[3]

Take the case of Ted B.* In 1971, when he was 16 years old, Ted began taking vitamin A because he had heard it could help the acne on his face. By the end of a few weeks, he was taking 200,000 units daily. (Nutritionists recommend 5,000 units a day in our diet.) He kept this up for two years. As his 18th birthday approached, he became weak, and then weaker. His appetite went way down, he lost 10 pounds, his gums began to bleed easily and so did his nose. His skin began to itch and flake over most of his body, his hair began to fall out, and he developed daily headaches, nausea and vomiting.

Soon Ted had involuntary leg twitchings, and finally the unbearable happened: his eyeballs began to move uncontrollably. Frightened, he dragged himself to the local hospital where the doctors measured the amount of vitamin A circulating in his blood. It was close to 100 times the normal amount! The diagnosis of chronic vitamin A poisoning was quickly made, and Ted quite willingly stopped taking his supplements.

On the 9th day of his hospital stay, Ted's abdomen swelled up with enough fluid that the doctors had to drain some of it out through a large needle inserted into the abdominal cavity. Fortunately, this problem did not recur. By the 30th hospital day, Ted felt recovered and was sent home. His system had not completely restored the level of minerals lost from his bones, but this too would eventually return to normal.

Who Is Responsible?

Where did Ted Bates get the idea to take all that vitamin A? The medical report doesn't tell us, but it is not hard to imagine the answer. Many popular books about "nutrition" recommend vitamin A for acne and a whole host of other problems. The books vary in recommended dosage, but they have one thing in common. Almost none of them warns the reader that too much vitamin A can be harmful. Moreover, there is a general philosophy among vitamin promoters that if a little bit is good, more is likely to be better.

Vitamin promoters certainly encourage people to diagnose and treat themselves with all sorts of things. Did you know that there are more than 2,000 books in print which suggest nutritional remedies for just about

*To spare unnecessary embarrassment, we have changed the names and some of the identifying details of victims mentioned in this book by first name only; but the medical facts are presented as they appeared in the medical journals which reported them. Where a person's full name appears, however, the victim or his family made the case public through a lawsuit or public testimony. In such cases, we have made no changes.

every condition known to humans? Did you know that "health food" stores alone sell more than $65 million of such books each year?

"Books are your silent sales force," advises the Denver-based Nutri-Books Corp., the largest distributor of "health-related books and magazines." Its 12-page booklet, *Building Your Nutritional Food Business with Books and Magazines,* advises retailers that:

> Books are the "cutting edge" of growth and direction for the nutritional foods industry. Millions of dedicated users of health food and supplements were persuaded to make their first nutritional purchases by the books of Adelle Davis, Dr. Carlton Fredericks, Dr. Richard Passwater, Dr. Lendon Smith, Dr. Earl Mindell, Gayelord Hauser and many other authors . . .
>
> Books and magazine covers are designed like billboards. They reach out and "grab" the customer . . .
>
> They tell your customers what your products will do for them. They explain the ways your products can be used. Very often this is information you may not be able to give—or may not be permitted to discuss . . .
>
> Sell a pound of wheat germ and it satisfies the customer's need. Sell a book and it *creates* a whole new set of needs in your customers.

What do you think would happen if you went to your local health food store and asked what to take for acne? I'll bet that most clerks would recommend one or more of the store's products. I'll also bet that they'd tell you nothing about limiting your dosage to avoid trouble.

Do you think that health food store clerks have any training in nutrition? Most of them get their information from the very same books and magazines they sell in the stores—publications that are chock full of unproven and sometimes dangerous advice. Some clerks take courses. Guess who gives the courses. Mostly companies that sell vitamins. Some companies suggest that dosage of certain vitamins be limited, but others do not. And some companies suggest that food supplements can bring about all sorts of miraculous cures.

Clerks also read magazines like *Prevention, Let's Live, Health Quarterly, Better Nutrition, Today's Living, Bestways, Health Express* and *Body Forum.* These magazines[4] promote all manner of unproven and questionable nutrition ideas. They, too, suggest that everyone needs supplements.

A few popular talk show guests make regular rounds on radio and TV to promote their unproven and sometimes far-fetched nutritional theories. For more than ten years, major health food industry groups have sponsored *Nutrition for Living,* a syndicated radio-TV talk show heard on many stations. Its host is a chiropractor, and most of its guests are food faddists.

Retailers are quite aware of the power of the press. "If I get three phone calls asking for the same product within one hour of opening," reports a

California proprietor, "I trot across the street and pick up a copy of the *National Enquirer*. Usually, whatever my customers are asking for is featured in that paper."[5]

The current rage in healthfoodland is the use of hair analysis to determine whether you need supplements. Many health food stores and magazine ads tell how to get one. Just clip some hair from the back of your neck, send it with $35 to a laboratory, and you will receive a computer printout telling which vitamins and minerals you supposedly need to take.

Why is this a rip-off? First of all, there are no vitamins in hair (except at the roots below the skin). Second, mineral deficiency cannot be diagnosed by hair analysis because medical scientists have not yet determined what the lower limits of normal are for minerals in hair. And third, the analyses are not being performed accurately because the technique of doing them has not yet been perfected. Hair analysis is not recognized as a valid test for vitamin or mineral deficiency by Medicare, Blue Shield and other insurance companies.

What about pharmacists? Are they likely to give you good advice about vitamins and minerals? Most pharmacists learn quite a bit about vitamins during their training. When they enter the world of commerce, however, they learn that food supplements are one of the most profitable of all products to sell in their stores. Although most pharmacists are capable of giving good advice, they are also content to carry and sell whatever supplements are popular. Chain drugstores tend to push vitamins with great vigor.

Some drug companies—most notably Lederle and Hoffmann-La Roche —advertise heavily to the public. Their ads suggest that most of us need vitamin supplements to face life's stresses safely. The National Advertising Division of the Council on Better Business Bureaus recently began to exert pressure against this type of advertising.[6]

Many medical doctors also play a role in promoting overuse of vitamins, particularly when patients complain of being depressed or overtired. Instead of finding out what is upsetting you (or referring you to someone who will), doctors too often recommend vitamins as placebos. This type of medically prescribed supplementation seldom if ever involves potentially dangerous dosages, but it does add considerably to public confusion about the need for vitamins.

Government Protection—Limited!

Can't the U.S. government protect people from false and dangerous promotional claims for vitamins and minerals? Well, it tries. The U.S. Food and Drug Administration (FDA) can block interstate commerce of unproven drug products. It can seize products which are hazardous or misbranded with false healing claims. Examples of products it has attacked are laetrile and pangamic acid ("B-15"). But the FDA has been stopped by Congress and the courts from requiring that high-dosage vitamin supplements be labeled and regulated as drugs.

Although the FDA is empowered to prosecute when false claims occur on product labels, it has no power to prevent the making of false claims through broadcasts and publications. Such claims are protected by the U.S. Constitution's First Amendment provision for freedom of speech and expression (including freedom of the press).

This book provides the facts you need to protect your health and your pocketbook from supplement salesmen.

References

1. Bellow, S.: To Jerusalem and Back. New York, Viking Press, 1976, p. 162.
2. Passmore, R., *In* vitamin C debate (Anderson and Passmore vs. Pauling and Szent-Georgyi). Nutrition Today 13:6-33,* March/April, 1978.
3. Metabolism 21:1171, 1972.
4. Herbert, V. and Barrett, S.: Vitamins and "Health" Foods: The Great American Hustle. Philadelphia, George F. Stickley Co., 1981.
5. Natural Foods Merchandiser, Dec. 1981, p. 13.
6. NAD Case Report, May 15, 1982, p. 15.

---

*Throughout this book, where numbers separated by a colon follow the name of a journal, they represent the volume and page numbers.

2

Danger In The Bottle

*Sola dosis facit venenum
(Only the dose makes a poison).*
—A centuries-old rule of pharmacy and medicine

While his mother did her last-minute packing for a family camping trip, 4-year-old Erin S.[1] hid under the dining room table and swallowed 40 of what he thought were small, brightly-colored candy animals. But he was soon in deep trouble. The little turtles, fish, owls and squirrels were potent *pills,* each representing a day's dose of vitamins A, B_1, B_2, B_6 and B_{12}, niacinamide, folic acid, pantothenic acid and the mineral, iron. Poor little Erin, a victim of both vitamin A and iron poisoning, ended up having his stomach pumped and spending two days in the intensive care unit of the University of Kansas Medical Center in Kansas City, Missouri.

How common are cases like this? Figures for *acute* poisoning from large single doses of vitamins or minerals can be found in the annual reports of the National Clearinghouse for Poison Control Centers, an agency operated by the U.S. Food and Drug Administration's Bureau of Drugs. In 1979, according to a recent issue of its *Bulletin,*[2] there were 144,000 "ingestion cases" called in by doctors, hospitals and a few members of the general public. Listed under "vitamins and mineral products" and "iron preparations" are a total of 4,707 cases, 3,793 involving children under 5 years of age. Of the 4,707 cases, 402 suffered toxic symptoms and 145 visited a hospital for treatment.

These numbers should be considered *minimum* figures. For every case called in to poison control centers by worried doctors and parents, ten times as many are handled by family doctors who do not report them— and not all centers report their cases to the National Clearinghouse.

6

The Book That Killed One Child and Crippled Another

Ryan Pitzer was not as lucky as Erin S. Ryan was one of twins. His parents had looked forward with great eagerness to his arrival. His mother, in particular, tried very hard to insure his good health. A fan of the late Adelle Davis and other supposed nutrition "authorities," she paid close attention to what she ate during her pregnancy.

Ryan and his brother both had pleasant dispositions. They ate well and would fall asleep soon after each feeding. One day, when the twins were 10 weeks old, they both became quite irritable. After ruling out various other possibilities, Mrs. Pizer concluded they were having "colic" and sought a solution in Adelle Davis's book, *Let's Have Healthy Children*. On page 242, the book suggests giving potassium supplements and reports how 653 colicky babies experienced "dramatic improvement" when given from 1,000 to 3,000 mg of potassium chloride by mouth.

Trusting the book, Mrs. Pitzer then offered both boys the recommended dosage of potassium from a bottle obtained at a health food store.[3] His brother spit it out, but Ryan did not. According to the official report of the county medical examiner,[4] Ryan received two doses of potassium chloride totaling 3,000 mg along with breast milk on the first day. On the following morning, his symptoms recurred and he was given 1,500 mg more. A few hours later, he became listless and stopped breathing. Despite resuscitation and intensive hospital treatment, he died of potassium intoxication about 36 hours later. It was calculated that Ryan had received at least four times the dose needed for treatment had he been deficient in potassium.

Wishing to protect other parents from a similar tragedy, the Pitzers filed suit against the book's publishers, the estate of Adelle Davis, and later the manufacturer of the potassium supplement. The suit also demanded that remaining copies of the book be withdrawn from the shelves—which they were. In 1981, "without admitting liability," the publishers paid $25,000 and the estate paid $75,000 to settle the suits against them.[5] The case against the manufacturer is still being litigated. If it goes to trial, the outcome may have significant impact upon the way that potentially dangerous supplements are marketed in the future.

In 1976, the estate of Adelle Davis paid $150,000 to settle out-of-court a suit brought by the mother of Eliza Young, a little girl whose growth had been stunted by "generous amounts" of vitamin A as recommended in *Let's Have Healthy Children*.

The Importance of Dose

In 1973, the Food and Nutrition Board of the National Academy of Sciences published the 590-page second edition of *Toxicants Occurring Naturally in Foods*. In the introduction, Dr. Frank Strong declares:

Nutritious food is essential for life. It is also a mixture of thousands of chemicals, any one of which in sufficient amount, would be harmful, perhaps fatal to the consumer. This holds for essential nutrients such as zinc, copper, methionine [an essential amino acid] and vitamin A. Human beings cannot live without them, but in excess, they are very toxic.

Food also contains safe doses of many non-essential chemicals which would be harmful if present in large amounts. According to Harvard University's Dr. Fredrick Stare,[6] the average American in one year eats potatoes containing a total amount of solanine, which, if concentrated into a single dose, could kill a person. Yet potatoes are one of our preferred sources of carbohydrate—and rightly so.

Kelp, a form of seaweed, is being recommended as a "health food" for self-treatment of thyroid conditions. Self-treatment for a potentially serious condition is never wise. Moreover, the American Dietetic Association[7] warns that too much kelp can cause arsenic (and possibly iodine) poisoning!

Hidden Dangers

In *Toxicants Occurring Naturally in Food,* in their chapter on vitamin toxicity, Drs. K. C. Hayes and Mark Hegsted note that the distinction between enough and too much of essential nutrients is not easily made by the average consumer—or indeed in some cases by physicians and nutritionists.

Although a few doctors were aware as early as 1930, it was not until about 1960 that the large majority recognized the dangers of prolonged overdosing with vitamin D. The symptoms of chronic vitamin D poisoning resemble several other conditions and illnesses. This is also true of vitamin A intoxication, which some doctors recognized as early as 1950. But it was not until about 1970 that the average physician understood how to look for it. Vitamins A and D, being fat-soluble, can accumulate in the liver and fatty tissues and build to toxic levels when taken in excess for prolonged periods of time. Later in this book we explore the adverse effects of excess amounts of these and other vitamins.

Can people feel when they are taking enough nutrients to build up gradually to toxic levels? Not usually! The human body has a marvelous protective capacity called "homeostasis"—the ability to maintain balance within the body's complex biochemical and physiological functioning. This includes considerable ability to cope with temporary shortages and excesses of nutrients.

Strong warnings that excessive daily vitamin and/or mineral intake is usually needless and may be harmful have been issued by the FDA, the American Medical Association (AMA), the National Research Council of the National Academy of Sciences, Ralph Nader's Health Research Group, the National Nutrition Consortium and many other scientific and professional organizations. Not long ago, the Consortium[8] stated that:

Taking large amounts of vitamins provides no benefits to the body and can be dangerous . . . A person who takes vitamins may think mistakenly that his or her nutritional needs have been cared for and that there is no need to plan appropriate food choices. Again this assumption is false . . .

The most subtle hazard of vitamin pills is that in taking them, some people get a false sense of security about their nutritional health.

Many people—including some doctors—have such confidence in vitamins that early signs of toxic build-up may not be recognized as related to vitamin intake.[9]

Vitamin "Addiction"

Did you know that a few vitamins can actually act like addicting drugs? In 1974, Dr. Philip White,[10] Director of the AMA Department of Foods and Nutrition, reported that large doses of some vitamins can create an unnatural dependency:

A drug dependency, if you will; stopping the regimen then results in a "withdrawal" situation—a self-induced deficiency. We know that this can happen with massive doses of vitamin C; we strongly suspect it can occur with the B-complex vitamins also.

Supplement Use vs. Abuse

Should anyone take dietary supplements on a regular basis? Possibly. We discuss this topic in Chapters 21 and 24. Are there any medical conditions which actually need high dosages (megadosage) of vitamins for their treatment? Yes, there are a few, but all of these conditions should be medically diagnosed and treated under a doctor's supervision.

In 1977, Dr. Samuel Vaisrub[11] wrote a guest editorial for the *Journal of the American Medical Association*. Titled *Vitamin Abuse,* it states:

It may be argued, of course, that misuse (of vitamins) is not necessarily abuse. It may be said that megavitamin therapy is a reassuring placebo (dummy pill), an expensive but harmless luxury, and as such, need cause no concern. Unfortunately, this is not the case. Megavitamin therapy can be harmful. Not only is it an insult to the pocketbook, it is also a threat to health. When consumed in excessive amounts, almost any vitamin can cause mischief.

Unfortunately, a few hundred physicians believe in "megavitamin therapy" with huge dosages of vitamins for conditions in which there is no evidence that vitamins can help. Mary M. was the victim of such a physician. At the age of 52, she entered a hospital because of malaise (general ill feeling), abnormal heartbeat, a skin rash all over her body, swelling around her eyes and in her legs, and recurrent fevers as high as 105°F. According to the medical report,[12] Mary had taken at least 40 tablets per day for 4 months of vitamins B_1, B_2, B_6, B_{12}, C, D and E, along with folic acid, pantothenic acid, copper, magnesium, calcium phosphate and carbonate, alfalfa, biotin and lecithin.

Tests done during Mary's hospital stay revealed a widespread inflammation of her blood vessels. Her heart was inflamed, her lungs contained abnormal amounts of fluid, and her kidney function was below normal as a result of inflammation of its arteries (necrotizing arteritis). Thinking that Mary's trouble might be a sensitivity reaction to something, the doctors persuaded her to stop taking the various vitamins, minerals and other "food supplements" and treated her with two anti-inflammatory drugs. Mary gradually improved and appeared to be completely recovered after four months of treatment.

What caused Mary's temporary but almost fatal illness? In this case, the doctors could not be absolutely certain. Hypersensitivity to drugs is known to cause allergic inflammation of the blood vessels, and Mary was taking no other drug substances except the "vitamin" preparations. The medical report concluded that, although Mary's difficulty could have resulted from an undiscovered and unrelated cause, "it is possible that vitamin abuse led to vasculitis (blood vessel inflammation) in this patient. As megavitamin 'therapy' is common, we hope this description will stimulate the reporting of similar cases."

Cases of individuals clearly harmed by megavitamin therapy are described throughout this book.

References

1. Marks, N.: We Must Keep Those TV Commercials From Harming Our Children. Today's Health, Aug. 1972, pp. 9-10.
2. Bulletin, National Clearinghouse for Poison Control Centers, Aug. 1981. U.S. Dept. of H.H.S. (formerly H.E.W.).
3. Medical World News: Popular Health Books Face Legal Hurdles, July 23, 1979, p. 40.
4. Wetli, C. V.: Letter to FDA Commissioner Donald Kennedy, Ph.D., April 25, 1978.
5. Portley, P.: Letter dated Dec. 9, 1981.
6. Stare, F. and Whelan, E.: Panic in the Pantry. New York, Atheneum, 1977, p. 100.
7. Journal of the American Dietetic Association 66:277, 1975.
8. FDA Consumer: Nutrition Group Warns on Vitamin Overuse, April, 1978, p. 3.

9. Taylor, K.: Rational Drug Therapy, Vol. 9, 1975, pp. 1-9.
10. Schultz, D.: The Verdict on Vitamins. Today's Health, Jan. 1974, p. 54.
11. Vaisrub, S.: JAMA* 238:1762, 1977.
12. Archives of Pathology and Laboratory Medicine 106:48, 1982.

---

*JAMA is the abbreviation for the *Journal of the American Medical Association.*

3

Science vs. Quackery

*If I set out to prove something, I am no real
scientist. I have to learn to follow where the facts
lead me. I have to whip my prejudices.*
　　　　　　　　　　　—Lazzarro Spallanzani[1]

Lazzarro Spallanzani, an 18th century biologist, is still honored for
proving that microorganisms exist and for disproving the theory of "spontaneous life" that had dominated "scientific" thought up to his time. He
established his truths by designing and carrying out a logical series of
experiments.

The scientific method, now refined to high degree, requires that each
step leading to a conclusion be proved by ruling out every other explanation. Findings offered in evidence must then be verified by other independent researchers. The scientific method calls for "controlled" experiments,
and those involving tests on humans should be done with special "double-
blind" techniques to avoid confusing psychological effects with biological
actions.

How Medical Theories Are Tested

A controlled test of a substance—such as a medication or nutrient—is
one in which the people being studied are divided into groups that are
roughly equivalent in age, sex and medical history (if pertinent). One
group is given the substance being tested, while another group (the control
group) is given a placebo (dummy or "sugar pill") which looks like the
real thing but contains no active ingredient. "Double-blind" means that
neither the researchers nor the people being tested know who is getting the
substance being tested. This insures that preconceived ideas or biases do
not lead to faulty observations by either party. Bottles containing the test
substance are labeled with code numbers known only to a third party who

does not reveal which substances are which until the rest of the experiment has been completed.

The tremendous progress in medicine and nutrition of the past 100 years could not have been made without the insistence of scientists NOT to place weight on personal testimonials. There are two reasons for this. First, "nature will lie to you if it can." Most ailments are self-limited and disappear spontaneously. Therefore careful, controlled testing is required to separate the effect of a proposed remedy from the natural course of the ailment. Second, many people who take placebos feel better because they believe they are taking a positive step. This is known as the "placebo effect." It is a very real and sometimes powerful effect which can make people believe that something has helped them when it actually has not.

Striking examples of the placebo effects have occurred in experiments to test the value of high-dose vitamin C for the common cold. In one study, hundreds of volunteers who received a placebo but thought they had been given vitamin C claimed that they felt unusually well. In another study, participants who received 1,000 mg of ascorbic acid daily appeared to have fewer and less severe colds than those taking the placebo. However, when asked which treatment they thought they were receiving, most guessed correctly because the vitamin C had a tart taste. Participants who had received vitamin C *but thought otherwise* had no apparent benefit from the vitamin. The subject of vitamin C and colds is discussed in detail in Chapter 13.

How to Recognize Quackery

> *Quackery and idolatry are all but immortal.*
> —Oliver Wendell Holmes[2]

Just because a person has an M.D. or a respectable Ph.D. after his or her name, should that person be entitled to your complete confidence? Does medical training or other doctoral education in a biological science render such a person immune to faulty judgment? No! There will always be a few highly educated individuals—including some who even make significant contributions to human knowledge—who develop irrational attitudes toward certain facts. One example was Dr. Andrew Ivy, a medical educator who abandoned his medical school post and wasted the rest of his career promoting the quack cancer remedy, krebiozen.

How can you tell when a trained professional is unreliable? This is a crucial question because libraries, bookstores and paperback book racks carry dozens of misleading books written by people with doctoral degrees. In *The Health Robbers,*[3] Dr. Philip Alper, Associate Professor of Medicine, University of California Medical Center, San Francisco, suggests four ways to tell when someone has abandoned scientific medical thought:

1) If he claims to have a special or secret machine or formula

2) If he makes blanket statements that surgery, x-rays or drugs do more harm than good

3) If he claims that the medical profession is persecuting him or afraid of his competition

4) If he uses testimonials from patients or flamboyant advertising to promote his practice.

In the same book, Dr. Victor Herbert presents a list of 17 tips to help spot a food quack—trained or not. The most telltale sign is the suggestion that everyone needs to consume vitamins, "health foods," or both. You should also be skeptical about anyone who promotes the idea that vitamins, minerals or other "nutritional" methods can cure serious diseases such as cancer or arthritis. While dietary adjustment (particularly weight loss for overweight individuals) may help in the treatment of some conditions, dietary *cures* are virtually nonexistent except in cases of classical deficiency diseases like scurvy, rickets, pellagra, etc.

Be Skeptical of "Persecutory" Claims

Those who promote quackery often try to represent themselves as scientists ahead of their time. When challenged, they remind us of scientific pioneers who were ridiculed. Dr. Herbert calls this the "Galileo Ploy." Don't let what happened more than 100 years ago fool you into thinking that the same thing is likely today! The ideas of these pioneers *were* accepted as the scientific community developed its logical rules for the testing of new ideas. Nowadays, valid new methods are likely to be accepted quite quickly. But methods not backed by *evidence* are another matter.

Do you believe—contrary to the medical establishment—that high-dose vitamins can really protect you from colds, the flu, arthritis, heart attacks, cancer or the effects of inhaling smog? Do you think that the medical establishment, our government, and the biomedical and nutrition scientists at our nation's great universities could be engaged in a conspiracy to hamstring the "health food" industry and "protect" big food companies? I do not.

Political Activity

Dr. George P. Larrick for many years guided the U.S. Food and Drug Administration's progress in protecting the public from health hazards in foods and drugs. In 1965, in the twilight of his distinguished career, Dr. Larrick[4] had this to say:

> The most widespread and expensive type of quackery in the United States today is the promotion of vitamin products, special dietary foods and food

supplements. Millions of consumers are being misled concerning their need for such products. Complicating this problem is a vast and growing "folk-lore" or "mythology" of nutrition which is being built up by pseudo-scientific literature in books, pamphlets and periodicals. As a result, millions of people are attempting self-medication for imaginary and real illnesses with a multitude of more or less irrational food items. Food quackery today can only be compared to the patent medicine craze which reached its height in the last century.

Shortly before Dr. Larrick retired as FDA Commissioner, the agency began trying to develop regulations to reduce public confusion about food supplements. In the early 1970s, after 10 years of study, the FDA proposed new marketing rules to combat this confusion. Many deceptive claims would be banned, supplement strengths would become more standardized, and doses higher than 1½ times the Recommended Dietary Allowances (RDAs) would be regulated as "over-the-counter" drugs. All would continue to be available without a doctor's prescription—except for vitamins A, D and folic acid (a B-vitamin). Because high dosages of these three nutrients can be quite hazardous, a doctor's prescription would be required to obtain them.

The FDA's proposed marketing rules were developed with the advice of leading scientific authorities including the Food and Nutrition Board of the National Academy of Sciences and the Council on Foods and Nutrition of the American Medical Association. But the health food industry and its faithful followers exploded with anger at what they called a threat to "freedom of choice." Industry organizations charged that the FDA was threatening the right of people to buy "non-harmful food supplements" of their choice. They accused the agency of trying to dictate laws based on "opinion —not facts."

Leading the fight was an organization called the National Health Federation (NHF). This group was founded in 1956 by Fred J. Hart, not long after he was ordered by a U.S. District Court to stop distributing phony electrical devices with false claims that they could diagnose and treat hundreds of diseases. Over the years, NHF has promoted a wide variety of unproven and questionable "health" methods and has opposed several very important and proven public measures. Dr. Stephen Barrett,[5] a consumer advocate who monitors NHF's activities closely, reports that 13 of its leaders have been in legal difficulty and 5 have even received prison sentences for questionable "health" activities. Dr. Barrett calls NHF "an unhealthy alliance of promoters fighting for the right to cheat, and victims fighting for the right to be cheated."

And fight they did. As soon as the proposed vitamin regulations were announced, NHF organized a letter-writing campaign which produced more than a million letters to Congress urging passage of a law to stop the

FDA's regulations. NHF had fewer than 20,000 members at the time, but they were assisted by "health food" storekeepers, chiropractors, and also by "health food" magazines with a combined readership of several million. Many Congressmen received more letters about vitamins than about Watergate—the super scandal that brought about the resignation of a President of the United States! Testifying before Senator Ted Kennedy's Subcommittee on Health, Dr. Barrett[6] noted:

> People who wrote did so in the belief that they were fighting for both better health and consumer protection. The sad fact is that the FDA, not the health-food industry, is trying to help them. In matters of health, there should be no tolerance for deception.

Faced with what appeared to be a massive grass-roots consumer effort, the majority of Congressmen sponsored legislation that would virtually remove food supplements from FDA jurisdiction. U.S. Senate Bill S-2801, introduced by Senator William Proxmire and referred to as the "Vitamin Bill," became the rallying point. Here's how some of the leading opponents and proponents lined up for testimony on this bill to Senator Kennedy's subcommittee:

FOR RESTRICTING FDA AUTHORITY

National Health Federation

Bob Hoffman, one of NHF's leaders, who is also president of York Barbell Co., a company that had supplement products seized for misbranding at least five times between 1961 and 1974.

Rodale Press, publisher of *Prevention* magazine. Prevention takes in over $10 million a year for food supplement advertising. The ads carry no health claims, but false and misleading claims for supplements are abundant in the magazine's articles, editorials and letters to the editor.

National Nutritional Foods Association, a trade association representing health food retailers, distributors and producers.

Council for Responsible Nutrition, organization of manufacturers and distributors of food supplements sold through "health food" stores.

Carlton Fredericks, a writer and lecturer on nutrition topics. Though lacking formal training in either nutrition or medicine, he recommends nutritional remedies for a wide variety of ailments. In 1945, he was even convicted of unlawful practice of medicine in connection with giving advice to "patients."

International Academy of Preventive Medicine, an organization founded in 1971 to provide a forum for the discussion and promotion of unproven methods.

Professor Linus Pauling

Professor Roger Williams

AGAINST RESTRICTING FDA AUTHORITY

American Dietetic Association
American Academy of Pediatrics
American Society for Clinical Nutrition
Institute for Food Technologists
Society for Nutrition Education
American Medical Association
U.S. Food and Drug Administration
Consumer's Union
Ralph Nader's Health Research Group
American Pharmaceutical Manufacturing Association
American Association of Retired Persons
National Retired Teachers Association
Professor Alfred E. Harper, Chairman, Committee on Dietary Allowances, Food and Nutrition Board, National Research Council/National Academy of Sciences
Philip Handler, President, National Academy of Sciences

As it turned out, Senate Bill S-2801 never came to a vote by itself, but Senator Proxmire managed to push it through the Senate by attaching it to an unrelated but popular bill. The bill's harmful effects were softened somewhat by a compromise made through the efforts of Representative Paul Rogers, but a version did pass—much to the detriment of American consumers.

Unknown to Congress and the FDA, a large percentage of those who wrote protest letters to Congress were not merely confused *users* of vitamin supplements. They were also *sellers*. Hundreds of thousands of people work as "distributors" engaged in person-to-person sales for large companies like Shaklee, Amway and Neo-Life. We strongly suspect that these people—who take in hundreds of millions of dollars each year selling unnecessary supplements—formed the core of the letter-writing campaign.

Where Can You Get Reliable Information?

If you have a question, your personal physician is probably the most convenient person to ask. You may have heard that "doctors don't know anything about nutrition." Dr. Fredrick J. Stare,[7] founder and former Chairman of Harvard University's Department of Nutrition, responds to this charge as follows:

> The fact is that most physicians know far more about nutrition than they get credit for. Doctors know that there is no such thing as a "nutritionally perfect food." They know that moderation and variety are the keys to good nutrition. They know that nutrition is an important part of recovery from

many severe illnesses. They know that overweight in the presence of other risk factors for heart disease is an added hazard . . . They also know that the woods are full of food faddists and nutritional charlatans whose scare tactics and sensational claims often sway the uninformed.

Most doctors are willing to answer nutrition questions or to refer you to someone else who will—most likely a registered dietitian (R.D.). These professionals are specially trained to translate nutrition research into healthful, tasty diets. Compared to physicians, they usually know less about biochemistry, physiology and metabolism, but more about the nutrient content of specific foods.

A number of organizations evaluate and publish accurate information about nutrition. They include:

• The Food and Drug Administration will answer inquiries and has available a variety of educational materials about nutrition and nutritional quackery. Its consumer affairs offices, located in 30 major cities, can furnish speakers for interested groups. The FDA is also interested in receiving complaints about food supplement products which are sold with false claims or inadequate directions for use. Its address is 5600 Fishers Lane, Rockville, MD 20857.

• The U.S. Department of Agriculture can answer questions and provide literature on nutrition and diet. Write: Food and Nutrition Information Center, USDA National Agricultural Library, Room 304, 10301 Baltimore Blvd., Beltsville, MD 20705, or telephone 301-344-3719 between 8:00 AM and 4:30 PM, EST.

• The USDA Extension Service of each land-grant university can answer questions about nutrition. Home economists at USDA county cooperative services can answer questions about food preparation. Your local telephone directory can tell you if your community has either of these two services available.

• The Department of Health and Human Services (HHS, formerly HEW) offers a broad range of nutrition publications available from the Health Services Administration of the U.S. Public Health Service, Washington, DC 20852 and the U.S. Government Printing Office, Pueblo, CO 81009.

• State health departments and some local health departments can be excellent sources of information about nutrition.

• The American Society for Clinical Nutrition is composed primarily of medical specialists in the field of nutrition. Its address is 9650 Rockville Pike, Bethesda, MD 20014.

• The AMA Department of Foods and Nutrition has pamphlets available and can answer questions. Its address is 535 N. Dearborn St., Chicago, IL 60610. State medical societies may also be helpful.

• The American Dietetic Association has a variety of publications and can answer questions. Its address is 430 N. Michigan Ave., Chicago, IL 60611. State and local dietetic associations are usually eager to be helpful. Dial-A-Dietitian services are available in a number of cities.

• The Institute of Food Technologists issues scientific summaries and position papers on topics related to food processing. Its address is 221 N. LaSalle St., Chicago, IL 60601.

• The Nutrition Foundation, 888 17th St., N.W., Washington, DC 20006, issues both popular and technical publications.

• Accredited colleges and medical schools with nutrition departments may be excellent sources of information.

• The American Council on Science and Health has a special interest in chemical and nutritional issues. Membership, open to anyone, costs $35/year. Several times a year, ACSH publishes reports based upon thorough review of current scientific evidence on particular topics. It also publishes a bimonthly newsletter, maintains a speakers bureau, and has a syndicated radio program. Its address is 1995 Broadway, New York, NY 10023.

References

1. Spallanzani, L. (1729-1799), quoted in Familiar Medical Quotations, (M. Straus, Ed.). Boston, Little, Brown, 1968, p. 525.
2. Holmes, O., quoted in A New Dictionary of Quotations (compiled by H. L. Mencken). New York, A. A. Knopf, 1942, p. 998.
3. Barrett, S.: The Health Robbers—How To Protect Your Money And Your Life, 2nd Ed. Philadelphia, George F. Stickley Co., 1980, pp. 83-84.
4. Larrick, G. P., quoted by R. L. Smith in "The Vitamin Healers." The Reporter, Dec. 16, 1965, pp. 18-25.
5. Herbert, V. and Barrett, S.: Vitamins and "Health" Foods: The Great American Hustle. Philadelphia, George F. Stickley Co., 1981, pp. 116-122.
6. Barrett, S.: The Unhealthy Alliance—A Report on the National Health Federation. Allentown, PA, Lehigh Valley Committee Against Health Fraud, 1974.
7. Stare, F. J. and Aronson, V.: Dear Dr. Stare: What Should I Eat? Philadelphia, George F. Stickley Co., 1982, pp. 17-18.

4

Common Beliefs—How True?

In 1972, a nationwide survey, sponsored and jointly funded by seven U.S. government agencies including the FDA, was published through the National Technical Information Service.[1] Entitled *A Study of Health Practices and Opinions,* the study revealed that 75 percent of American adults believed that extra vitamins provide extra energy and well-being, and 20 percent even thought that arthritis and cancer are caused by vitamin and mineral deficiencies in the diet. *These ideas are false!* Only calories provide energy. And the effects of deficiency—called "deficiency diseases"—are specific and well known. Arthritis and cancer are not among them.

Vitamins as "Health Insurance"

To help in dietary planning, scientists have developed a set of general nutrition guidelines known as the Recommended Dietary Allowances (RDAs). These are the levels of intake of essential nutrients considered adequate to meet the needs of healthy persons. (We discuss this in detail in the next chapter.) Vitamin and mineral promoters have instilled into the minds of Americans a "miss-no-bets on your health" philosophy consisting of two parts:

1. *Make sure you have enough!* This appeal is based on the argument that you might have malnutrition and not know it. It has not been difficult for vitamin pushers to persuade Americans that a danger of deficiency exists. We can measure for ourselves how much gasoline we need per average week or for a trip. All we need to know is how far we will be driving and how many miles per gallon the car uses under such circumstances. We can watch the gasoline being pumped into the car and measure the amount in the gas tank. But there is no direct way for us to measure the amount of nutrients entering our body or how they are being used. For this information we must rely on facts gathered by others—and there's the rub. Our "measurement" has to be based on whom we trust and believe rather than on what we can see for ourselves. As indicated in Chapter 1, vitamin pushers are supersalesmen.

2. *More is better!* ("More" means more than the RDA.) This is based on the notion that since small amounts of nutrients are good, more may be even better. "More" may be just a bit over the RDA for "insurance," or it may involve very high quantities—10 or more times the RDA—known as "megadoses." To ward off the potential customer's worry about taking 10 or even 100 times the RDA of a nutrient, vitamin salespeople may reassure that their products are "just concentrated food." These words are happily swallowed by millions. But the overwhelming majority of professionally trained nutritionists say NO, nutrients are not concentrated food, and over-dosing on them is NOT NATURAL!

"Go back to nature!" has been a rallying cry of "health-organic-natural" food enthusiasts and the suppliers who profit from their enthusiasm. They worship the eating of "natural" food, but never stop to think how unnatural it is to concentrate nutrients like vitamin A or zinc and to swallow them in pill form every day. Biochemists and nutrition scientists say this is unnatural because centuries of evolution have never equipped animals or humans to take massive concentrates of any vitamin or mineral. Experts would say that, for normal animals or humans, Mother Nature abhors long-time large excesses or shortages of any essential nutrient. This is because over thousands of years, our whole physiological and biochemical make-up has been programmed by heredity to expect and to flourish best with a balanced and varied diet, *with vitamin and mineral intakes determined by their content in food.*

Is There Great Individual Variability?

A 1971 book by Dr. Roger Williams focuses mainly on the argument that people vary so greatly in their daily needs for vitamins that some might need many times the RDA for a certain vitamin. Dr. Williams calls this "biochemical individuality." He claims, for example, that a 20-fold (2,000%) variation exists for vitamin C. But the predominant scientific viewpoint is that normal variations in vitamin requirements exist but are not great. The normal range for vitamin C, for example, does not exceed plus or minus 30 percent.[2] RDAs are set considerably higher than average requirements in order to allow for individual variation—which is nowhere near what the health food industry would have you believe.[3] Dr. Williams, co-discoverer of pantothenic acid, is highly respected for his early research in nutrition, but his current ideas about the need for vitamin supplementation are rejected by the overwhelming majority of medical and nutrition scientists.

There is a well-known, scientifically established minimum level of daily intake for each vitamin below which almost every human being will eventually fall victim to deficiency disease. There also appears to be a maximum for each vitamin above which almost all humans will suffer damage if taken for a long time. In this connection, Dr. Victor Herbert[4] states:

> Promoters of exaggerations of "individual variability" forget that this argument cuts both ways (i.e., there is a wide individual variability in toxicity), so that less of an excess of a given vitamin or mineral may produce toxicity in patient A than would be required for toxicity in patient B.

"Natural" vs. "Synthetic" Vitamins

Not all, but many vitamin companies make and sell "natural" vitamins and promote them with unfounded claims of being much better than the synthetic. Some even claim that synthetic vitamins have toxic effects whereas natural ones have none. Ronald Deutsch[5] gives perhaps the best explanation of why people are susceptible to these unwarranted beliefs in his excellent book, *Realities of Nutrition*:

> Why do many people become suspicious of a man-made vitamin? Possibly because the word synthetic is often misused. Synthetic rubber, for example, is not a reproduction of rubber made from trees; it is something that merely looks and acts similarly. The term synthetic tends to be used loosely by some industries, but not in nutrition, where it means an exact reproduction of a molecule.

Professor Charles Glen King,[6] co-discoverer of vitamin C, testified as an expert at the December 1971 Hearings on Health Foods held by the New York City Consumer Affairs Department. Lambasting claims for "natural" vitamin C, he charged that it is "clearly misleading" to claim special values for a vitamin that has been isolated from rose hips, acerola cherries or citrus "as if there was some magic in their origin."

"Natural" vitamin C—supposedly made from rose hips—has been subjected to particular ridicule by scientists because it actually contains only a tiny amount of the "natural" substance. For example, Adolph Kamil,[7] Assistant Clinical Professor of Pharmacology, University of California School of Pharmacy, has reported his experiences in the early 1970s when he visited two manufacturers of "natural vitamins" in California:

> These companies make capsules, tablets and other dosage forms sold under some of the most famous brand names found in "health food" stores . . .
> During the visits, it became clear that many vitamin products labeled "natural" or "organic" are not really what I had imagined those terms to mean.
> For example, their "Rose Hips Vitamin C Tablets" are made from natural rose hips combined with chemical ascorbic acid, the same vitamin C used in standard pharmaceutical tablets. Natural rose hips contain only about 2% vitamin C, and we were told that if no vitamin C were added the tablet "would have to be as big as a golf ball." A huge stock barrel contain-

ing raw material for tablet manufacture was labeled "Rose Hips—Adjusted to contain 50% Ascorbic Acid." Nevertheless, the labels on the bottles read by the consumer were titled simply "Rose Hips Vitamin C." Would you have guessed that the amount of vitamin C coming from rose hips was but a tiny fraction of the amount added as a chemical?

Similarly, the B vitamins turned out to be mostly synthetic chemicals added to yeast and other natural bases.

Even Linus Pauling, the advocate of high-dosage vitamin C, agrees that there is no difference between synthetic and natural vitamin C. In his 1971 book, *Vitamin C and the Common Cold,* he states:

> There is only one vitamin C. It is the substance L-ascorbic acid, which is also called ascorbic acid . . . There is no advantage whatever to buying "All-natural Vitamin C," "Wild Rose Hip Super Vitamin C," "Acerola Berries Vitamin C," or similar preparations. In fact, there is the disadvantage that you would waste your money if you bought them, rather than the ordinary ascorbic acid . . .
>
> The dealer also misleads his customers by suggesting that ordinary ascorbic acid is different from "all-natural vitamin C, from organically grown rose hips imported from Northern Europe." The words "organically grown" are essentially meaningless—just part of the jargon used by health-food promoters in making their excess profits.

The Various Tocopherols: Much Ado About Nothing

There are actually a few synthetic vitamins whose structure is slightly different from their natural counterparts—but these differences are of no practical significance. Most of the fuss made by the "health food" industry concerns vitamin E, which occurs naturally as a mixture of eight closely-related substances called "tocopherols." To distinguish them from one another, each of the tocopherols has been given a Greek letter prefix: alpha-, beta-, gamma-, etc. Synthetic alpha-tocopherol is a 50:50 mixture of two structures called "d" and "l" isomers. Like your left and right hands, these isomers are identical in every respect except that one is the mirror image of the other. All natural tocopherols occur as the d-form.

Natural d-alpha-type vitamin E is biologically the most active tocopherol and is 20-30 percent higher in potency than the synthetic dl-alpha mixture. Because synthetic dl-mixtures are cheaper to manufacture, they are used in many supplement products. The FDA requires that vitamin E products be labeled according to their biological strength—in International Units (IUs) or Tocopherol Equivalents (TEs). Thus all vitamin E products labeled 100 IU should be equally potent.

Some faddists claim that high doses of natural E (d-isomer) are non-toxic or less toxic than the synthetic (dl-isomers) mixture. Dr. John Bieri, Chief of the Nutritional Biochemistry Section, National Institute of Arthritis, Metabolism and Digestive Diseases, is a leading expert on vitamin E. Recently[8] he informed me of a surgeon who had reported just the opposite experience. Patients getting 2,000 IU of *natural* alpha-tocopherol complained of headache and nausea, while those getting 2,000 IU of *synthetic* alpha-tocopherol did not.

Natural vs. Synthetic Vitamin A

To further confuse the public, many vitamin faddists have, in recent years, insisted that the "natural" vitamin A is more beneficial and less toxic than the synthetic. Vitamin A exists spatially in what are called "cis" and "trans" isomer forms. Natural vitamin A exists as two very similar structures, vitamin A_1 in animals and vitamin A_2 in fish liver oil. "Natural" A has an all-"trans" structure. Synthetic A is a 50:50 mixture of cis and trans isomers, which faddists claim is inferior. However, in 1954, Nobel Prize winner Dr. George Wald[9] pointed out that the human body changes the all-trans form to a cis-trans mixture so that the difference between synthetic and natural vitamin A is insignificant within the body.

Natural vs. Synthetic Vitamin D

Vitamin D is available to humans in two slightly different structural forms (vitamers). "Natural" vitamin D_3, cholecalciferol, is formed by the action of sunlight on 7-dehydrocholesterol which is present in the deep layers of human skin. Vitamin D_3 is also found in rich amounts in fish liver oils and in very small amounts in such animal products as liver, egg yolk and butter. "Synthetic" vitamin D_2, ergocalciferol, is made by man by irradiating ergosterol with ultraviolet light. Ergosterol is a plant sterol naturally present in many foods including rhizomes, cottonseed and wheat germ oil, and especially yeast. Most vitamin D in tablets, capsules and fortified milk is synthetic D_2.

All evidence indicates that synthetic vitamin D_2 and natural D_3 are equally potent. According to the Food and Nutrition Board of the National Academy of Sciences,[10] for example, both are equally potent in preventing rickets (a vitamin D deficiency disease) in children.

"Natural" advocates also claim that D_3 is also less toxic than the synthetic D_2, but there is no scientific evidence to support this view. In fact animal experiments in rats, monkeys and pigs suggest just the opposite.[11,12]

Dr. Carl J. Reich, a practicing physician who advocates megavitamin therapy, claims that although long-term use of 20,000 IU of D_2 (400 times the RDA) can cause calcium deposits in the kidneys, this does not happen if natural D_3 is used.[13] But Professor Hector DeLuca of the University of Wisconsin, an internationally recognized authority on vitamin

D, disagrees: "Dr. Reich's experience is clinical . . . I believe he does not have sufficient evidence of a controlled nature."[11]

"Our Depleted Soils Produce Inferior Foodstuffs." Right?

Wrong! Our soils ar not "depleted." This is just propaganda from those who want you to buy vitamins and "organic" foods. Home gardeners who do not analyze their soil for many years (especially for iron and phosphorus) might develop problems with soil deficiency. But commercial farmers cannot afford to allow their soils to become deficient! The American Medical Association Council on Foods and Nutrition[14] sums up the situation this way:

> Soils on which crops are grown in this country are analyzed frequently and are adequately fertilized to prevent nutritional depletion. No disease or abnormality in man, except endemic goiter due to a deficiency of iodine, has been traced to deficiency in soil.

If any nutrient needed by a plant is absent from the soil, the plant just will not grow. If any nutrient is present but in short supply, the crop yield will be less per acre and the plants produced may be smaller—but they will have normal levels of vitamins. (Levels of a few minerals may be decreased if the soil is deficient, but this is of no significance for people who eat properly.)

Ronald Deutsch[15] aptly explains why it is logical to believe that the nutrient content of fruits and vegetables is primarily determined by heredity. A carrot does not make vitamin A precursor (building block) "as a generous gesture to humans, it produces the stuff for its own growth and survival. Likewise an orange makes vitamin C for its own benefit and wheat makes thiamin for its own health."

Are "Organic" Fertilizers Superior to "Chemical" Fertilizers?

The U.S. Plant, Soil and Nutrition Laboratories at Cornell University and similar prestigious facilities have compared food plants grown on soil fertilized with manure or humus with plants grown on acres treated for years only with manufactured fertilizers. Analysis of the foods showed that their nutrient content is the same. This is not at all surprising because plants do not actually get nourished by organic molecules. Organic fertilizer must first be broken down by soil bacteria into simple nitrates, ammonia and phosphates— the same inorganic chemicals found in chemical fertilizers.

In case some of the chemical facts mentioned in this chapter sound complicated or confusing, don't struggle too hard to understand them. Just remember that your body doesn't much care whether the nutrients it gets are labeled "natural," "organic," or anything else. If it gets enough—as most of our bodies do from our food—it will do just fine. It is not necessary to become a biochemist in order to achieve good nutrition—any more than you need to become a mechanic in order to become a good driver. If you eat properly, your body's chemistry will automatically do the rest.

References

1. NTIS Publication #PB-210978: A Study of Health Practices and Opinions. Springfield, VA, National Technical Information Service, U.S. Dept. of Commerce, 1972.
2. Tracey, M.: Human Nutrition. Nutrition Today 13:13, Nov./Dec., 1978.
3. Herbert, V. and Barrett, S.: Vitamins and "Health" Foods: The Great American Hustle. Philadelphia, George F. Stickley Co., 1981, p. 6.
4. Herbert, V.: Nutrition Cultism. Philadelphia, George F. Stickley Co., 1981, p. 125.
5. Deutsch, R.: Realities of Nutrition. Palo Alto, CA, Bull Publishing Co., 1976, p. 253.
6. King, C. G.: Interview in *House and Garden* magazine, July, 1971, p. 5.
7. Kamil, A.: Nutrition Reviews, Vol. 32, Suppl. No. 1, p. 34, July, 1974.
8. Bieri, J.: Personal communication to author, July 9, 1980.
9. Wald, G.: *In* The Vitamins, Vol. I, (W. H. Sebrell and R. S. Harris, Eds.). New York, Academic Press, 1954.
10. Food and Nutrition Board: Recommended Dietary Allowances, 8th Ed. Washington, D.C., National Academy of Sciences, 1974.
11. DeLuca, H.: Personal communication to author, July 9, 1980.
12. Hayes, K. C. and Hegsted, M.: Toxicity of Vitamins, Chapter 11 *in* Toxicants Occurring Naturally in Foods, 2nd Ed. Washington, D.C., National Academy of Sciences, 1973.
13. Reich, C.: Toxicity of Vitamin A & D Questioned. Letter to the Editor, Nutrition Today 15:36, March/April, 1980.
14. AMA Council on Foods and Nutrition: JAMA 218:397, 1971.
15. Deutsch, R.: Family Guide to Better Food and Better Health. Des Moines, IA, Meredith Corp., 1971, p. 163.

5

What Is A Vitamin?

*Diseases like rickets and scurvy are very likely
caused by a lack in the diet of very tiny,
even trace amounts, of "accessory food factors."*

The above statement was made by English biochemist and nutrition pioneer Frederick Hopkins in a lecture in London in 1906. It was the very first proposal of the basic concept of vitamins. Six years later, Casimir Funk, a Polish biochemist working in England, suggested the name "vitamine" for all such accessory food factors. Funk had noted that crude extracts of rice hulls which cured the disease beriberi contain a chemical grouping chemists call an "amine." His term was derived by combining the Latin *vita-* ("necessary for life") with the word "amine." Later, when it was found that some vitamines were not amines, the "e" was dropped to make "vitamin."

By 1912, none of the vitamins had yet been chemically isolated in pure form. But their presence was increasingly suspected from evidence that lack of "accessory food factors" was responsible for the dreaded disorders, scurvy, rickets and beriberi. Between 1912 and 1937, a span of only 25 years, painstaking research into such deficiency diseases uncovered all but one of the vitamins now known. (B_{12} was found in 1948.) Later in this book we describe the discovery of each vitamin and the diseases caused by its lack.

Key Definitions

A *vitamin* is an organic (carbon-containing) substance required in tiny amounts to promote one or more specific and essential biochemical reactions within the living cell. For the definition to fit, lack of the substance for a prolonged period of time must cause a specific deficiency disease which is quickly cured when the substance is resupplied.

27

A *catalyst* is a substance that initiates or speeds up a chemical reaction but remains unchanged while performing its task many times.

An *enzyme* is a protein substance that acts as a catalyst for one or more specific biochemical reactions essential for life and health.

An *apoenzyme* is a protein which is almost an enzyme but has a missing part.

A *coenzyme* is the "missing" non-protein part that combines with the apoenzyme to form a complete enzyme. A good way to visualize this is to think of the enzyme's protein part (the apoenzyme) as a key which cannot turn a lock or a power switch because one of its teeth (the coenzyme) is missing.

Important Vitamin Facts

There are 13 known vitamins for humans. Four are fat-soluble (A, D, E and K) and nine are water-soluble (C and the eight "B-complex" vitamins: thiamin, riboflavin, niacin, B_6, pantothenic acid, B_{12}, biotin and folic acid).

All vitamins are catalysts, and in normal dosage, most of them act as coenzymes. This means that they usually do not get used up by the reactions they promote—which explains why they are required in only tiny amounts.

Vitamins, unlike fats, proteins or carbohydrates (and alcohol), have no caloric value—and supply no energy to the body.

Most vitamins must be obtained from food because the human body cannot manufacture them. A few vitamins, however, are made by the body, but not in adequate amounts. Vitamin D is supplied in part by the action of sunlight on a cholesterol derivative in the skin. Humans can obtain a small fraction of their niacin needs by the body's conversion of the amino acid, tryptophan. Most humans get most or nearly all of their needed vitamin K from that made in their intestinal tract by beneficial bacteria which also usually make part of the biotin and pantothenic acid that we need.

What Happens to Vitamins in Your Body?

After absorption, each vitamin is distributed to its target tissues and enters cells which need it. Any surplus is first used to maintain the optimum (ideal) level in the circulating blood serum, and the rest is either excreted or stored. The B-vitamins have no large storage sites, and vitamin C is stored in modest amounts in the white blood cells and blood platelets. Only the fat-soluble vitamins are stored in substantial amounts. Excess vitamin A is stored in the liver to a maximum reserve of 500,000 IU; excess vitamin D is stored in the liver; vitamin E is stored in the fatty tissues with a normal body pool of about 5,000 IU; and vitamin K has limited storage in the liver. Excess water-soluble vitamins are excreted in the urine along with their chemical breakdown products, but none of the fat-soluble ones is excreted intact. These must be broken down by complex chemical reactions before their end products are excreted in urine or bile.

Can you tell if you are vitamin deficient? Not likely! Some vitamin deficiency states may be a diagnostic challenge even for experienced physicians. Most symptoms found in vitamin deficiency are also found in other disorders. For example, tender and bleeding gums, which are a sign of scurvy, are also found in gum disease (periodontal disease) due to chronic infection. It certainly would be unfortunate if you let a friend or health food store clerk persuade you to load up on vitamin C instead of getting professional help to prevent loss of your teeth from continued infection.

What Quantities of Vitamins Do Experts Recommend?

The main guidelines used by nutritionists are called "Recommended Dietary Allowances (RDAs)." These are the recommendations of a panel of scientific experts called the Food and Nutrition Board (FNB) of the National Research Council, a subdivision of the National Academy of Sciences. RDAs are defined as:

> the levels of intake of essential nutrients considered, in the judgment of the Committee on Dietary Allowances of the Food and Nutrition Board on the basis of available scientific knowledge, to be adequate to meet the known nutritional needs of practically all healthy persons.[1]

It is important to note that RDAs are *average* daily amounts, not *minimum daily requirements,* and are deliberately set to exceed the estimated requirements of most individuals. Note too that the RDAs are guidelines for healthy population groups. Such problems as premature birth, inherited metabolic disorders, infections, chronic diseases, and the use of medications, may require special dietary and therapeutic measures. These situations, which are discussed in Chapter 21, are not covered by the RDAs.

The first set of RDAs was published in 1943 at the request of the U.S. government for help with nutritional preparedness during World War II. Revisions incorporating results of newly acquired scientific data have been published every four or five years, the latest being the 9th edition in 1980. Current RDAs are listed in Appendix B.

How Are the RDAs Determined?

Dr. Alfred Harper,[2] chairman of the group that produced the 8th edition of the RDA, has pointed out that the RDA Committee considers several types of data:

1) Evidence is gathered on how human dietary requirements may change with age and changes in body physiology. Included for consideration are experiments, by many research groups, on human volunteers to determine how low the intake of a vitamin may be before the first symptom of deficiency or related abnormality appears.

2) Average requirements are estimated and a safety factor is added to allow for individual variability.

3) Allowances are made for incomplete absorption of some nutrients.

4) Other special circumstances are considered.

RDAs do not allow for the nutrients that might or might not be lost during food processing, cooking or other types of food preparation. This means that you cannot take the values from a list of the vitamin content in raw foods and expect it to be what you get after storing and cooking the food. Rather, RDAs are the average daily amounts which should be present in your foods as actually eaten.

U.S. RDAs

"U.S. RDAs" are a slightly simpler system of nutrient measurement developed by the U.S. Food and Drug Administration for reporting nutrient content on food labels. U.S. RDAs generally represent the highest level of the RDA for each nutrient in each life-cycle category of the RDA table (see Appendix B). The current U.S. RDAs are based on the 1968 RDAs rather than the 1980 values; but they are still a useful guide to the nutrient contents of foods.

Estimated Safe and Adequate Intakes

Traditionally, RDAs have been established for essential nutrients only when sufficient data were available to make specific recommendations for the various age and sex groups included in the RDA table. In 1980, the Food and Nutrition Board established "estimated safe and adequate intakes" for three vitamins (vitamin K, pantothenic acid and biotin), six trace minerals (copper, chromium, fluoride, manganese, molybdenum and selenium), and the electrolytes, sodium, potassium and chloride. The data upon which these suggested intakes are based are less complete than those for nutrients for which the RDAs are established. For this reason, they are presented as ranges of intake rather than single values for the various age-group categories.

A Two-Edged Sword

The discovery of vitamins—substances which in tiny amounts work wonders in our bodies—was a wonderful scientific achievement which certainly can benefit our health. But it has also provided promoters of quackery with new opportunities. In the next chapter, we discuss how calling something a "vitamin" can help boost its sales.

References

1. Food and Nutrition Board: Recommended Dietary Allowances, 9th Ed., 1980, p. 1.
2. Harper, A.: Nutrition Today, March/April, 1974, p. 15.

6

Non-Vitamins and Phony Vitamins

Science does not progress in a straight line. Many ideas which appear reasonable are discarded as new evidence shows them to be incorrect. As nutrition developed, some substances were discovered which appeared to have vitamin activity for some organisms—but were later judged not to be essential nutrients for man. Food faddists still promote some of them as "vitamins" or "miracle drugs." In this chapter, we classify them as "non-vitamins."

There are also some substances promoted as "vitamins" for which no vitamin activity has ever been claimed or even suspected by respectable nutrition scientists. Since their "vitamin" labeling is strictly a sales gimmick, we call them "phony vitamins."

NON-VITAMINS

Carnitine—"Vitamin B_T"

In 1948, Fraenkel[1] found that the mealworm (*Tenebrio molitor*) required a then unknown substance to live, a substance Fraenkel found in yeast. He named this substance vitamin B_T (T=Tenebrio). Today its chemical name is carnitine, from the Latin word, *carnis,* meaning flesh (muscle). Carnitine is abundant in animal and human muscle tissues, and the human body can make it from the amino acid lysine. We know that it is involved with fat metabolism and special fat synthesis in muscle cells. But it is *not* a dietary essential and has no rational use as a supplement for adult humans. Evidence exists that premature or very young infants may have limited ability to synthesize carnitine, but a diet appropriate for their age will supply the amount needed.

Bioflavonoids—"Vitamin P"

Bioflavonoids are being touted as essential for good health and resistance to colds and flu. But they fail all the tests of being vitamins for humans.

In 1936, the world-renowned biochemist and co-discoverer of vitamin C, Dr. Albert Szent-Gyorgyi, reported that extracts of lemons and red peppers seemed to have an increased anti-scurvy effect when added to vitamin C supplements for guinea pigs. He suggested that some substances in the extracts might be acting to decrease excessive capillary bleeding in animals suffering from scurvy. The substances were later identified as a mixture of flavones and flavonols, and the mixture is now called bioflavonoids. However, research by others has shown that they do not do what Szent-Gyorgyi proposed.

For a short time, the mixture was classified as "vitamin P," but this name was withdrawn when later evidence showed that it is not essential in humans.[1] Some tests[2,3] of vitamin C against the common cold have also found bioflavonoids to be of no value in prevention or treatment—either alone or combined with vitamin C. Nor have bioflavonoids been found useful in humans for the treatment of any other condition.[4]

Choline and Lecithin

Choline is a vitamin for some animals, but according to the Food and Nutrition Board,[5] the human body can readily make sufficient choline. It is therefore not classified as a vitamin for humans. Choline is abundant in foodstuffs and is a basic part of the structure of lecithins and other phospholipids. Choline can also be converted in the body to acetylcholine, a vital controller of nerve impulses. However, it has never been shown to be associated with a specific deficiency disease in humans.

Use of choline to improve the failing memory of older persons was suggested many years ago, but no acceptable evidence has been offered to support this idea. A study done on eight elderly volunteers (ages 64 to 86 years) was reported in 1979 by Dr. Kenneth Davis[6] of the Veterans Administration Hospital, in Palo Alto, California. His research team found no improvement in memory during a period when choline supplements were given.

None of the several varieties of lecithins is classified as a vitamin for humans because the human body can make them. "Health food" industry spokesmen claim that lecithin supplements "keep blood cholesterol in solution" and prevent it from forming deposits on the walls of arteries. But there is no scientific evidence to support this claim.

Para-aminobenzoic Acid (PABA)

This substance is simply a small structural part of the B-vitamin, folic acid. It is a vitamin for bacteria, but *not for humans*. This means, according to Dr. Victor Herbert,[7] that it could actually worsen bacterial infections in some people by helping the bacteria to grow!

34

Inositol and Rutin

Inositol is quite abundant in foodstuffs, the average human daily intake being about 1,000 mg. It is not a vitamin for humans since the body is able to make it when needed. Most animals can also make inositol within their bodies. Rutin, chemically related to the bioflavonoids, is also a non-vitamin for humans. It is illegal for supplements to be labeled with any nutritional claims for inositol, rutin or bioflavonoids.[8]

"Vitamins" Q and U

So-called "Vitamin Q" is a substance isolated in 1972 by Dr. Armand Quick and claimed to be an aid in blood clotting. However, it is not recognized as a vitamin for humans.

"Vitamin U," also known as metanoic acid, was reported as having been isolated from dairy products by a Russian scientist, and claims were made that it could cure ulcers. But there is no evidence that it is essential to humans and therefore it, too, is not a vitamin.

Miscellaneous Substances

The 1980 edition of the RDA book[5] lists a number of other substances in food which may benefit experimental animals but for which no evidence exists that they are required in the human diet. The substances include linoleic and arachnodonic acids and taurine (required for cats), and myoinositol (required for gerbils and some species of fish). The book also lists some other substances known to be growth factors for lower forms of life but not required in the diets of higher animals (vertebrates) or humans. These substances include asparagine, Bifidus factor, biopterin, chelating agents, cholesterol, coenzyme Q (ubiquinones), hematin, lipoic acid (thioctic acid), nerve-growth factors, nucleotides and nucleic acids, various peptides and proteins, pimelic acid, various polyamines, and pteridines (other than folic acid). No essential nutrient function for two other substances, chlorophyll and orotic acid, has ever been reported in reliable scientific literature.

Will More Vitamins Be Found?

In *Realities of Nutrition,* science writer Ronald Deutsch urges you to place no stock in claims that substances like those discussed above are essential to your diet:

> *One thing is certain*: the health-food maker or eccentric healer is not able to identify vitamin needs which the nation's major universities, clinics and

laboratories cannot confirm. The scientific demand for hard evidence is not, as some claim, due to cronyism, a passion for some form of exclusivity; it is born of a responsibility that must insist on reality.

In *Vitamins and "Health" Foods: The Great American Hustle,* Dr. Victor Herbert presents a convincing argument that no more vitamins will be found:

The last one was discovered in 1948, and three decades of intensive research have not uncovered any more. Moreover, patients have now lived for many years on just intravenous solutions which contain the known nutrients. If there were an undiscovered vitamin, these patients would have shown evidence of a deficiency disease.

PHONY VITAMINS

Laetrile ("Vitamin B$_{17}$")

Every three or four months I see a woman with an advanced and usually inoperable breast cancer that has been present for months or years while the patient was receiving no treatment except laetrile. I note no tendency for the frequency of such cases to diminish.

—Dr. George Crile[9]

This tragic statement from a longtime breast cancer specialist at the famous Cleveland Clinic illustrates quackery's greatest danger—that of luring cancer patients away from treatment that could have cured them or prolonged their lives. Writing in *The Health Robbers,* two American Cancer Society officials[10] summarize the problem this way:

Cancer quackery is big business, with an estimated yearly income in the billions. It is also cruel business, for its customers come in desperate fear. Those customers who come while undergoing good medical care will buy only empty promises. But those who delay or abandon medicine's best, will purchase death.

Laetrile's History

Laetrile was extracted from apricot pits in the 1940s by E. T. Krebs, Sr., a California physician, but the substance had been known to chemists for over 100 years. Krebs, who was associated with the promotion of a number of other questionable remedies, came across laetrile while searching for a way to improve the flavor of bootleg whiskey. Laetrile's chief ingredient is mandelonitrile-glucosido-glucoside, a substance which breaks down in the intestines to give off cyanide. Krebs trademarked his extracted substance, "amygdalin."

During the 1950s, Krebs and his son Ernst, Jr., began to promote amygdalin, first as "Laetrile" and later as "vitamin B_{17}." They speculated 1) that laetrile might attack cancer cells, but not normal cells, if cancer cells contain more of an enzyme capable of splitting off cyanide within them; and 2) that normal cells could detoxify cyanide faster than cancer cells. Neither of these events actually takes place, but laetrile promoters soon claimed that the Krebs' speculations were facts.

Despite the fact that laetrile has been known, tested and used for more than 25 years, there is no scientific evidence that it has any actual or potential value in the management of cancer. Nor does amygdalin meet the criteria for being a vitamin for humans. Millions of people have lived long, healthy lives without ever getting even 1 mg of amygdalin. Eliminating it from the diet of humans for a year—or for 10 years—would not produce a deficiency disease.

If you are interested in further details of the laetrile story, be sure to read *Laetrile: The Political Success of a Scientific Failure* in the August, 1977 *Consumer Reports,* and *Laetrile: The Making of a Myth* in the December 1976-January 1977 issue of *FDA Consumer.* A third article, *Laetrile: The Fatal Cure,* in the October 1977 *FDA Consumer,* tells of two women, one with breast cancer and the other with uterine cancer. Both had a good chance of recovery with surgery, but chose laetrile instead— and were dead within nine months.

The Sad Case of Chad

Nutrition Cultism, a 1980 book by Dr. Victor Herbert, describes in much more detail the deceptive ways that laetrile is promoted. The book also provides case histories of several laetrile victims, some hurt by using laetrile and some poisoned by eating crushed apricot kernels. One of the saddest cases is that of Chad Green. In 1978, at the age of three, Chad was receiving the latest medically approved chemotherapy for childhood leukemia at Massachusetts General Hospital. The first series of treatments put Chad into remission (which means that the cancer was stopped, but not cured). Before the next treatment series was to start, however, Chad's parents embraced the laetrile cult and informed the hospital that Chad would not return. Within a few weeks. Chad's leukemia relapsed into the active state. The doctors notified state authorities who took Chad under legal custody and ordered him to be returned to the hospital. A second series of chemotherapy treatments again produced a remission.

During the hospital stay, however, the doctors were horrified to learn that for about three months, Chad's parents had been treating him daily with laetrile, 45,000 units of "emulsified vitamin A," and enemas containing digestive enzymes (which could damage Chad's intestines). Checking Chad's blood, they found that its vitamin A level was 10 times normal and that its cyanide and cyanate levels were in the toxic range. Elevation of an enzyme in the blood (SGOT) indicated that liver damage was taking place. The doctors also noted that the treatment given to Chad by his parents had caused him to suffer irritability, insomnia and abdominal distress.

Even when told of these facts, Chad's parents had such faith in their "nutritional and metabolic therapy" that they kept the child home and continued to administer it. In January 1979, Judge Guy Volterra ordered the parents to stop home "treatment" and to return Chad to the hospital. But they took him instead to the laetrile clinic of Dr. Ernesto Contreras in Tijuana, Mexico, where he died nine months later.

The Federal Court Struggle

Because no proof exists that laetrile helps cancer patients, it is illegal to import it into the United States or to market it in interstate commerce. But several years ago, a confused judge (Luther Bohannon) of the U.S. District Court in Oklahoma ordered the FDA to stop interfering with the importation of laetrile for cancer patients classified as "terminal." He ruled that their "constitutional rights" should prevail over the FDA law requiring proof of safety and effectiveness before a drug can be marketed. Judge Bohannon also set up a system whereby anyone with an affidavit from a physician can legally import a six-month supply of laetrile for personal use.

The FDA, of course, appealed the case. The Federal Appeals Court upheld the lower court, reasoning that "safety and effectiveness" have no reasonable application to "terminal patients." But in June 1979, the U.S. Supreme Court disagreed. Recognizing that there is no way that patients can accurately be judged as "terminal," the Supreme Court ruled that individuals with fatal illnesses, such as cancer, still deserve protection from fraudulent cures. Unfortunately, the affidavit system set up by Judge Bohannon will continue in operation until a number of other issues in this case finish winding their way through the courts.

A Decisive Test

In response to political pressure, laetrile was recently tested in humans at the Mayo Clinic and three other major cancer centers under sponsorship of the National Cancer Institute. According to Dr. Charles Moertel[11] of the Mayo Clinic's Cancer Center, the laetrile used was amygdalin derived from apricot pits, but identical in chemical structure to that of the major Mexican producer, and was given in the manner and dosage levels used by "laetrile practitioners."

One hundred seventy-eight patients were treated with laetrile plus a "metabolic therapy" program consisting of diet, enzymes and vitamins. All of these patients had cancers for which no standard treatment was known, but the great majority of these patients were still in good general condition. None was totally disabled, and one third had not received any previous chemotherapy.

Laetrile failed miserably in this test. Not one patient was cured or even stabilized, and none had any lessening of cancer-related symptoms. Several patients experienced symptoms of cyanide toxicity or had blood levels of cyanide approaching the lethal range. Dr. Arnold S. Relman,[12] editor of *The New England Journal of Medicine,* commented on these results as follows:

> Laetrile, I believe, has had its day in court. The evidence, beyond reasonable doubt, is that it doesn't benefit patients with advanced cancer, and there is no reason to believe that it would be any more effective in the earlier stages of the disease. Some undoubtedly will remain unconvinced, but no sensible person will want to advocate its further use and no state legislature should sanction it any longer. The time has come to close the books on laetrile and get on with our efforts to understand the riddle of cancer and improve its prevention and treatment.

Pangamic Acid ("Vitamin B$_{15}$")

In 1949, a U.S. Patent was issued to Dr. E. T. Krebs and his son for another substance extracted from apricot kernels which they named "pangamic acid." This name was chosen because the Krebs' thought it was present in all seeds (which it is not)—*pan* means universal, and *gamy* means seed or reproduction. Later they obtained a U.S. trademark for the name "vitamin B$_{15}$." In May 1978, the FDA[13] stated its position:

> The FDA considers "vitamin B$_{15}$" to be a food additive for which no evidence of safety has been offered. It therefore is illegal for the substance to be sold as a dietary supplement. No new drug application for pangamic acid has been submitted or approved by the FDA, and the substance cannot be legally marketed as a drug.

The FDA's position has been upheld in three federal court cases, but B$_{15}$ continues to be marketed in some "health food" stores along with books which claim falsely that it can help a wide variety of conditions including heart disease, aging, fatigue, diabetes, cancer, glaucoma, schizophrenia, allergies, breathing problems and inflammation of the liver. Some proponents even claim that B$_{15}$ is recognized as a vitamin in several countries whose scientists have set Recommended Dietary Allowances for it, but this claim is also untrue.

In a lengthy review of this matter, Dr. Herbert[14] points out that the Krebs' promoted pangamic acid only for horses in the 1950s, and that little public attention was paid to it until Krebs, Jr.'s stepson, P. W. Stacpoole, succeeded in getting a long article published in a second-rate scientific journal after the *American Journal of Clinical Nutrition* had rejected the article as scientifically unworthy. Stacpoole's article retold a large number of anecdotal reports, mainly from Russian sources, of people supposedly helped by pangamic acid. Probably inspired by the article, *New York* magazine issued a cover story suggesting it as a cure for just about everything. Almost overnight, the magazine later reported, "It became impossible to find the product on any dealer's shelf in the metropolitan area for a full week."

Of course, the fact that B_{15} is neither a vitamin nor a nutrient was not made clear to the magazine's readers. Nor was the fact that "pangamate" is not a single substance, but a variety of substances, one of which, Dr. Herbert believes,[15] may actually cause cancer!

References

1. Weininger, J. and Briggs, G., *in* Modern Nutrition in Health and Disease, 6th Ed. (R. Goodhart and M. Shils, Eds.) Philadelphia, Lea & Febiger, 1980, pp. 279-281.
2. Tebrock et al.: JAMA 162:1227, 1956.
3. Franz et al.: JAMA 162:1224, 1956.
4. Consumer Reports: The Medicine Show. Mount Vernon, New York, Consumers Union, 1974.
5. Food and Nutrition Board: Recommended Dietary Allowances, 9th Ed., 1980.
6. Davis, K.: American Journal of Psychiatry, Oct., 1979; cited in Science News 116:264, Oct. 20, 1979.
7. Herbert, V. and Barrett, S.: Vitamins and "Health" Foods: The Great American Hustle, Philadelphia, George F. Stickley Co., 1981, p. 15.
8. FDA Drug Bulletin, Dec., 1973.
9. Crile, G., quoted in Science 193:982-985, 1976.
10. Wood, G. and Presley, B.: The Cruellest Killers. *In* The Health Robbers (S. Barrett, Ed.). Philadelphia, George F. Stickley Co., 1980.
11. Moertel, C. et al.: New England Journal of Medicine 306:201-206, 1982.
12. Relman, A.: *Ibid.,** p. 236.
13. FDA Consumer, May, 1978, p. 28.
14. Herbert, V.: Nutrition Cultism. Philadelphia, George F. Stickley Co., 1980, pp. 107-118.
15. Herbert, V.: *Ibid.,* pp. 119-120.

Ibid., for *Ibidem* (Latin for "in the same place") refers to the reference work cited just above.

7

Vitamin A Can Help or Harm

The nutritional cure for night blindness—one of the earliest symptoms of vitamin A deficiency—has been known for thousands of years. Eber's Papyrus, an ancient Egyptian medical treatise of about 1,500 B.C., recommends eating roast ox liver or the liver of black cocks to cure night blindness.[1] The famous Greek philosopher Hippocrates prescribed raw ox liver as its cure. As recently as 1955, "medicine men" in Central Africa were observed using chicken liver for the same purpose.

Of course, neither the ancients nor the modern medicine men knew what ingredient in liver did the curing. Now we know that some animal livers contain 15,000 IU of vitamin A per ounce and are second only to fish livers in being the richest natural source of this vitamin. (In comparison, a cup of whole milk contains about 300 IU of vitamin A.) Fish liver, which can contain more than 500,000 IU per ounce, is so rich that it has caused severe poisoning.

Mysterious cases of poisoning among Arctic explorers who ate polar bear liver began being reported almost 400 years ago.[2] Each account describes toxic symptoms that began a few hours after eating 4 to 8 ounces of cooked polar bear liver. The victims become drowsy, then irritable, and finally cried out with severe headache and vomiting. The next day their face, hands and/or feet became red and swollen. Within a few days, the skin in these areas began to peel off in sheets. The men recovered in 8 to 10 days. It was not until 1943 that the mystery of these poisonous reactions was solved when researchers[3] found that polar bear liver contains the astounding vitamin A content of 350,000 to 500,000 IU per ounce. Thus some hungry Arctic explorers actually consumed *millions* of units at a single sitting!

As recently as 1970, Dutch doctors[3] reported a violent illness which struck 11 fishermen who had eaten between one and ten ounces of fried halibut liver. Five hours later, all 11 got sick, most having the symptoms described above. The sailor who ate ten ounces received at least ten million units of vitamin A.

How Vitamin A Was Discovered

Recognition of the substance that was later named vitamin A stemmed from a 1912 report by Sir Frederick Hopkins, the renowned biochemist who subsequently received a Nobel Prize for this work. Professor Hopkins determined that something present in small amounts in milk was required for growth by rats. He first called it "milk factor." During the next three years, Dr. Elmer McCollum and his team of researchers at the University of Wisconsin identified "milk factor" in butter, egg yolk and cod liver oil and its name was changed to "fat-soluble A." In 1920, Dr. J. C. Drummond proposed that the names of "accessory food factors" be simplified by employing Funk's term "vitamine" without the final "e" and adding the letters A, B, C, etc., as other vitamins were found in the future. In 1930, it was discovered that compounds called carotenes, found in vegetables and similar in structure to vitamin A, are converted in our body to vitamin A.[4] The chemical structure of vitamin A was established in 1931, and it was synthesized in pure form in 1947. Its current scientific name is "retinol."

The pioneer discoveries of Hopkins and McCollum were made by studying and varying animal diets. The earliest modern medical report of human vitamin A deficiency disease, called "hypovitaminosis-A" or "avitaminosis-A," probably was that of Dr. C. E. Bloch, Professor of Pediatrics, University of Copenhagen, Denmark. Between 1910 and 1920, Dr. Bloch made extensive studies of Danish children. Among them were many who had impaired growth and xerophthalmia (a severe disease of the eye which can lead to blindness). Suddenly in 1917, these cases began to clear up quickly. Why?

Dr. Bloch, who had long suspected that xerophthalmia was related to nutrition, soon deduced the correct answer. In December 1917 the Danish government had begun to ration butter. Every Dane was to receive one-half pound per week. Prior to that time, butter was a prized export. Most families could not afford to buy it, so they ate lard or margarine (made from imported oils) instead. Nobody knew at the time that these fats contained no more than slight traces of Vitamin A.

When German submarines blockaded Danish ports in 1917, butter could no longer be exported and the cheaper, less nutritious oils could not be imported. So the Danes got to eat the butter themselves. Professor Bloch conducted further experiments to search for "fat-soluble A" and published his findings[5] in the United States in 1924.

What Does Vitamin A Do For Us?

Vitamin A plays many important roles in human health and bodily function. It is needed as a coenzyme in at least six essential enzyme systems.[6] It helps maintain the health of the skin and all inner linings of the body (the epithelial tissues which line the stomach, intestines, bladder, nose, mouth, throat, windpipe and other air passageways). Vitamin A is essential for vision and the integrity of some parts of the eye's structure. It is converted within the body from retinol (an alcohol) to retinal (an aldehyde) which then forms several light-sensitive pigments essential to the eye's retina (the back part of the eye that receives the image).

Vitamin A aids in the resistance to infections. It is essential for proper development of bones; and is needed for proper sperm formation in men and maintenance of a healthy fetus in women. Vitamin A is also involved in the adrenal cortex wherein the vital cortisone-type hormones are manufactured.

Food Sources of Vitamin A

Vitamin A is found as the preformed vitamin (retinol) almost exclusively in animal and fish products, the richest sources being livers. (But beware of fish livers, which may contain too much!) The next best sources of retinol are whole milk, butter, cheese and margarine (which nowadays is always fortified). Most seafoods contain lesser amounts.

Vitamin A is also obtained indirectly from the carotenoids (called pro-vitamin A) in most vegetables and some fruits. Carotenoid pigments, which are typically red, orange or yellow, are widely distributed in plant tissues, but some of them have no vitamin A activity. Beta-carotene, the most important provitamin A, is converted in the human body to vitamin A with about a 40 to 50 percent yield. Among the richest sources of beta-carotene are carrots, spinach and turnip greens and palm oil. The next best include dark yellow squashes, pumpkin, sweet potatoes, tomatoes, broccoli and beet greens. Lesser sources of carotenoids include most fruits, summer squash, zucchini squash, beans, cabbage, corn, peas and many kinds of nuts. Most Americans get about half of their vitamin A as retinol and the rest as beta-carotene.

How Much Vitamin A Do We Need?

The U.S. RDA for vitamin A is 5,000 International Units (IU). The Food and Nutrition Board's Recommended Dietary Allowance (RDA) for vitamin A, as listed in the 9th (1980) edition of its guide, is 800 Retinol Equivalents (RE) for adult women and 1,000 for men. A "Retinol Equivalent" is the same as 5 of the old International Units. RDAs for infants, children, pregnant women and lactating women, are listed in Appendix B.

Recent studies[7] on human volunteers have established that the minimum daily dosage to keep adults free of all deficiency symptoms and to maintain adequate blood levels of vitamin A is 1,650 to 2,000 IU. At a daily usage rate of 2,000 IU of vitamin A and a liver storage of 400,000 to 500,000 IU, a well-nourished adult who received no vitamin A would take 100 days to use up half the reserve. Any amount of vitamin A ingested over what we need will be stored by the liver which releases a constant amount for use by the body tissues. When so much vitamin A is taken that it builds up beyond the liver's storage capacity, the excess spills into the blood in an unregulated way and becomes poisonous to the tissues.

Nutrition scientists have spent a great deal of effort for many years to develop reasonable and prudent recommended dietary allowances for vitamins. But a few scientists and hordes of pseudoscientists still urge the public to consume vitamin A at many times the RDA. Linus Pauling suggests that many people may require as much as 25,000 IU of vitamin A daily—5 times the RDA for adult men. He implies that this dosage is harmless to all. However, it is not! Chronic vitamin A poisoning is noted in the medical literature at dosages of "only" 25,000 IU per day for several months.

Tumor-like Symptoms[8]

At age 30, Estelle M. developed high blood pressure and her doctors prescribed antihypertensive drugs to maintain her pressure within the normal range. Two years later another doctor told her to take 25,000 IU of vitamin A and 800 IU of vitamin E daily. She was supposed to check back with this doctor to see if these vitamins were still needed, but she never did so. After eight months on this regimen she began to have episodes of blurred vision which became worse over the next month. Then she was startled by occasional blinding flashes of light in her eyes. But she continued taking 25,000 units of vitamin A daily for three years.

Finally, unable to bear her frightening symptoms, Estelle entered a large university medical center where her blood pressure was found to be elevated despite faithful use of her medication. Examination of her eyes revealed swelling (papilledema) near both optic nerves and some bleeding at the back of the right eye. Her brain and spinal fluid pressure were abnormally high. These findings are suggestive of brain tumor, but fortunately for Estelle, her doctors made the correct diagnosis of chronic vitamin A poisoning. They persuaded her to stop her supplements and within five days her blood pressure returned to normal. It took six months for her eyes to return to normal.

Many "nutrition promoters" suggest that dosages of 25,000 are harmless and appropriate for the treatment of a wide variety of ailments. Estelle's case indicates that this is a treacherous belief! Some people who take 25,000 units of vitamin A (5 or 6 times the RDA) will build their body stores to toxic levels over a period of months.

Retarded Growth[9]

In 1951, when Bonnie S. was born, she weighed nearly seven pounds and was normal in every way except that one of the open seams (fontanels) in her developing skull seemed wider than normal to her doctor. At that time, doctors often prescribed extra vitamin D for a few weeks to increase bone growth in children. However, in addition to vitamin D, Bonnie was given fish liver oil rich in vitamin A as well as a multivitamin pill containing vitamins A, B, C, D and E. So little Bonnie received a daily total of 30,000 units of vitamin A and 3,000 units of vitamin D (7½ times the RDA).

When Bonnie was four months old, her doctor noticed that the abnormally wide fontanel was not closing on schedule. So for the next two months her daily vitamins were increased to 80,000 units of A and 11,000 of D. By six months, Bonnie became very irritable, lost her appetite and developed a swelling on the side of her right foot. More worrisome, her entire skull bone began to get soft and thin, a condition called craniotabes. Since vitamin D often corrects this condition in infants, her vitamin dosages were increased even further.

By age 6½ months, Bonnie was extremely irritable and cried out in great pain whenever she was touched or when she tried to move her arms or legs. When x-ray films revealed abnormal bone development, she was transferred to a large university hospital. There, Bonnie's bones were so painful that the nurses had to carry her around on a pillow.

Chronic vitamin A poisoning was suspected and confirmed by a blood test, and her vitamins were stopped. She became less irritable within a few days, her appetite improved within one week, and her skull soon became firmer. Sent home with a moderate dosage of vitamin D to help restore bone development, she improved markedly within the next two months. Follow-up examination at age 15 months showed no abnormalities. She was a healthy, happy child—finally.

Love or Child Abuse?[10]

When Jerry K. was nearly 2½ years old, he was living with his grandmother. He was an extremely active little fellow who would race and jump around the house, often knocking down furniture as he went by. So Grandma took Jerry to a doctor who believes in megavitamin therapy for children. A year later Jerry's "hyperactive" behavior became so bad that he was taken to a private clinic. Here a number of tests were run which showed everything normal except his liver function.

On his fourth birthday six months later, Jerry could scarcely enjoy his birthday party. He was extremely irritable, his legs hurt when he walked, and he cried out in agony when touched by the other children. Four months later his alarmed grandmother took him to a large university hospital. The staff there noted extreme irritability, arm and leg pain, deep sores at the corners of Jerry's mouth, a heart murmur and an enlarged liver. Liver enzymes were abnormally elevated and a bone scan revealed abnormal metabolism taking place in his bones.

These findings suggested to the doctors that excessive vitamin A intake could be the cause of Jerry's distress. They ordered a vitamin A blood analysis and found, to their astonishment, that his blood contained 20 times the normal amount. Jerry's grandmother denied giving the boy any vitamins, but one of the doctors happened to learn from Jerry's nursery school teachers that the grandmother owned a "health food" store and that Jerry brought a bottle of vitamin pills to school each day and ate them like candy.

Jerry was kept in the hospital for one month and allowed no vitamin supplements. His symptoms slowly disappeared as his vitamin A blood level fell. He was discharged to a foster home.

More Wasn't Better![11]

By the time David H. was 13 years old, he had read just about every book about flying aces of both World Wars and had seen several movies about aviation heroes. He decided that, most of all, he wanted to become an airline pilot. He had heard that good night vision was very important to pilots and that vitamin A was good for it. So he started moderately by taking a daily multivitamin containing the RDA of vitamin A. Then, worried that his night vision wasn't super enough, he started taking 25,000 units of Vitamin A plus 1,250 units of vitamin D. After 13 more months he upped his dosage to 50,000 or 100,000 units of Vitamin A a day. After 21 more months with no adverse effects, he raised his daily intake to 200,000 units.

One month later, shortly after his 16th birthday, he began to notice increasing muscle and joint tenderness which became so severe that he couldn't shake hands. Though he tried to hide his discomfort from others, his parents noted a marked change in his behavior and insisted that he enter a hospital to see what was wrong.

When first asked by the doctors whether he took any vitamins, David said "No." But when confronted with the fact that his x-ray films showed abnormal bone formation, he finally revealed what he had done. He was persuaded to stop his vitamin supplements, of course, and had an uneventful recovery during the next few months.

Laid Low by Liver[12]

Do you think it possible that a person could be harmed by eating two much of a wholesome food? Early in 1979, Mrs. L. became the proud mother of twin daughters, Lucy and Lois, and vowed she would provide them with the finest care. When they reached seven months of age, however, she became wracked with worry. Lucy had suffered three episodes of vomiting within two days and had become increasingly irritable. Examination by the doctor revealed that the soft spot on top of her head was bulging outward abnormally—indicating that the brain was under abnormal pressure. Further studies in the hospital indicated that her vitamin A blood level was four times normal. About a week later, her twin sister Lois was admitted to the hospital and found to have the same problem.

Mother was shocked and bewildered. How could this happen to her babies? She had prepared all her own baby foods to avoid "additives" she thought were present in commercially prepared baby foods. She had cooked and canned the babies' carrots and squash which the girls began eating at two months of age. At age three months, she began providing meat by using chicken liver. This seemed to be an ideal choice because it was easy to cook, homogenize and freeze. The girls were given two ounces each day for a few days, then 4⅓ ounces daily for four months because they liked it so much.

The twins' well-intentioned mother did not realize that just one ounce of chicken liver contains 2,800 IU of vitamin A, and thus for four months each twin had been getting 12,000 IU from the liver (plus 2,000 IU from fortified milk, 2,000 IU from a vitamin pill and smaller amounts from yellow vegetables). This totals at least 16,000 IU a day, more than seven times the RDA for infants. Fortunately, the twins' condition improved when their vitamin A intake was restored to normal.

Liver is a fine dietary source of many minerals and vitamins. However, because its vitamin A content is high, it is not prudent to eat too much of it. Infants receiving chicken liver should not eat it as the major meat in their diet. They should be at least 6 months old and have no more than two ounces weekly. Beef liver (15,000 IU of vitamin A per ounce) is nutritious, but should be limited to once-a-week for adults (less often for those with high cholesterol levels). Fish liver should not be eaten by humans because its vitamin A content varies from 200,000 to 1 million units, depending on the type of fish, its size, and the season of the year.

A Famous Case[13]

Franklie L. was born in the Spring of 1937 and at age two months was a rosy-cheeked infant bursting with good health. His devoted mother had read from many sources on child care and sought the advice of her pediatrician, but she was also an enthusiastic believer in vitamins. When Frankie was 2½ months old, she began giving him a teaspoon of halibut liver oil daily (containing about 40,000 units of vitamin A—much more than is in cod liver oil) despite the doctor's instruction to give not more than six drops. After all, she thought, what could be more wholesome and "natural" than vitamins and the oil of a fish?

By the time Frankie was six months old, he had developed an extravagant liking for fish liver oil and was occasionally allowed to drink directly from the bottle. His mother was happy that the boy liked something "obviously so good" for him. At age 14 months, however, Frankie's appetite began to fail and he gradually became too listless to play. At age 22 months, following a tonsillectomy, doctors noted that he was anemic, his liver and spleen were enlarged, the ends of his fingers had become club-shaped, and most of his hair had fallen out.

At age 30 months, because of continuing anemia and enlarged spleen, Franklie was brought to a respected medical center where the diagnosis of chronic vitamin A poisoning was made. Naturally his mother was advised to stop the fish liver oil, which she did, and the boy's health returned almost to normal during the next six months. (She noted, however, that for two months he developed a craving for butter and carrots, both sources of vitamin A.) A follow-up examination two years later indicated that Frankie's liver and spleen were still a little enlarged and his fingers were still slightly clubbed.

Frankie's case, published in 1944, is famous in the world of medicine because it is the first documented case of chronic vitamin A poisoning in a human. The first cases in human adults were not reported until ten years later.

A Case of Acute Poisoning[14]

In 1971 Wendy R. was living with her husband in a large city in South Africa. At age 28, she turned men's heads as she passed with her beautiful red hair and fair skin sprinkled with a few freckles. But she envied other women who had nice even brown suntans. A good tan might also hide some of her freckles, she thought—but her skin was so very sun-sensitive.

While working in the office of a medical school, Wendy heard that the doctors were planning a clinical trial of a new sunburn preventive. She obtained a bottle of the product and read its instructions to take two 25,000 unit vitamin tablets once a day for three days before exposure to the sun. If there was any real burning sensation after sunbathing, the label said, start taking two tablets every 30 minutes until the skin can be slapped without discomfort.

Wendy took two tablets daily for three days and then took a one hour sunbath. Four hours later, her skin began to burn, so she began taking 50,000 units every half-hour as instructed by the label. Since the burning pain prevented her from sleeping, she was able to continue this dosage faithfully until the next afternoon—ingesting a total of 1,300,000 units of vitamin A during a 27-hour period!

Her reward? Nausea, intense headache, dizziness so bad she could not stand up, uncontrollable eyeball movements (nystagmus), and severe blistering of the skin on her back and thighs. Doctors at the school, of course, quickly identified the problem as acute vitamin A poisoning. She recovered completely, but not before her skin peeled off in large sheets from most of her body and some of her beautiful red hair fell out.

The Carrot Juice Junkie

In 1968, Gerald G. was a nutrition officer in a government department in England. Vitamins were readily available to him through a government dispensary. Somehow he became convinced that daily supplements of vitamin A would relieve some of his minor ailments and prolong his life, so he began taking 50,000 to 100,000 units daily. In mid-1969, even though warned against it by dispensary personnel, he suddenly increased his dosage to more than 300,000 units daily. He then raised it gradually during the next three months to 5 *million* units a day—over 1,000 times the RDA—until severe symptoms of acute vitamin A poisoning, including widespread itching, forced him to seek medical care. During this final 3-month period, Gerald consumed an estimated 300 million units of vitamin A!

Medical examination revealed that his liver was hard and enlarged, and his blood vitamin A content was more than 30 times normal. His doctors warned him about the dangers of excessive vitamin A and cut off his access to vitamin A from the dispensary. But Gerald just could not believe that anything as "wholesome" as a vitamin could really have made him sick. After brooding a few days about the injustice of being disallowed his favorite vitamin, he persuaded his wife to prepare fresh carrot juice daily using a blender. He began drinking a quart of it daily, obtained from 2 to 3 pounds of blended carrots.

Over the next year, Gerald gradually increased his juice intake to one gallon per day. This meant that he was getting over 10,000 units of vitamin A daily and was accumulating excess amounts of carotenes in his body tissue. (The excess carotene turned his skin yellow—a condition called carotenemia.) After four years of this practice, he died of liver failure caused by vitamin A poisoning resulting primarily from his enormous earlier intake of the pure vitamin. At the time of his death, according to medical reports,[15,16] Gerald had severe scarring (cirrhosis) of his liver.

Gerald G. was only 48 when he died. His fanatical 6-year addiction to vitamin A surely sets some kind of record. That he survived such massive dosage as long as he did must stand as a testimonial to the magnificent capacity of the human body to adjust to extremes of nutrition abuse.

A Close Call

Scientists have long known that the amount of vitamin A supplied to the offspring is related to the mother's vitamin A intake during pregnancy. In rats, both excessive intake and deficiency of vitamin A in the mother can result in deformed offspring. The RDA provides for extra vitamin A during pregnancy (5,000 IU instead of 4,000). But some faddists have recommended more.

Louise R. may have been a victim of this advice.[17] Her mother, while pregnant, had made what she thought was every effort to eat right and follow all the "best" rules including advice in a new popular paperback book by Adelle Davis. Many of her female friends were so enthralled by this book that they talked of little else for several months.

For a few days after Louise's birth, pride and thankfulness filled the hearts of Louise's parents and grandparents. But at one month of age, the child became progressively listless and began to lose weight. A pediatrician who visited was startled to find a large bluish mass protruding from Louise's tiny vagina.

Into a large West Coast university medical clinic went Louise. There, extensive examination found that she had an extra urine-carrying tube (ureter) running from her left kidney to her vagina. Partial blockage of this tube had caused the left kidney to stop functioning. Fortunately, doctors were able to relieve the blockage and kidney function returned to normal three months later.

What had caused this problem? Louise's doctors were aware of a case reported in Italy[18] of a baby dying of similar complications and whose mother had taken large daily doses of vitamin A. They were also aware of reports of similarly deformed newborn animals born of females who, during pregnancy, had been fed huge doses of vitamin A by research workers. Questioning of Louise's mother revealed that she had taken 25,000 units of vitamin A daily during the first three months of pregnancy and 50,000 units thereafter. So Adelle Davis and vitamin A might well have been the culprits in Louise's close call with death.

How to Avoid Trouble with Vitamin A

All of these case reports indicate how dangerous large amounts of vitamin A can be. They also indicate the variety of ways in which people have been exposed to such large dosages. Arctic explorers have simply been unlucky victims of circumstance. Children have been hurt by the actions of well-meaning relatives who themselves had been misled by faddists. Teenagers and adults have overdosed themselves on the theory that "if some is good, more is better." In some of these cases, the diagnosis was made more difficult because the victim was either too embarrassed to admit making a mistake or had trouble believing that vitamins can be toxic in high dosages. Both children and adults have been harmed by eating excessive amounts of foods rich in vitamin A. Worst of all, some victims have been misled by advice from licensed physicians.

The list of toxic effects of vitamin A reported in scientific journals[19-22] is quite long: loss of appetite; weight loss; loss of hair; anemia; blurred vision; retinal bleeding; protruding eyeballs; extreme drying and thickening of the skin; widespread itching; great pain and tenderness of the arm and leg bones, especially in children; abnormal bone growth; bleeding tendency; cracking of the lips; mouth ulcers; increased brain and spinal fluid pressure with headache and papilledema (mimicking brain tumor); irritability in children; and birth defects in children born to mothers who took megadosages of vitamin A. Curiously, vitamin A *deficiency* can produce some similar problems: bleeding tendency;[13] birth defects;[21,22] skin difficulty;[1] and increased brain and spinal fluid pressure.[23]

How can you and your loved ones avoid trouble with excess vitamin A? Very simply. *Remember that all fat-soluble vitamins when taken in excess can accumulate in the body to reach toxic levels.* Unless advised otherwise by a physician, you should assume that the RDA intake levels of Vitamin A listed in Appendix B of this book are sufficient to assure maximum health benefits. This amount is easily obtained from a balanced diet which includes green and yellow vegetables, fruit, a reasonable amount of dairy products, eggs, and occasional portions of liver or other organ meats. Don't go overboard on foods exceedingly rich in vitamin A or carotenes. But more important, don't supplement with megadoses of vitamin A. Never take 25,000 or more units of vitamin A daily or give more than 10,000 units to a small child, even if a doctor advises you to do so. If you encounter such advice, get a second opinion!

References

1. Lui, N. and Roels, O.: *In* Modern Nutrition in Health and Disease, 6th Ed. (R. Goodhart and M. Shils, Ed.) Philadelphia, Lea and Febiger, 1980, p. 142.
2. Richardson, J.: The Polar Regions. Edinburgh, Black Publishers, 1861, p. 71.
3. Nater, J. P. and Doeglas, H. M. G.: Acta Dermatovener (Stockholm), English Ed., 50:109, 1970.
4. Moore, T., Biochemical Journal 24: 692, 1930.

5. Bloch, C.: Journal of Dairy Science 7:7-10, 1924.
6. Kutsky, R.: Handbook of Vitamins and Hormones. New York, Van Nostrand Reinhold, 1973.
7. Hodges, R. and Kolder, H.: *In* Summary of Proceedings, Workshop on Biochemical and Clinical Criteria for Determining Human Vitamin A Nutriture (Chairman, J. G. Bieri). Washingon, DC, National Academy of Sciences, 1971, pp. 10-16.
8. JAMA 226:674, 1973.
9. Pediatrics 8:788, 1951.
10. JAMA 238:1749, 1977.
11. Annals of Internal Medicine 80:44, 1974.
12. Pediatrics 65:893, 1980. (Note: The reported estimate of vitamin A of 36,000 units is erroneous. The correct figure is 12,000.)
13. American Journal of Diseases of Childhood 67:33, 1944.
14. American Journal of Clinical Nutrition 26:575, 1973.
15. Proceedings of the Nutrition Society (London), 34:44A, 1975.
16. Dr. D. H. (pathologist): Personal communications to author, 1975-76.
17. Obstetrics and Gynecology 43:750, 1974.
18. Pilotti, G. and Scorta, A.: Minerva Ginecologica (Torino, Italy) 17:1103, 1965.
19. Moore, T.: *In* Section X of The Vitamins, 2nd Ed. (W. H. Sebrell and R. S. Harris, Eds., Vol. 1) New York, Academic Press, 1967.
20. Hayes, K. C. and Hegsted, D. M.: *In* Toxicants Occurring Naturally in Foods, 2nd Ed., Section on "Toxicity of Vitamins." Washington, D.C., National Academy of Sciences, 1973, pp. 235-353.
21. Darby, W. J.: Medical Clinics of North America, 48:1203, 1964.
22. AMA Drug Evaluations, 2nd Ed. Acton, Mass., Publishing Sciences Group, 1973.
23. Roels, O. A.: Biochemical systems. *In* The Vitamins, 2nd Ed., *op. cit.,** pp. 180-190.

---

op. cit., for opere citato (in the work cited), refers to the fact that additional information about a book is found in a reference above.

8

Vitamin D Can Help or Harm

The word "rickets" is derived from the Greek word "rakhitis," meaning "diseased spine." Ancient writings indicate that rickets in children and osteomalacia (bone softening) in adults were observed long ago. An early clue to the cause of adult osteomalacia was provided by a Dr. Bardsley who cured it in 1807 with cod liver oil.[1] During the last half of the 19th century, many children in the industrial cities of England suffered stunted growth and crippling deformities of their bone characteristic of rickets. These cities were notorious for being blanketed with such heavy smoke that even strong winds could clear the sky only momentarily. In 1890, a Dr. Palm was the first to observe and suggest a connection between sunlight and childhood rickets.

The next big advance came in 1919 when Mellanby reported a technique for producing rickets in young animals and then curing it with cod liver oil. In 1922, McCollum and co-workers reported success in partially separating the active ingredient from cod liver oil and named it "vitamin D." Two years later, the University of Wisconsin biochemist, Steenbock, announced that the anti-rickets vitamin could be produced by irradiating certain foodstuffs and even live animals with ultraviolet light. For this discovery, he later received a Nobel Prize.

Forms of Vitamin D

Vitamin D is a general term for a family of compounds which exhibit vitamin D activity. The two major forms are natural vitamin D_3 and synthetic vitamin D_2. What happened to D_1? Well, "vitamin D_1," which was studied during the early years of vitamin D research, was later found to be a mixture. So the term "vitamin D_1" was abandoned along with most of the research involving it. The scientific name for natural vitamin D_3 is cholecalciferol, which is formed by action of sunlight on a cholesterol derivative in the skin; and that for vitamin D_2 is ergocalciferol, made by ultraviolet radiation of ergosterol, a plant sterol plentiful in yeast. Vitamins D_2 and D_3 are equally potent in humans.[2]

By 1924 it was clear that the anti-rickets, anti-osteomalacia vitamin (D_3) in cod liver oil and formed by sunlight on skin is essentially the same as the vitamin (D_2) formed by ultraviolet irradiation of ergosterol. But it was not until 1931 that pure, crystalline vitamin D_3 was isolated from cod liver oil by a long, laborious process. The exact chemical structure of vitamin D_3 was eventually determined in 1936 by the German scientist and Nobel Prizewinner, Adolf Windaus. Soon Steenbock's method of ultraviolet radiation was tried on ergosterol to produce Vitamin D_2 commercially. This is the chief way of producing vitamin D nowadays for fortifying foods like milk, and for producing supplement capsules.

Functions of Vitamin D

Vitamin D is essential for normal bone growth and development. Together with the parathyroid hormones, it regulates phosphorus and calcium metabolism and promotes calcium absorption from the intestines. Vitamin D maintains normal blood phosphorus and calcium concentrations so long as excessive intakes of the vitamin are not taken for long periods. It promotes normal bone calcification and helps provide needed inorganic phosphates for the body by activating the enzyme, alkaline phosphatase. After prolonged shortage of calcium in the diet, vitamin D comes to the rescue by keeping the blood calcium from dropping too low and threatening the heart muscle which depends on proper calcium concentrations. To do this, however, vitamin D (aided by parathyroid hormone) must stimulate the mobilization of calcium from bones, and this can lead to brittle bones (osteoporosis) or bone softening (osteomalacia).

What happens if someone whose diet is low in vitamin D seldom sees the sun? A growing infant or child will develop rickets. Without sufficient vitamin D, there will be inadequate absorption of calcium from food, calcium will be mobilized from bones, and abnormal deposits of calcium will be made in some bones. Vitamin D and parathyroid hormone are also needed to harden (calcify) the soft "osteoid" tissue in growing bones. Unless rickets is corrected very early by a vitamin D supply, its victims will become permanently crippled.

In 1968, it was discovered by Dr. Hector DeLuca's group at the University of Wisconsin that vitamins D_2 and D_3 actually have little biological effect within the body. They must first be converted by successive actions of two specific enzymes, one in the liver and one in the kidneys, into 1,25-dihydroxy-vitamin D_2 or D_3, hormone-like substances,[3,4] Adults who lack vitamin D or who lose the ability to convert it to its most active forms will develop many biochemical imbalances; but primarily they lose calcium and develop osteomalacia, a softening of the bones which causes great pain and results in abnormal bending and other bony deformities. This condition is different from osteoporosis, a defect in bone structure which is common in elderly women, but can also occur in pregnancy.

"Super Vitamin D"

For years, medical experts have been puzzled by cases of osteoporosis which do not improve with calcium and vitamin D supplementation. These stubborn cases are not rare. In 1979, the Mayo Clinic reported on 52 women with this problem who were from 54 to 75 years old. X-ray examinations showed that all of them had abnormally low spinal bone (vertebral) density, and that each had suffered at least one fractured vertebra. All were in negative calcium balance, losing more calcium each day in their urine and feces than they were getting in a normally adequate diet, but calcium and vitamin D supplements had not helped them. When 27 of these 52 patients were compared with 27 women the same age who did not have osteoporosis, it was found that the osteoporotic patients absorbed much less calcium from their food. They also had lower blood levels of parathyroid hormone and 1,25-dihydroxy-vitamin D_3, the active form of vitamin D that had been discovered by Dr. DeLuca's elegant research. (Parathyroid hormone is needed to activate the kidney enzyme which completes production of 1,25-dihydroxy vitamin D_3.) So the Mayo Clinic team led by Dr. Lawrence B. Riggs[5] decided to see whether treatment with this "super vitamin D" could help.

Twenty-four of the patients were given tiny doses of "super-D" for 7 days while 13 patients were given a placebo. All 37 received the same diet providing 1 RDA for calcium and vitamin D. The "double-blind" experiment showed that 21 of the 24 patients getting "super-D" had good increases in calcium absorption and the other three improved when their dosage was doubled. Those receiving the placebo showed no improvement. The 1-week treatment was repeated after one month and again after six months, at which time all 24 of the treated patients were in positive calcium balance—with increased calcium absorption and no more loss of calcium from their bones. Additional treatment will be needed from time to time.

I wonder how many of these improved patients, as they left the Mayo Clinic to return home, realized their good fortune in not having sought treatment at the hands of spine manipulators or other quacks. I also wonder how many realized the debt and the respect we all owe to Dr. DeLuca, Dr. Riggs and the many other true heroes of nutrition and medical science.

How Much Vitamin D Do We Need?

One international unit (IU) of vitamin D is defined as the activity contained in 0.025 micrograms (μg) of cholecalciferol (vitamin D_3). The

1980 Recommended Dietary Allowance is 10 μg (400 IU) for infants, children, adolescents, and pregnant or lactating women. This is reduced to 7.5 μg (300 IU) from age 19 to 22 and 5 μg (200 IU) after the age of 22 years. The Food and Nutrition Board[6] also advises that:

> Although vitamin D can readily be formed by the action of sunlight on the skin, the amount formed is dependent on a number of variables, including length and intensity of exposure and color of skin. One report (Loomis[7]) concluded that heavily pigmented skins can prevent up to 95 percent of ultraviolet radiation from reaching the deeper layers of the skin, where vitamin D is synthesized. In areas where sunlight is limited seasonally or where there is considerable atmospheric pollution, ultraviolet energy from the sun may be insufficient for adequate formation of vitamin D in the skin.

Black children who live in areas with minimal sunlight would thus be more likely than white children to develop rickets, but fortification of milk with vitamin D has largely eliminated this disease in the United States. It is noteworthy that black children can tolerate higher daily dosages of vitamin D than white children. Loomis also reported that to cure a case of rickets required only 900 units of vitamin D daily for several weeks for white children, but 1,500 IU per day for black children. Yet some white children develop symptoms of borderline vitamin D poisoning on 1,500 IU of vitamin D per day. For healthy children, black or white, one RDA of 400 IU from diet and/or sunlight is sufficient to prevent rickets.

Is 400 units of vitamin D enough for adults? Yes, it is adequate except for abnormal conditions, such as lack of parathyroid hormone, inability to absorb fats and fat-soluble vitamins, or inability to convert vitamin D to its active forms.

Food Sources of Vitamin D$_3$

The richest sources of natural vitamin D$_3$ are the livers or liver oils of most salt-water fish, some containing as much as a million IU per ounce. Medium rich foods are tuna, salmon, herring and egg yolk. Lower levels of vitamin D are found in grains, vegetable oils, butter, cheese, milk (rich source if fortified with D$_2$), and livers of beef, pork and lamb. Remember, though, most adults obtain all or most of their vitamin D requirement from the action of sunlight on the skin.

A Two-Edged Sword

In 1928, Hess and Lewis[8] reported the spectacular cure of 12 children with rickets by treatment with 5 mg of irradiated ergosterol (the Steenbock process). However, dosages were guesswork to those pioneers, so the children got between 50,000 ad 150,000 IU of vitamin D daily for 3 to 6 weeks. Mild toxic effects were observed in all 12 children, and severe toxic reactions occurred in 3 of them.

Despite this early warning, it took 30 years before reports of vitamin D poisonings began to decline. Because vitamin D could cure bone-softening and rickets, the idea flourished that it might benefit all forms of arthritis. Between 1930 and 1960, thousands of arthritic patients were treated with large doses of vitamin D—50,000 IU per day and often much more. No benefit to their arthritis was ever proved.

Archie W. was one of those cases.[9] In 1938, at age 51, he was struggling to keep up his medium-sized farm on the fertile soil of a large Mideastern state. During that year he began to feel arthritic pain and stiffness which slowly worsened and gradually involved his ankles, knees, shoulders, wrists, elbows, fingers and hips. Three years later, doctors at a large eastern teaching hospital examined Archie and diagnosed rheumatoid arthritis. Examination showed no kidney damage and blood pressure was normal. Seven blood tests including those for calcium and phosphorus levels were normal. He was treated with 12 injections of a gold salt at weekly intervals and sent home with his arthritis somewhat improved. He returned to the same hospital for a checkup three years later in 1944, and again his weight and blood tests were normal.

At home, Archie was frustrated by the failure of the big clinic to do more to alleviate his arthritis. He was able to do only a minimum of farm work. Upon his repeated complaints early in 1945, his family doctor prescribed a half-million units of vitamin D daily. Archie's arthritis improved steadily, so he kept taking this huge daily dosage for another 18 months without telling his doctor. He finally stopped in September 1946 because he developed really worrisome symptoms.

First there were severely itchy skin eruptions that spread to many parts of Archie's body. His fingernails became quite tender and developed yellow deposits under the nails. He began to experience nausea, loss of appetite, and excessive urination even at night. In December 1946, three months after stopping the vitamin D supplements, Archie (now 59 years old) returned to the original hospital clinic. Here, examinations revealed that he had lost 33 pounds in one year (to a mere 125 pounds) and was anemic. His blood calcium level was very high. Calcium deposits were apparent in his eyes and under his skin in many places. Tests revealed serious kidney impairment with probable damage from calcium deposits.

The diagnosis for Archie was vitamin D poisoning. He was advised to begin a low-calcium diet with no milk or cheese. A minimal amount of cream and butter was allowed, and he was told to force himself to drink 4 quarts of fluids daily. He improved very slowly during the next two years. After 20 months, the calcium deposits in his eyes had nearly cleared and his blood calcium level and blood count were back to normal. However, his kidney function remained poor. With the help of one son who returned to the homestead, Archie still worked his farm, but he never fully recovered and could work only an hour or two a day.

A Trio of Tortured Tots

About the year 1960, three infants were growing up in the same neighborhood in a large Italian city. Lucia, Marissa and Alessandro were respectively 7, 8 and 20 months old. Though the three were healthy and had received proper vitamin supplementation since birth, each mother decided her child needed extra vitamin D above what the doctor had ordered. So for one month Lucia was given, instead of the recommended 400 units per day, a daily average of 83,000 units. Marissa got the moderately high dosage of 8,700 units each day for 4 months while Alessandro was overloaded with 200,000 units per day for 15 days. The duration of overdosing varied because it stopped abruptly when each child was taken to the excellent pediatric clinic in that Italian city.

Doctors at the clinic diagnosed all three as suffering from vitamin D poisoning. All three showed loss of weight, extreme thirst and constipation. Marissa, who had received the lowest overdosage, did not suffer any of the following, but Lucia and Alessandro did: fever, paleness, dry skin, loss of appetite, and neurological symptoms such as instability and extreme restlessness.

Fortunately, the clinic doctors knew the proper treatment. First, all vitamin D supplements were stopped. Then each infant was given a cortisone type of hormone. All three recovered fully—Marissa took only 6 days, Lucia took 15 days, and poor Alessandro was not well until the 25th day of treatment. The physicians who published this report[10] included the records of nine other infants admitted to their clinic with vitamin D intoxication between 1960 and 1964.

Last School Bell for Stevie[11]

Stevie M., at age three, was an exceptionally bright and active lad. He felt fine, but he was judged to have a borderline case of rickets because x-ray examinations of his wrists showed poor bone density, and the bones of his skull felt "peculiar" to his family doctor. A daily dose of two capsules of vitamin D totaling 100,000 units was prescribed for just a few weeks, but his parents were anxious to speed the correction of Stevie's problem. Without telling his doctor, they began giving Stevie two tablespoons of cod liver oil plus a variable amount of multivitamin drops per day in addition to the prescribed capsules. Altogether, Stevie received an average of 150,000 units of vitamin D daily for the next 2½ years. Oddly enough, there seems to have been no medical effort made to see if the bone development returned to normal after a few months of this therapy.

Nine months after the start of the vitamin D treatment, Stevie became nauseated, restless and irritable. His parents stopped giving him multivitamins, but continued the vitamin D capsules and cod liver oil for the next 1½ years. Stevie remained irritable and could sleep only five hours a night. Because of increasing stiffness in his legs and arms, he did not participate in the school's physical activities.

At age 5½ years, Stevie entered an orthopedic hospital at a large university medical center. Examinations revealed a dangerously high blood calcium level. X-ray films showed deranged bone growth in his feet, hands, wrists and the ends of the long bones, as well as the base and vault of his skull. Abnormal calcium deposits surrounded the joints of his feet, hips, hands, ankles and shoulders and were suspected in his kidneys. Kidney function was poor, and this, if permanent, could lead to high blood pressure and heart trouble. The diagnosis was vitamin D intoxication of long duration. Strict orders were given to stop all the vitamin D supplementation.

At intervals of 7, 8 and 10 months, Stevie returned to the hospital for x-ray checkups. The x-ray films now showed a decrease in the abnormal bone growth at the joints with partial return to normal bone growth. At age 6 years, his skeletal development was that of a 4-year-old.

A few months later, the boy's family placed him under the care of a pediatrician. Now he was suffering from fever, swelling of the face and abdomen. There was blood in his urine, and his blood pressure was quite high at 180/120. He was hospitalized and treated for a respiratory infection, but the presence of kidney damage was also apparent. During this hospital stay, drugs brought Stevie's blood pressure down to normal and then controlled it. X-ray pictures showed that 15 months without any vitamin D supplement had greatly improved his bone density pattern. After several weeks Stevie went home; but his family, disobeying the doctors' warning that he needed strict bed rest, sent him to school.

About two months later, Stevie, now 7 years old, returned to the university orthopedic hospital. His blood pressure was back up to 190/130, his heart was enlarged, and his kidney functioning had worsened. He was ordered home with advice that his condition was grave, that he should have a low protein diet without milk, and lots of rest. But once again, the family ignored the doctors and sent Stevie to school.

During the next five weeks, the boy worsened, developing widespread bleeding into the skin, oozing of blood from his nose, and great difficulty in breathing. A local doctor rushed him to a hospital but little Stevie—so healthy at age 3—died soon after readmission to the hospital. Autopsy revealed enlargement of the heart, atherosclerotic deposits in the main artery from his heart (aorta), bleeding into the walls of the stomach and small intestine, and an enlarged, fatty liver. Of great significance were the calcium deposits in the lungs, intestinal walls, adrenal glands, and most seriously, the kidneys. The official cause of death: Vitamin D poisoning from massive daily intake, especially for one year between ages 3 and 4, resulting in abnormally high absorption of calcium and phosphorus with calcification of soft tissues, most critically in the kidneys. Progressive kidney failure had caused the high blood pressure, the heart damage and fatal outcome. Poor Stevie would answer the school bell no more.

The Heart of Hilda's Trouble[12]

As a 12-year-old, Hilda G. could outrace her 14-year-old brother to a ledge high up in the Austrian Tyrolean hills. But at age 50 years she started to notice a dull pain in her left hip which got progressively worse. Her doctors diagnosed the condition as degenerative destruction of the hip joint caused by interruption of nerve supply to the area. When she was 58, vitamin D was prescribed along with other drugs.

After a month of treatment, Hilda decided to use vitamin D only. Without telling her doctors, she stopped the other medication and took 100,000 units of vitamin D daily for the next 17 months. After 8 months of high-dose vitamin D, she began to experience increasing fatigue, weakness and loss of weight. Later she developed loss of appetite, severe thirst and occasional vomiting. After 16 months, she began to suffer from breathing difficulties, swelling of her lower legs and racing heartbeat (tachycardia); she occasionally passed out for several seconds at a time. Her doctors found that treatment with digitalis, the usual drug for her kind of heart condition, made her worse.

Finally, 18 months after starting the high-dose vitamin D, Hilda was taken to a large hospital. Doctors found her to be severely weakened, dehydrated, short of breath, and in a generalized state of wasting. An electrocardiogram (EKG) indicated seriously impaired heart function. Other findings included an enlarged liver and severe anemia. Very high amounts of urea (body waste) in the blood indicated kidney damage, and high blood calcium levels indicated the likelihood of kidney injury. Analysis of her urine showed further evidence of kidney damage.

The doctors stopped Hilda's daily dosing with vitamin D and began intensive heart and circulation therapy, even before all the entrance examinations were completed. They treated her anemia with vitamin B_{12} and iron supplements. Her attacks of unconsciousness persisted, but the EKG revealed that they were caused by electrical disturbances of the heart. She was given a special drug for this, and after several weeks had no more "collapses."

After treating Hilda's heart impairment and anemia, the doctors then tried to reverse the widespread damage caused by the excessive vitamin D. They employed a super-cortisone hormone therapy, and put her on a calcium-free diet. They also gave her intravenous fluids, antibiotics and blood transfusions. After several weeks, Hilda's anemia and kidney function improved, but acidosis (acidic blood) due to remaining kidney trouble still caused her heart to race periodically. She died of heart failure on the 70th hospital day.

Autopsy revealed calcium deposits throughout her kidneys, in her heart muscle and in the lining of the aorta. There were even calcium deposits in her thyroid gland and hip joints. The final diagnosis: vitamin D poisoning causing widespread abnormal calcification especially in the kidneys; and heart failure secondary to kidney failure.

Hilda G., the robust hill-climber in her youth, could not rise above the mountainous disaster of too much vitamin D for too long.

Blue Baby Barbara[13,14]

Can the growing fetus be harmed if a pregnant woman takes megadoses of vitamin D? Some people with an unusual medical condition (lack of parathyroid hormone) actually need and are not harmed by high-dose vitamin D. Barbara's mother is such a person. In 1964, she began taking 50,000 units of vitamin D and some calcium lactate daily on her doctor's advice. Barbara was born in 1971. Almost from the start, she had a bluish tint to her skin and other symptoms of impaired circulation. Congestive heart failure was diagnosed, and heroic medical measures over the next several days brought enough improvement to send her home.

When Barbara was 6 months old, heart specialists visualized the inside of her heart by a special x-ray examination. To their horror, they found several serious anatomical malformations in the heart and the large arteries connected to the lungs. One of these arteries was too narrow to allow normal blood flow. Also revealed was a serious defect in the thin wall between the right and left sides of the heart; and the left side of the heart was enlarged.

At the age of 18 months, Barbara underwent heart surgery, but the repair was only partially successful. She was able to live normally, but the doctors knew that she would have increasing heart trouble as she grew. She was checked every year by a heart specialist. By the time she was four, the right side of her heart was enlarged, and blood flow through the defective lung artery had almost stopped. Barbara now showed some physical weakness. Open heart surgery was done in the hope of correcting most of this difficulty, but she died a few hours after the operation was completed.

The doctors who reported this case thought it possible that Barbara's condition had been caused by her mother's excessive intake of vitamin D, but they realized, of course, that a single case of this type is not conclusive. Nevertheless, it should be kept in mind that animal experiments support this speculation. In 1966, Friedman and Roberts[15] showed that very large doses of vitamin D could produce defects in the large arteries of animals. In 1977, the research team of Kamio, Kummerow and Imai[16] reported that large vitamin D doses added to the food of newly weaned pigs for 3 months resulted in atherosclerosis with an abnormal thickening of the lining of the aorta. Dr. A. F. Kummerow[17] later reviewed many other studies which, together with his group's study, indicate that excessive vitamin D is injurious to the inner wall of arteries in or near the heart.

Bungled British Babies[18]

Early in 1955, the Ministry of Health asked the British Pediatric Association to investigate a possible link between vitamin D supplements given infants in Great Britain and the rising number of cases of hypercalcemia (high blood calcium level). During a 2-year period ending in the spring of 1955, 204 cases were reported to the Pediatric Association. High blood calcium levels can spell serious trouble—including erratic deposits of calcium in soft tissues and joints, as well as abnormal bone development and kidney damage.

During World War II, the British government had begun a supplement program based on a British Pediatric Association recommendation that all infants (except prematures) be given a daily dose of cod liver oil equivalent of 700 units of vitamin D. However, this was followed soon by fortification of babies' dried milk and cereals with vitamin D and the addition of 1,000 units per quart of milk, as endorsed by the British Ministry of Food. The 1955 study revealed that each day, the average British infant took in about 700 units of vitamin D from cod liver oil plus 1,700 units from dried milk made into formula (or 800 units from whole milk), plus 1,500 units from cereal. Thus, daily intake averaged between 3,000 and 4,000 IU of vitamin D and could indeed be the cause of the high blood calcium.

Therefore in 1956, the British Pediatric Association recommended to the government that vitamin D fortification of all foodstuffs except milk be stopped and the amount added to milk be much reduced. This was done, and the cases of high blood calcium ceased. Use of cod liver oil for infants was continued because it also provided much needed vitamin A.

How little vitamin D given daily can cause trouble? In 1938, Jeans and Stearns[19] demonstrated that bony skeletal growth in infants occurred best on daily supplements of 340 to 600 units of vitamin D, but that 1,800 to 2,000 units caused *less* growth than dosages as low as 135 units. This suggests that 2,000 IU of vitamin D is the threshold of toxicity for most children. In 1974, the Food and Nutrition Board[20] concluded that amounts of vitamin D above 2,000 IU per day for prolonged periods have produced high blood calcium levels in infants and calcium deposits in the kidneys of infants and adults.

Summary of Adverse Effects

Remember that vitamin D is fat-soluble and that excess amounts are not readily excreted but accumulate in the body. Vitamin D cannot be excreted as such in the urine but must be slowly broken down by the liver. Excess vitamin D can cause loss of appetite, nausea, headache, excessive urination, diarrhea or constipation, weakness, fatigue, hypochromic anemia, kidney damage from calcium deposits, increased nitrogen waste products, calcium deposits in other soft-tissue organs, injury to arterial walls, high blood pressure, elevated blood cholesterol and mental depression. The possibility of other relationships between excess vitamin D and cardiovascular disease has been suggested.[21-23] A very rare form of supersensitivity to vitamin D has been reported[24] in children.

The threshold for adverse vitamin D effects appears to be about 1,200 IU per day for white children and about 2,000 IU for black children. For adults the lowest safe daily intake is unclear, but except for special medical conditions (such as lack of parathyroid hormone), the evidence points to prolonged daily intakes above 2,000 IU of vitamin D as posing considerable risk for most people.

Natural vitamin D_3 is just as toxic and harmful upon excessive intake as is the synthetic vitamin D_2 at the same dosage level, despite the claims to the contrary made by a few megavitamin practitioners.

Vitamin companies should provide a multivitamin product with one RDA dosage of every vitamin except vitamin D. Such a supplement would be useful for some elderly people, but inclusion of too much vitamin D is potentially dangerous.

References

1. DeLuca, H. F.: *In* Modern Nutrition in Health and Disease, 6th Ed. (R. Goodhart and M. Shils, Eds.) Philadelphia, Lea and Febiger, 1980, p. 160.
2. Food and Nutrition Board: Recommended Dietary Allowances, 9th Ed., Washington, D.C., National Academy of Sciences, 1980, p. 60.
3. Blunt, J. W. *et al.*: Biochemistry 7:3317, 1968.
4. DeLuca, H. F.: Federation Proceedings 33:2111, 1974.
5. Gallagher, J. C., Riggs, B. L., et al.: Journal of Clinical Investigations 64: 729, 1979.
6. Food and Nutrition Board: Recommended Dietary Allowances, 9th Ed., *op. cit.*, p. 61.

7. Loomis, W. F.: Science 157:501-506, 1967.
8. Hess, A. F. and Lewis, J. M.: JAMA 91:783, 1928.
9. Journal of Clinical Endocrinology 8:895, 1948.
10. Rivista Clinica Pediatria 77:3-16, 1966.
11. Archives of Diseases in Childhood 36:373, 1961.
12. Weiner Klinische Wochenschrift 78:463, 1966.
13. Lancet 2:1258, 1972.
14. Personal communication from child's pediatrician, Sept. 24, 1977.
15. Friedman, W. F. and Roberts, W. C.: Circulation, 34:77, 1966.
16. Kamio, A. *et al.*: Archives of Pathology and Laboratory Medicine 101: 378, 1977.
17. Kummerow, F. A.: American Journal of Clinical Nutrition 32:58-83, 1979.
18. British Pediatric Association: Report on Infant Hypercalcemia, British Medical Journal 2:149, July 21, 1956.
19. Jeans, P. C. and Stearns, G.: Journal of Pediatrics 13:730, 1938.
20. Food and Nutrition Board: Recommended Dietary Allowances, 8th Ed. Washington, D.C., National Academy of Sciences, 1974.
21. Knox, E. G.: Lancet 1:1465, June 30, 1973.
22. Linden, V.: British Medical Journal 3:647, Sept. 14, 1974.
23. Dalderup, L. M.: Lancet 2:92, July 14. 1973.
24. Taussig, H.: Annals of Internal Medicine 65:1195, 1966.

9
Vitamin E Can Help or Harm

The scientific name for vitamin E is tocopherol, but it occurs as a mixture of eight related substances, the most biologically active one being alpha-tocopherol.

Discovery

In 1922, Professor Herbert Evans and Katherine Bishop[1] reported the presence of a micronutrient in vegetable oil concentrates that would cure sterility in rats fed a rancid lard diet. They first called it Factor X and then the anti-sterility vitamin. Pure vitamin E was not obtained until 14 years later. In 1923, Evans and co-workers found Factor X not only in butterfat and meat, but also in grains such as wheat, oats and alfalfa. In 1924, Mattill and co-workers confirmed Evans' work by finding Factor X in lettuce and yeast. In 1925, Dr. Evans adopted the name *vitamin E,* as had been suggested the year before by Professor B. Sure.

Up to 1935, all research on vitamin E had been done using partially purified wheat germ oil concentrates. But in 1936, the research team of Herbert Evans, Oliver Emerson and Gladys Emerson[2] isolated the first pure, biologically active vitamin E from wheat germ oil. They determined that part of its chemical structure is an alcohol and named it alpha-tocopherol. *Tocos* is Greek for childbirth; *phero* means "to bear," and *ol* indicates an alcohol. Alpha, the first letter in the Greek alphabet, was chosen as the prefix to indicate that it is the first in a series.

In 1938, the American chemist, Fernholz, determined the exact molecular structure of natural alpha-tocopherol and the Swiss chemist, Paul Karrer, synthesized it as a mixture of its mirror image isomers. Later, the Evans team isolated several other naturally occurring tocopherols. By 1956, eight different ones were known, all but the alpha having relatively low vitamin potency. They were given Greek alphabet prefixes, alpha, beta, gamma, and so on.

What Does Vitamin E Do for You?[3-6]

Vitamin E is an essential nutrient for higher animals, including humans.[7] It is known to act as an antioxidant[8] and may also work as a coenzyme (especially in muscle cell and bone metabolism).[9] Antioxidants are essential to prevent destructive attack by oxygen on the essential unsaturated fats in cell outer membranes.

Humans need very little vitamin E daily for at least four possible reasons. It is not easily excreted; it is used up very slowly while performing most of its jobs; it can be regenerated from its oxidized form by vitamin C; and the human body has at least four other antioxidants available, one or more of which can substitute for vitamin E in most of its functions (see Chapter 14).

Together with these other antioxidants, vitamin E contributes to the following: protects and maintains the cell walls of red blood cells and most other tissue cells (even fragile walls of tiny structures inside cells); protects essential unsaturated fatty acids from oxidation to peroxides; and helps maintain normal muscle metabolism. In animal studies, vitamin E deficiency impairs the health of blood vessels, heart muscle, kidney tubules and liver, and results in brain softening (encephalomalacia). Vitamin E deficiency increases fetal loss during pregnancy, and, in the male, impairs the production of sperm (see Chapter 14). Vitamin E also protects vitamin A from oxidation destruction. A 1980 report of Drake and Fitch[10] states that vitamin E is required for red blood cell formation in monkeys and pigs but suggests that it is not normally required for this purpose in humans.

Food Sources of Vitamin E

Vitamin E is found in practically all foodstuffs but is especially plentiful in vegetable oils, particularly wheat germ oil. In vegetable oils and margarine, the vitamin E content ranges for 10 to 80 IU per ounce. The second richest sources of vitamin E are olives, peanut oil, chocolate, cabbage, asparagus, wheat germ, soybeans and spinach, with a content ranging from 1 to 11 IU per ounce. Vitamin E is found in smaller amounts—0.1 to 1 IU per ounce—in just about all vegetables, in many fruits, and in eggs, butter, cheese, cornmeal, oats, wheat and meats.

Amounts Needed

The Recommended Dietary Allowance (RDA) of vitamin E ranges from 4.5 IU for infants to 10 IU for men and 15 IU for pregnant women (see Appendix B for details). Balanced diets supplying 1,800 to 3,000 calories per day provide a total vitamin E biological activity in the range of 10 to 20 IU; and, if such diets are high in fat, they furnish about 25 IU daily.

As of 1980, the RDAs for vitamin E are expressed in alpha-tocopherol equivalents. ("α" is the symbol for alpha, and 1α-TE equals 1.5 IU.) Synthetic vitamin E is a mixture of related but spatially different structures (isomers) and is usually listed on supplement labels as "dl-alpha-tocopherol acetate." Because the synthetic mixture has only about two-thirds the potency of natural d-alpha-tocopherol, manufacturers are required to put more of it in a pill or capsule to comply with its labeled strength.

Most human tissues and organs contain tocopherol.[11] However, by far the bulk of the stored vitamin E is in body fat. Researchers have measured the total tocopherol content of a wide variety of tissues from a number of healthy humans soon after their accidental deaths. They found that an average, well-nourished, 150-pound adult stores about 5,000 mg (7,500 IU) of vitamin E—enough to last 16 months if used up at the rate of 15 units a day.

Deficiency in Humans[4-7]

Vitamin E deficiency symptoms in humans traceable only to an inadequate diet have never been reported except in premature infants who, while in the womb, are unable to get vitamin E from their mothers. (Unlike most vitamins, vitamin E cannot cross the placenta to get from the mother's blood stream to the infant's in adequate amounts.) Premature infants are therefore prone toward hemolytic anemia (breakdown of red blood cells) and bleeding tendency (see Chapter 21).

In adults, evidence of deficiency has been observed only in patients with longstanding inability to absorb fat during the digestive process.[12-14] No specific clinical symptoms were observed in such persons, but laboratory studies reveal increased fragility of red blood cells, increased urinary excretion of creatine (indicating muscle loss), and deposition of ceroid pigment (aging pigments) in the muscles of the small intestine.

There are two obvious reasons why healthy adults do not become deficient in vitamin E: 1) not much is required; and 2) the vitamin is so widely distributed in food that it is virtually impossible to select a diet adequate in all other nutrients which does not contain some vitamin E. About 20 years ago, the pioneer vitamin E researcher M. K. Horwitt[12,13] and several of his colleagues made a vigorous attempt to produce vitamin E deficiency through dietary restriction. According to their famous "Elgin Studies" report, they tested 19 human volunteers with special low-vitamin E diets (about 3 IU per day) for 4½ years. During the experimental period, the volunteers showed no sign of deficiency except for slight changes in their red blood cells detected by blood tests. Some cases of anemia in young children who had severe protein-calorie malnutrition and low levels of blood vitamin E have responded to treatment with tocopherols.[10]

Deficiency in Animals[6,15]

A deficiency of vitamin E can be produced in young animals, with symptoms varying considerably from species to species. For experimental animals such as mice, rats, guinea pigs and hamsters, diets can be prepared with zero or near-zero vitamin E content. Animals on such diets can suffer a multitude of disorders including: impairment of sex organs and fertility, weakening and withering of muscles, fragility of red blood cells, interference with red blood cell formation, bleeding tendency, and damage to the liver, brain and heart muscle.

The most striking of these problems is reproductive failure—the observation that led Professor Evans to discover vitamin E in 1922.[1] With E-depletion, females lose their litters and males suffer reversible damage to the testicles with low sperm count. This finding has been used to mislead the public. Severe vitamin E deficiency causes loss of *fertility,* not sexual performance, but vitamin superpromoters claim that extra vitamin E improves *sexual performance* (virility) in humans. This is doubly untrue. Even if the findings in rats were always applicable to humans—which they are not—the fact is that E-deficient animals readily engage in sexual intercourse. Moreover, long-term high-dose vitamin E can cause degeneration of the testicles and low sperm counts in male experimental animals and infertility in females![16-19,21]

How Much Vitamin E Can Humans Tolerate?

Today many vitamin enthusiasts are taking 500 units daily of vitamin E supplements. Capsules of vitamin E providing as much as 1,000 units are readily available in drug and "health food" stores. How many vitamin E true believers are swallowing three such capsules every day? How safe is vitamin E when 20 or more times the Recommended Daily Allowance is taken?

Medical journals of the past 30 years contain many reports of patients who took vitamin E at dosages over 300 units daily for many months with no apparent ill effects.[12,23-26] There seem to be some people capable of tolerating vitamin E doses as high as 1,600 IU per day for a few months,[25,26] but only time will tell whether long-term exposure to 800 to 1,600 IU per day, will reveal problems detectable only after several years of usage.

A study done by Farrell and Bieri[24] at the National Institutes of Health is often cited as evidence for the relative safety of vitamin E. These researchers recruited 28 healthy adults who had been taking vitamin E supplements regularly and 100 volunteers who had never ingested vitamin E except in food. Of the 28 vitamin E users, 9 were taking 100 to 200 IU daily, 13 were taking 400 IU, and 6 were taking 600 to 800 IU per day. Their duration of usage ranged from four months to 21 years, with the average being about 3 years. A medical questionnaire revealed that none of the 28 users had experienced any ill effects. Then 20 blood tests were performed on the 28 vitamin E users and on the 100 non-users. Test results for the vitamin E users were all normal and close to those of the non-users, except that the vitamin E group had an average of 8 percent higher blood cholesterol.

It should be noted that the Farrell-Bieri study is not evidence that vitamin E up to a daily dosage of 800 IU is safe for everyone, because only persons who experienced no undesirable side effects from vitamin E supplementation were included. The study did not consider people who had tried vitamin E supplements and *quit because of ill effects*. The study is useful only to the extent that it shows that some human adults can ingest up to 400 IU and probably up to 800 IU of vitamin E daily for at least one year without observable ill effects (except for dents in their pocketbooks).

Two scientifically controlled trials of megadose vitamin E show adverse effects. Professor Alan C. Tsai and co-workers[27] recruited 200 volunteers among college students. Half of them were given bottles of 600 IU vitamin E supplements labeled only with an identifying code while the other half were given placebos (dummy pills) also labeled only in code. The procedure was "double-blind"—neither the volunteers nor the doctors knew who were getting the vitamin E. The trial lasted four weeks. All participants answered questionnaires the day before the experiment started and on its final day. From the answers, Dr. Tsai's medical team concluded that megavitamin E supplements at 600 IU daily did not affect work performance, sexuality or the feeling of well-being, and did not cause muscular weakness or gastrointestinal disturbances. However, blood tests revealed a small but significant increase in blood triglycerides in women as well as some reduction of thyroid hormone in both sexes. This finding that megadose E can lower thyroid hormone might be worthy of further investigation because high dosages of vitamin E have been shown to cause thyroid gland damage in several kinds of experimental animals.[28-30]

Another double-blind trial was conducted by Dr. Terence W. Anderson[31] who gave the huge daily dose of 3,200 IU of vitamin E to 18 patients with angina pectoris (a heart condition) for 8 to 9 weeks. Another 18 got a placebo. Three patients who got the vitamin suffered repeated bouts of diarrhea and one had severe intestinal cramps after 6 weeks which stopped while taking 400 IU daily for a few days but returned after dosage of 3,200 IU was resumed. This experiment demonstrates how individuals vary in tolerance to large doses of vitamins.

Among the less dangerous but uncomfortable symptoms reported[20,31-35] at dosages of 400 to 1,600 units per day are the following: nausea, diarrhea, rapid pulse, itchy rash, headache, extreme fatigue, muscle weakness, inflammation and cracking of the mouth, and blurred vision.

Some promoters of vitamin E supplements claim that only synthetic vitamin E has harmful effects in high doses and that "natural" E is harmless at any dose. This certainly is not true. In fact, one physician recently reported to vitamin E authority, Dr. John Bieri, that patients getting 2,000 IU of natural alpha-tocopherol had gotten headaches and nausea while others getting synthetic E had not.[36]

Why can many people tolerate high-dose vitamin E? Dr. Bieri recently advised this author: "If there are pharmacological effects due to vitamin E, they should be demonstrated with 400 IU per day. Any more than this is totally wasteful—90 percent or more passes through the gut unabsorbed."[36] However, even at 400 IU daily intake, there will be a gradual accumulation of vitamin E in the body, mostly in fatty tissues, but with the risk of harmful levels arising in other organs after sufficient time.

Harmful Effects in Humans

Because the discovery of vitamin E revealed that it is essential for fertility in animals, the medical world enthusiastically tried using it to treat all kinds of reproductive disorders during the 1930s and 1940s. Pure vitamin E was not available, so wheat germ oil concentrates were used. Attempts to prevent miscarriages and to cure menstrual disorders and infertility (in both men and women) were all unsuccessful. After pure vitamin E became commercially available in 1946, it was used in these trials, also without success (see Chapter 14). Many of these trials revealed harmful effects from megadosage.

Scientific summaries of the harmful effects of megadose vitamin E in humans and animals have been published by Drs. Hayes and Hegsted,[37] Victor Herbert,[38] M. H. Briggs,[39] and H. J. Roberts.[40] Table 1 summarizes the adverse effects of vitamin E in humans, and Table 2 lists those produced in experimental animals.

A Case of Easy Bleeding[41]

At 55, Eddie L. suffered a severe heart attack (myocardial infarction) due to partial blockage of blood supply to part of his heart. He was treated with anti-clotting drugs and seemed to improve over the next two months.

Table 1. Possible Harmful Effects of High-Dose Vitamin E in Humans*

*Nausea[20,33,36]	*Risk for women of infertility or
*Diarrhea[20,31,32]	spontaneous abortion on dosages
*Headache[33,36]	above 1,500 IU[47]
Rapid pulse[20]	*Suppression of thyroid gland[27]
Itchy Rash[20]	*Risk to men of sore and enlarged
*Extreme fatigue[32-35]	breasts from estrogen-like effect[43]
*Muscle weakness[32-34]	Risk of fatty liver development[54-56]
*Blurred vision[33]	Risk of increased blood fats
*Inflammation and cracking at	(triglycerides)[27,40]
corners of mouth[32]	Increased blood cholesterol[57-59]
Serious crisis for persons with	*Creatine in urine, indicating possible
high blood pressure[20,48]	muscle damage[32-35]
Danger above 150 IU daily to	Danger to diabetics taking insulin
persons with rheumatic heart	or oral anti-diabetes drugs[48]
disease[48]	Interference with iron medication
Danger to heart patients taking	used to treat children with iron-
digitalis[48]	deficiency anemia[60]
Increased risk of bleeding for	*Increased risk of blood clots,
persons low in vitamin K (from	especially in women taking
long-term antibiotic therapy)[51,52]	estrogens[40,42,43]
Lowered resistance to infections[63]	*Risk of internal bleeding in persons
Risk to vegetarians by blocking con-	taking anti-clot drugs like
version of carotenes to vitamin A[53]	warfarin[41,51,52]

*Denotes risks discussed in the text of this chapter.

Table 2. Reported Adverse Effects of High Dosage Vitamin E in Animals*

*Testicular damage and degenera-	Lowered resistance to infection[61]
ation[16,19,21]	Thyroid gland damage[28-30]
*Female infertility, damage to sex	Blocking of conversion of vegetable
organs[17,18,49]	carotenes into vitamin A in the
Bone weakening[29,68]	body[64,65]
Increased fat and cholesterol in the	Increased risk of lung cancer in some
blood and/or liver[54-56]	animals[62]
Blocking of vitamin K, causing	Feminizing effect on male
internal bleeding[29]	animals[66,67]

*Denotes risks discussed in the text of this chapter.

In July, he returned to the hospital because of "skipped beats." Tests showed that his "prothrombin time" was between 16 and 17 seconds. (This is a test of ease of blood clotting. Normal clotting time is 12 to 14. The desirable range while undergoing treatment is 20 to 24 seconds. A longer time means an increased risk of internal bleeding.) Further tests showed that Eddie's blood cholesterol was high at 324 mg% (normal is 150 to 250), and that his blood triglycerides (non-cholesterol fats) were at least four times normal at 800 mg% (normal is 10 to 190). An electrocardiogram showed some irregular heart contractions due to previous damage. Eddie was sent home on drugs for each of these problems. His heart irregularity was under control, and his prothrombin time was in the desirable range.

In September, Eddie's clotting time was quite high at 31.4 seconds, indicating danger of internal bleeding, so his anti-clotting drug (warfarin) was temporarily stopped until his prothrombin time went down to 19 seconds. However, two months later he was in real trouble. Purple, black and blue patches appeared on his arms and abdomen, caused by many pinpoint hemorrhages (petechiae) from leakage of blood out of capillaries. Also, his urine was red—a development that startled Eddie. A severe two-day constipation problem also alerted doctors to the possibility of bleeding deeper in the abdominal regions. His clotting time tested as much too long at 36.6 seconds. They took him off the anti-clotting drug at once.

The doctors then questioned Eddie very thoroughly and he admitted that about two months earlier, he had been persuaded by friends to read a book about vitamin E which influenced him to take 1,200 units per day! The doctors told him to stop the supplements which he did reluctantly. Twenty-four hours later, his clotting time had shortened to near the desired level. Within a few days, the bleeding spots began to clear up and Eddie was sent home with his dose of warfarin slightly reduced. Before leaving the hospital, Eddie asked about vitamin E and the doctors told him high-dose vitamin E increased warfarin's anti-clotting potency so much that he risked internal bleeding. Eddie was worried because he believed that the vitamin E was necessary for continued well-being.

Eddie's doctors made a deal with him. If he would not take any vitamin E for two months and take only the drugs they prescribed, they would later run an experiment in which he could take vitamin E supplements. During the next two months, Ed returned once a week for clotting time tests which stayed at 21 to 24 seconds, the desired range. When the two months were up, the vitamin E experiment was started with Eddie's consent and delight. As the doctors put it, his system was to be "challenged" with 800 units daily of vitamin E while he continued to take his prescribed medications.

It was not until the end of four weeks on the 800 units daily of vitamin E that Eddie's clotting time started to get longer. By the end of six weeks, it was close to 30 seconds and widespread bleeding under the skin could be seen. At last Eddie was convinced that his doctors were right and the vitamin E book was wrong—*that high-dose vitamin E is not safe for everyone.*

A Doctor's 90-Day Binge

In 1957, a 41-year-old physician and associate professor of medicine, Dr. Robert Hillman, decided to test the safety of daily high-dose vitamin E on himself. He began with a daily intake of 2,000 IU for 37 days. Then, despite some unpleasant symptoms, he increased his daily supplement to 4,000 units for the next 43 days. He took 6,000 units on days 81 through 92, and finished his binge with 3,000 on the 93rd and final day.

Dr. Hillman's report[32] states that during the 3-month experimental period, he experienced skin difficulty near the corners of his mouth, abdominal distress, diarrhea and vague muscle weakness and fatigue. Most of these symptoms occurred toward the end of the test period, and all disappeared within two weeks after the vitamin E was stopped.

Dr. Hillman was uncertain whether his symptoms were actually caused by the vitamin E, but the laboratory did report the abnormal presence of creatine in his urine throughout the experimental period. Creatine is made in the liver and is essential for proper functioning of muscles. This finding, together with similar findings in animals, suggests that in some people, excess amounts of vitamin E taken for long periods of time may impair muscle function—and that the appearance of creatine in the urine may be a telltale sign of such impairment. *This case is one of the strongest pieces of evidence ever published on the risks of high-dosage vitamin E.*

An Experimental Failure[33]

Earl's doctor despaired of helping the slowly worsening contraction of Earl's right hand. Over the past year, the deep fibrous layer under the skin of his palm had grown thicker and the fingers pulled into an unmovable, claw-like position. This condition is called Dupuytren's contracture. So Earl was sent to the orthopedic department of a large London hospital.

There the doctors decided to try a newly proposed treatment, first suggested in 1947, the use of 300 to 500 units of vitamin E daily for three to four weeks. Earl was given 100 mg (150 units) of pure alpha-tocopherol three times a day—a total of 450 units daily. After a few days, he began to feel progressively tired and had daily headaches. By the middle of the second week on the vitamin E therapy, he also experienced occasional mild nausea and sudden unexplained sweating. Half-way through the third week, he developed blurred vision and extreme fatigue and begged to be taken off the experimental treatment. The doctors stopped his vitamin E therapy and within three days, all of these uncomfortable symptoms cleared up.

Earl was one of 13 patients with Dupuytren's contracture treated with vitamin E at the London hospital during early 1949; doctors there reported that 6 of the 13 had to stop the treatment within the first three weeks because of symptoms similar to Earl's. Two of the six were so miserable that they stopped the vitamin E during the first week.

When Earl ended his vitamin E treatment at about the 19th day, the doctors saw no improvement in his contracted right fingers. Only one of the seven patients who finished the trial showed improvement with a slight straightening of the fingers.

Dr. Cohen's E-Weakening[34]

Early in 1972, Dr. Harold J. Cohen of Sylmar, California, decided to investigate possible beneficial effects of vitamin E. Having read many medical reports about vitamin E, he was not convinced that vitamin E supplementation produced much benefit but at least it seemed harmless. So he put several of his patients, as well as his medical partner and himself, on 800 units daily.

About a week later, Dr. Cohen began to suffer "an amazing weakness and sense of fatigue" which resembled that of severe influenza. He stopped the daily vitamin E and within a few days he felt normal again. Thinking that his symptoms had probably been caused by a flu-like virus, Dr. Cohen resumed taking 800 units of vitamin E. Two days later, his weakness and fatigue returned.

Dr. Cohen's medical partner left their office early two days in a row, because he felt "very tired and sick." So Dr. Cohen told his partner of his similar experience. The partner stopped taking the vitamin E supplement and felt normal again within two days. By this time, most of Dr. Cohen's patients who had been taking 800 units of vitamin E daily began calling in complaining of unusual fatigue and weakness. Some of these patients were able to tolerate the vitamin at 400 units daily with only a minimum of fatigue. The rest of the patient group stopped their vitamin E supplements altogether. Dr. Cohen reported:

> In the course of my day-to-day practice of general medicine, I see many people who have become obsessed with the megavitamin concept for "good health," and these people take literally handfuls of vitamins daily . . . Many of these young people have been coming into my office complaining of very severe fatigue. Very comprehensive work-ups are done . . . tests are inevitably negative, and the overpowering fatigue responds promptly to withdrawal of vitamin E.

Dr. Cohen commented further that among young patients he has seen, excess intake of vitamin E ranks second only to depression as a cause of fatigue!

Dr. Evan Shute[22] (a leading promoter of megadosage of vitamin E for a whole spectrum of diseases) and Dr. Samuel Ayers, Jr.,[23] responded to

Dr. Cohen's report with published letters stating they had never seen fatigue in the large numbers of patients for whom they prescribed vitamin E. However, in another letter,[35] Dr. Michael Briggs, an Australian physician, reported a double-blind experiment where eight healthy young men received either 800 IU of vitamin E or a placebo (dummy pill). Within three weeks, two of those taking vitamin E withdrew from the experiment because of extreme fatigue. Both of these individuals had amounts of creatine in their urine similar to those mentioned above for Dr. Hillman.

It seems clear that some individuals who take high dosage of vitamin E will experience severe fatigue.

Clara's Critical Clot[42]

When Clara was 55, she noticed a gradually worsening tenderness and pain in the calf of her left leg over a 10-day period. She put off seeing her doctor for another week and suddenly had severe pain on taking a full breath. At the hospital, her doctor along with staff doctors diagnosed thrombophlebitis (leg vein inflammation and clot) and suspected pulmonary embolism (displacement of a clot from the leg to the lung). Pulmonary embolism is life-threatening, but after treatment for several days with anti-clotting drugs, she was declared out of danger.

Before sending Clara home, the doctors inquired into her use of drugs and her diet. They learned that she had been taking daily supplements of 1,000 IU of vitamin E for about six months. Although vitamin E has been reported to have a slight anti-clotting effect in many persons, Clara's doctors fortunately knew of reports indicating that in some people high-dose vitamin E has the opposite effect. This seems especially true of patients with certain glandular disorders, blood vessel and heart disease, and especially for women taking birth control pills that contain the estrogen type of female sex hormone.

So the doctors sent Clara home with the advice not to take any vitamin E supplements. However, Clara didn't believe a vitamin could possibly be harmful, no matter what her doctors said. After being home for about six weeks and completely free of her leg pains, she became worried that she was missing that "optimum health" which some of the popular vitamin books claim was the reward of the faithful who take extra vitamins. So she started on vitamin E again, beginning with 400 units and a week later increasing the daily intake to 800 units. Four weeks after again starting her vitamin E supplements. Clara was stricken once more with severe leg pains which were diagnosed by her doctor as another attack of thrombophlebitis.

Once again, the doctors cured Clara by standard treatment methods and this time Clara was finally convinced that she was not a person who could safely take vitamin E supplements.

In 1978 and 1979, Dr. H. J. Roberts[42,43] reported on thrombophlebitis in 40 women and 6 men taking vitamin E supplements. Thirteen had taken more than 800 IU of vitamin E daily, 26 had taken between 400 and 800 IU per day, 2 had taken less than 400 IU, and 5 had taken varying undisclosed amounts. In 26 patients, pulmonary embolism was diagnosed or strongly suspected. Eighty-five percent of the 46 patients had taken vitamin E daily for longer than one year. The majority had no history of thrombophlebitis prior to starting vitamin E supplements. Following hospitalization, stopping the vitamin E supplements, and standard medical treatment including the use of anti-clotting drugs, all recovered, but two later suffered repeat thrombophlebitis after they resumed high-dose vitamin E supplements against medical advice. By 1981, Dr. Roberts' series[40] totalled more than 80 patients with thrombophlebitis, pulmonary embolism or both. Their average age was 62 years; four of them have recurrences after resuming vitamin E supplements.

Dr. Roberts suspects that vitamin E may encourage abnormal clotting in patients who already have metabolic, cardiovascular, or endocrine disorders which predispose to small-vessel disease, platelet aggregation and thrombosis, especially if estrogens are also taken.

The latest evidence indicates that for normal *healthy* humans, vitamin E in 400 to 1,000 IU dosages has neither an anti-clot nor a pro-clot effect unless estrogens are also being taken.

Hormonal Disturbances?

Trials on women and experimental animals conducted between 1930 and 1950 by German scientists have been described in a lengthy review by Robert Beckmann.[44] Another noteworthy German report was published in 1952 by Dr. H. O. Kleine,[45] a gynecologist, who concluded that vitamin E given in high doses for many months can damage the sexual organs of women. He warned that vitamin E should not be administered longer than 6 months (and less with younger women). He also advised that dosage should be limited to 300 mg (300 to 450 IU) with a total of no more than 6,000 mg over a 6-month period.

Both H. J. Roberts in 1979[43] and F. Kessler[46] in 1970 reported cases of vaginal bleeding in late menopause related to vitamin E supplements—400 IU per day in Dr. Roberts' case and 100 IU per day in Dr. Kessler's. Dr. Roberts also described three cases of enlarged, painful breasts in men taking vitamin E whose symptoms went away when the vitamin E was stopped. These observations suggest that megadose E may have a female hormone-like effect. Possibly related to this is the finding of Vobecky[47] and co-workers that women who aborted spontaneously had normal but slightly higher blood levels of vitamin E than women whose pregnancies ended in normal childbirth.

Proponents Warn of Danger

Individuals with high blood pressure can go into dangerous crises on vitamin E dosage even at the moderately high level of 400 units daily, according to Vogelsang and the Shute brothers.[20,48] They warn that hypertensive patients should not use any vitamin E supplements until their blood pressure is first controlled by medically supervised drugs.

W. E. Shute[48] also warns that there is considerable risk to heart patients who need and use digitalis if they take too high a daily dose of vitamin E. He states that it is also very dangerous for patients with rheumatic heart disease (RHD); careful physician supervision is essential with dosages even as low as 150 units per day. Dosages about 150 units may cause sudden congestive heart failure in RHD patients. Shute also warns that even moderate doses of vitamin E must be taken with caution by diabetics, preferably under a physician's supervision. He reports that whether diabetics are trying to control their diabetes with insulin injections or by oral anti-diabetic drugs like tolbutamide, excessive vitamin E can interfere.

Conclusion

Some years ago, so the story goes, a scientist decided to resolve the vitamin E controversy once and for all by doing a controlled experiment. First he would interview residents of a retirement community. Next he would select two groups comparable in every respect except that one took vitamin E and one did not. Then he would see whose health remained better. His project never got off the ground, for he could find no one who was not taking the vitamin.

Although this is not a true story, it is clear that millions of Americans are supplementing with vitamin E. In my opinion, this is unwise. There is certainly no reason to take vitamin E supplements to be sure you get enough in your diet. The daily requirements for individuals are so small, and vitamin E is distributed so widely in foods that it is virtually impossible to develop a deficiency unless you have a disease in which vitamin E absorption is defective. As noted in Chapter 21, such conditions are quite rare and should always be under medical management.

Vitamin E may be useful in treating a few other ailments under medical supervision—as discussed in Chapter 14. But people who take large doses of vitamin E with hopes of preventing or treating a wide variety of diseases for which no scientific evidence of benefit exists are taking a gamble. Cases of *serious* harm are not common, but why run an unnecessary risk? If, despite what I say, you are convinced that vitamin E supplementation helps you, at least keep your dosage no higher than 200 IU daily. Adverse effects are quite rare at that level.

References

1. Evans, H. and Bishop, K.: Science 56:650, 1922.
2. Evans, H., Emerson, O. and Emerson, G.: Journal of Biological Chemistry 113:319, 1936.
3. Horwitt, M.: *In* Modern Nutrition in Health and Disease, 6th Ed. (R. Goodhart and M. Shils, Eds.) Philadelphia, Lea and Febiger, 1980, pp. 181-190.
4. Horwitt, M. K.: Nutrition Reviews 38:105-113, 1980.
5. Kutsky, R. J.: Handbook of Vitamins and Hormones. New York, Van Nostrand Reinhold Co., 1973.
6. Combs, G. F.: Proceedings of the Nutrition Society (London) 40:187-194, 1981.
7. Food and Nutrition Board: Recommended Dietary Allowances, 9th Ed. Washington, D.C., National Academy of Sciences, 1980.
8. Tappel, A. L.: Vitamins and Hormones 20:493, 1962.
9. Bieri, J. G.: Nutrition Reviews 33:161-7, 1975.
10. Drake, J. R. and Fitch, C. D.: American Journal of Clinical Nutrition 2386, 1980.
11. Mason, K. E. and Horwitt, M. K.: *In* The Vitamins, Vol. V, 2nd Ed. (W. Sebrell and R. Harris, Eds.) New York, Academic Press, 1972, pp. 293-309.
12. Horwitt, M.: American Journal of Clinical Nutrition 8:451, 1960.
13. Horwitt, M. K., Century, B. and Zeman, A.: *Ibid.* 12:99, 1963.
14. Binder, H. J. and Spiro, H.: *Ibid.* 20:594, 1967.
15. Herting, D.: *Ibid.* 19:210, 1966.
16. Stahler, F., Hebstreit, E. and Fladung, K.: Archiv fur Gynakologie 170:142, 1940.
17. Czyba, J-C.: Comptes Rendus Hebdomadaires des Seances de l'Academie des Sciences (Paris) 261:536, 1965.
18. Yang, N. Y. J. and Desai, I. D.: Experientia 33:1460, 1977.
19. Czyba, J-C.: Comptes Rendus des Seances de la Societe de Biologie et de Ses Filiales (Paris) 160:765, 1966.
20. Vogelsang, A., Shute, E. and Shute, W.: Medical Record 203:279, 1947.
21. Piedrabuena, L. A.: Nutrition Abstracts and Reviews 40:48, 1970.
22. Shute, E. V.: California Medicine 119:73, 1973.
23. Ayers, S., Jr.: *Ibid.* p. 73-74, 1973.
24. Farrell, P. and Bieri, J.: American Journal of Clinical Nutrition 28:138, 1975.
25. Ayers, S., Jr. and Mihan, R.: New England Journal of Medicine 290:580, 1974.
26. Gillilan R., Mondell, B. and Warbusse, J.: American Heart Journal 93:444, 1977.
27. Tsai, A. C. et al.: American Journal of Clinical Nutrition 31:831, 1978.
28. Huter, F.: *In* Annotated Bibliography of Vitamin E: 1940-1950 (R. Harris and W. Kujawski, Eds.). Rochester, N.Y., Eastman Kodak Co., 1950, Abstract No. 797.
29. March, B. E. et al.: Journal of Nutrition 103:371, 1973.

30. Murphy, T. P. et al.: Poultry Science 60:1873, 1981.
31. Anderson, T. W.: American Journal of Clinical Nutrition 27:1174, 1974.
32. *Ibid.* 5:597, 1957.
33. Journal of Bone and Joint Surgery 31B:443, 1949.
34. New England Journal of Medicine 289:980, 1973.
35. *Ibid.* 290:579, 1974.
36. Bieri, J. G.: Personal communication, June 3, 1980.
37. Hayes, K. C. and Hegsted, D. M.: *In* Toxicants Occurring Naturally in Foods, 2nd Ed., Section on "Toxicity of Vitamins." Washington, D.C., National Academy of Sciences, 1973, pp. 235-253.
38. Herbert, V.: Proceedings of the Western Hemisphere Nutrition Congress IV-1974, Acton, Mass., Publishing Science Group, Inc., 1975, pp. 84-91.
39. Briggs, M. H.: Lancet 1:220, Feb. 9, 1974.
40. Roberts, H. J.: JAMA 246:129, 1981.
41. JAMA 230:1300, 1974.
42. Lancet 1:49, Jan. 7, 1978.
43. Roberts, H. J.: Angiology 30:69-76, 1979.
44. Beckmann, R.: Zeitschrift fur Vitamin, Hormon und Fermentforschung 7:281-376, 1955. (Part II of a 2-part review.)
45. Kleine, H. O.: Zeitschrift fur Geburtshilfe und Gynakologie 137:1-22, 1952.
46. Kessler, F.: JAMA 214:604, 1970.
47. Vobecky, J. S. et al.: International Journal of Vitamin and Nutrition Research 46:291, 1976.
48. Shute, W. E.: Dr. Wilfred E. Shute's Complete Updated Vitamin E Book. New Canaan, Conn., Keats Publishing Inc., 1975, pp. 163, 170, 185, 186.
49. Evans, H. and Burr, G.: Journal of Biological Chemistry 76:273, 1928.
50. Krasavage, W. and Terhaar, C.: Journal of Agricultural and Food Chemistry 25:273, 1977.
51. Horwitt, M. K.: American Journal of Clinical Nutrition 29:569, 1976.
52. Nutrition Reviews: 33:269, 1975.
53. Moore, T.: Biochemical Journal 34:1321, 1940.
54. Alfin-Slater, R. B. et al.: Abstracts of the IX International Congress of Nutrition, Mexico City, 1972, p. 191.
55. Martin, M. and Hurley, L.: American Journal of Clinical Nutrition 30:1629, 1977.
56. Yang, N. Y. J. and Desai, I. D.: Journal of Nutrition 107:1418, 1977.
57. Dahl, S.: Lancet 1:465, March 16, 1974.
58. Dahl, S.: Personal communication, Dec. 20, 1975.
59. Leonhardt, E. T. D.: American Journal of Clinical Nutrition 31:100, 1978.
60. Melhorn, D. and Gross, S.: Journal of Laboratory Clinical Medicine 74:789, 1969.
61. Cheville, N. and Monlux, W.: Journal of the American Veterinary Medical Association 147:1674, 1965.
62. Telford, I. R.: Annals of the New York Academy of Science 52:132, 1949.
63. Prasad, J. S.: American Journal of Clinical Nutrition 33:608, 1980.

64. Hickman, K. C. D., et al.: Journal of Biological Chemistry 152:301, 311 and 321, 1944.
65. Johnson, R. and Baumann, C.: *Ibid.* 175:811, 1948.
66. Levin, E., Burns, J. and Collins, V.: Endocrinology 49:289, 1951.
67. Booth, A., Bickoff, E. and Kohler, G.: Science 131:1807, 1960.
68. Yang, N. Y. J. and Desai, I. D.: Journal of Nutrition 107:1410, 1977.

10

Vitamin K Can Help or Harm

In 1929, the Danish biochemist Carl Peter Henrich Dam observed an unexpected bleeding disease in baby chicks being used in his pioneering studies of cholesterol. He determined that this bleeding was caused by deficiency of a previously unknown fat-soluble food factor—some kind of vitamin. During the next few years, several research groups reported evidence of a blood clotting factor in extracts of plants, especially green leafy vegetables and alfalfa. The same factor was also found in extracts of fish meal and animal sources, apparently obtained from plants they ate or made by bacteria living in their intestinal tracts. In 1935, Dam named it "Vitamin K" because the German word for clotting is "Koagulation."

Types of Vitamin K

Vitamin K comes in many forms. Vitamin K_1 (phylloquinone) is found naturally in plants. Vitamin K_2 (menaquinone), which has about 75 percent of the potency of K_1, is made by bacteria in the intestinal tract of humans and various animals. K_2 is actually a whole family of chemically related substances, including menaquinone-4 (MK-4) and MK-5 through MK-13. Vitamin K_3 (menadione) and K_4 (menadiol) are man-made. Vitamins K_1 and K_2 and menadione are fat-soluble. Vitamin K_4 is water-soluble but can be used by intestinal bacteria to make K_2.

In 1939, Professor Dam and a Swiss co-worker isolated pure vitamin K_1 from alfalfa. During the same year, Professor E. A. Doisy, an American, obtained pure K_1 from alfalfa and K_2 from fish meal, and showed them to be slightly but definitely different in structure. For this work and for the earlier discovery of human sex hormones, Dr. Doisy shared a Nobel Prize with Dr. Dam in 1943.

Food Sources of Vitamin K

The best dietary sources of vitamin K are green leafy vegetables such as turnip greens, spinach, broccoli, cabbage and lettuce. Other rich sources are soybeans, beef liver and green tea. Medium-rich sources are egg yolks, oats, whole wheat, potatoes, tomatoes, asparagus, butter and cheese. Lower levels are found in beef, pork, ham, milk, carrots, corn, most fruits and many other vegetables.

The Food and Nutrition Board's estimated safe and adequate intake of vitamin K is 70 to 140 micrograms (μg) per day for adults. Lesser amounts are needed by children. According to the Food and Nutrition Board,[1] a "normal mixed diet" in the United States provides 300 to 500 μg per day.

Why Is Vitamin K Essential?

Vitamin K is needed primarily for the blood clotting mechanism that protects us from bleeding to death from cuts and wounds, as well as from internal bleeding. The liver needs vitamin K as part of a co-enzyme to make prothrombin, a special protein upon which depends a whole series of biochemical steps that produce a clot when needed. Vitamin K is also involved with the proper maintenance of several other clotting factors.

Vitamin K deficiency in humans is extremely rare because K_1 is widely distributed in plant and animal foodstuffs—and because intestinal bacteria normally make 50 to 60 percent of what we need anyway.[2] There are, however, a few special situations where supplementation under medical supervision is appropriate:

1. *Newborn infants.* The placenta does a poor job of transporting vitamin K from the mother to the developing fetus. Furthermore, the newborn's gut is sterile for the first few days and thus contains none of the beneficial bacteria which produce the substances needed to make vitamin K. In normal infants, the prothrombin level may fall by the third day to 20 percent of normal. If the level falls below 10 percent, bleeding disorders can occur. It is now standard practice to prevent this problem by injecting newborns with a small dose of vitamin K.

2. *Low-K Adults.* Normal adults consuming a diet low in vitamin K for a few days rarely show blood prothrombin levels below 60 percent of normal. This is so because intestinal bacteria can supply all or most of what we need. However, there are some patients on intravenous feeding (with no vitamin K intake at all) who also receive antibiotics which destroy their helpful intestinal bacteria. After a few weeks, some of these patients may show blood prothrombin levels in the danger zone of 20 percent.

3. *Impaired Bile Flow.* Vitamin K, being fat-soluble, is normally absorbed from the intestine along with dietary fat. Since bile is needed for fat absorption, chronic obstruction of bile flow can interfere with the absorption of vitamin K so that supplementation is necessary.

4. Malabsorptive diseases, such as sprue, are associated with poor ab-

sorption of fat and excess loss of it in the stools (steatorrhea). Patients with these conditions may require supplements of vitamin K.

5. *Diet Faddists.* About 40 years ago, some cases were reported of people on severely restricted diets who developed a bleeding tendency and were found to have very low blood prothrombin levels. Medical intervention with oral vitamin K restored them to normal.

Can Vitamin K Harm?

Vitamin K is one of the few nutrients which food faddists never seem to promote. As far as I know, no cases of harm from self-administration of vitamin K have been reported in the scientific literature. However, there are some hazards associated with its administration by doctors.

Bertha's Bleeding Puzzle

In 1959, 80-year-old Bertha G. was admitted to the hospital with major abdominal surgery scheduled. All preliminary tests were normal except that her prothrombin time was somewhat long at 18 seconds (normal is 11-13), indicating a tendency to bleed. Her liver appeared to be in normal condition and was not enlarged. Two days later her prothrombin time was 15.5 seconds, not much longer than normal. On the third day, as a preventive against excess bleeding, Bertha was given 50 mg of natural vitamin K_1 and 150 mg of synthetic vitamin K_4 by injection. Surgery was performed on the fourth day. During the operation, her liver was observed and looked normal.

Bertha was given 30 mg of synthetic vitamin K_4 each day for the next 11 days plus 50 mg of vitamin K_1 from the 8th to the 11th day. These injections were administered despite the fact that her prothrombin time had returned to normal on the fourth day after surgery. On the 12th day, the nurses reported that Bertha was bleeding from her crotch area. An immediate check revealed that her prothrombin time was 29 seconds—more than twice normal—so that she was again in danger of serious bleeding. Liver function tests, run to see if Bertha's liver was able to make prothrombin, now showed some abnormalities.

The vitamin K injections were stopped and Bertha was given two transfusions of fresh blood to control her bleeding. Her clotting time improved during the next three weeks, and her liver function returned to normal about two months after that. The published medical report[3] does not divulge the ultimate success or failure of Bertha's surgery, but her survival for three months at age 80 suggests that it was successful. However, the report does indicate how doctors acquired an understanding in 1960 that even low doses of synthetic vitamin K_4 given for too long can *cause* bleeding instead of preventing it, and may also harm the liver.

Other Reports of Harm

Natural vitamins K_1 from food and K_2 made by human intestinal bacteria appear to be harmless at doses as high as 10 to 25 mg, even for premature infants, according to a lengthy 1961 review by the American Academy of Pediatrics.[4] But the two synthetics, K_3 and K_4, are a different story. As early as 1940, animal studies[2] showed that very large doses of vitamin K caused anemia, and in 1943 it was found that large doses of vitamin K_4 derivatives produced aplastic anemia, bleeding spots in the skin (petechial hemorrhages) and kidney damage. The danger of using K_3 or K_4 to correct bleeding in adults was pointed out in 1970 by J. A. Udall[5] in an article entitled "Don't Use the Wrong Vitamin K."

In 1973, Hayes and Hegsted[6] pointed out that newborn infants commonly have low prothrombin levels and, therefore, bleeding problems. Until the early 1960s it was customary to treat newborn babies, especially premature babies, with vitamin K. K_4 (trade name Synkavite) was the type used most often, but troubles were reported. In the mid-1950s, several medical teams published observations of dangerous effects on premature infants of large doses of K_3 and K_4. Hemolytic anemia (destruction of red blood cells) was reported[7] with dosages over 5 mg and kernicterus (brain damage from blood breakdown products) and death were reported[8] with 10 mg given three times daily for three days.

The American Academy of Pediatrics report also warns that high dosages of vitamin K_4 given to pregnant women prior to delivery can have the same adverse effects upon the newborn as does direct administration to the infant after birth. To prevent hemorrhagic disease of the newborn, the Academy advises using a single injected dose of 0.5 to 1.0 mg of K_1 or an oral dose of 1.0 to 2.0 mg. "The margin of safety is almost certainly greatest . . . and vitamin K_1 is therefore considered the drug of choice," says the report.

What should you, as a consumer, do about vitamin K? In my opinion, the best thing to do is to forget about it. There is no good reason to prescribe oral supplements of vitamin K for yourself. Nor should you try to out-think your doctor if you acquire a bleeding disorder or are having a baby.

References

1. Food and Nutrition Board: Recommended Dietary Allowances, 9th Ed. Washington, D.C., National Academy of Sciences, 1980, p. 69.

84

2. Olson, R.: *In* Modern Nutrition in Health and Disease (R. Goodhart and and M. Shils, Eds.) Philadelphia, Lea & Febiger, 1980, p. 178.
3. JAMA 173:502, 1960.
4. American Academy of Pediatrics, Committee on Nutrition: Pediatrics 8: 501, 1961.
5. Udall, J.: California Medicine 112:65, 1970.
6. Hayes, K. and Hegsted, M.: Toxicity of Vitamins, Chapter 11 in Toxicants Occurring Naturally in Foods, 2nd Ed. Washington, D.C., National Academy of Sciences, 1973.
7. Allison, A.: Lancet 1:669, 1955.
8. Laurence, B.: Lancet 1:819, 1955.

11

B-Vitamins Can Help or Harm

The "B-Complex" consists of eight B-vitamins which often work together in metabolic activities. They are thiamin (B_1), riboflavin (B_2), niacin (B_3), pyridoxine (B_6), B_{12}, folic acid, biotin and pantothenic acid. All are water-soluble and excreted fairly rapidly. They are usually nontoxic even when taken in large amounts; but some pose special dangers.

THIAMIN (VITAMIN B_1)[1-4]

More than 4,000 years ago in the Far East, many persons were reported to have suffered a slowly increasing weakness which made them unable to work. The people of Ceylon (now Sri Lanka) called the affliction beriberi from the Singhalese word "beri" meaning weak. It was not until 1890 that beriberi was recognized as a dietary deficiency. Now we know it is caused by a lack of thiamin.

Thiamin is abundant in the rice husks removed by the polishing process that makes white rice. In Asia, where rice is the staple in the diet, only the very poor escaped beriberi prior to 1920. They could not afford the white rice that everyone else was eating. Because the Japanese Navy served polished rice, many sailors became weak from beriberi until a researcher named Takaki[5] in 1887 reported curing them by adding dry milk or a little meat to their diet. In Java, in the 1890s, the Dutch physician, Eijkman fed polished rice to chickens who soon developed beriberi-like symptoms which he cured by adding some rice husks. Eijkman did not recognize that the curative factor in rice husks was an essential food factor but thought that the husks contained an antidote to a poison present in white rice.

The first to propose that the curative substance is a dietary factor was Grijns in 1901, who also cured beriberi in fowls by giving them rice polishings. In 1912, Casimir Funk,[6] a Polish biochemist working in England, prepared crude extracts of rice polishings which cured beriberi. In 1926, Jansen and Donath prepared the first pure crystalline thiamin in very tiny amounts. In 1934, the great American biochemist, Robert R. Williams prepared large enough quantities of pure thiamin to permit structural research and determined its exact chemical structure. In 1936, Williams and Cline succeeded in synthesizing pure thiamin identical to that in foodstuffs. Now chemical manufacturers make thiamin by the ton.

What Does Thiamin Do for You?

Thiamin, as the pyrophosphate or diphospho- derivative, joins with magnesium ion to form an essential coenzyme called cocarboxylase. This serves in several enzyme systems which catalyze important biochemical reactions, especially some needed to convert carbohydrates into energy or fat. As a coenzyme, thiamin is essential for the functioning of nerve tissue because it participates in the synthesis of acetylcholine, a key controller of nerve transmissions. Thiamin is also needed to maintain heart muscle tone, to help remove excess lactic acid formed by muscular activity, and to help maintain proper levels of ATP which is a source of quick energy for muscle and other vital cells.

How Much Thiamin Do Humans Need?

Based on tissue and red blood cell content and the amount discarded in the urine after ingesting 5 mg of thiamin, experts have found that the adult male is saturated with a daily intake of 1 to 2 mg and uses up less than 1 mg per day. The Recommended Dietary Allowance has been set at 1.1 mg for adult women and 1.5 mg for men.

Many companies are promoting "stress tablets" containing 5, 10 or even 15 mg of thiamin. Such doses can be appropriate for short-term treatment of severe thiamin deficiency, but are inappropriate and economically wasteful for healthy individuals. The RDA is about twice the minimum amount needed by the average person.

Over the past 40 years, experience with the treatment of humans and experiments with animals have indicated almost a complete lack of toxicity for thiamin taken by mouth. Taken orally, it is claimed to be safe in enormous amounts. Its relative safety, explain Hayes and Hegsted,[7] is "probably due to the fact that 5 mg is the maximum quantity that can be absorbed from a given (oral) dose." It has been reported that megadose thiamin can interfere with vitamins B_2 and B_6, causing deficiency symptoms.[8]

Since absorption is limited, it seems futile to self-medicate with daily doses of 100 mg thiamin—or even 10 mg—but such high potency tablets are being marketed. It even seems useless to take supplements providing more than 5mg of thiamin per tablet (the RDA is 1.5 mg). However, the FDA Advisory Panel[3] cites a case of a woman who was foolish enough to take 10,000 mg of thiamin and suffered irritability, headache, insomnia and weakness. On stopping the megadose thiamin, all symptoms cleared, but they returned when she took only 5 mg. This may be a case of sensitivity brought on by the severe abuse of taking thousands of times the RDA of a vitamin. Scientific studies of the behavior of such quantities in humans have not been reported.

Food Sources of Thiamin

Rich natural sources of thiamin are yeast, rice husks, wheat germ, soybean flour, liver and pork. Moderate concentrations are found in all lean meats (especially pork), as well as poultry, eggs, milk, and many seafoods including cod and salmon. Other moderate sources include oats, barley, brown rice, nuts, potatoes, asparagus, most beans, broccoli, peas, corn, cauliflower, plums, prunes and many other fruits and vegetables. Some fruits and vegetables contain lesser amounts of thiamin. Flour, cereals and other commercial grain products are now enriched to replace thiamin lost during the processing of wheat or rice. It is estimated[3] that in the United States, three-fourths of the dietary thiamin is obtained from vegetables, grains and lean meat, and one-fourth comes from enriched foods.

Thiamin Deficiency

Thiamin deficiency occurs most frequently in parts of the world where the diet still consists mainly of unenriched white rice and white flour. Thiamin deficiency is rare in the United States, probably because these products are enriched. In this country, thiamin deficiency occurs mainly among severe alcoholics. Others at risk include long-term kidney dialysis patients, and women suffering from prolonged vomiting during pregnancy.

The clinical signs of beriberi in adults involve primarily the nervous and cardiovascular systems. Most cases are mild, exhibiting altered reflexes and paresthesias (feelings of "pins and needles"), muscle weakness and cramps. More severe cases exhibit generalized swelling (edema), mental confusion, loss of appetite, uncoordinated gait, muscle wasting, increased pulse rate and enlargement of the heart.

Juvenile beriberi strikes infants whose nursing mothers subsisted chiefly on polished rice. It typically appears between the first and fifth month of life with infants showing a strange anguish called "silent crying" or a tendency to sudden death from heart failure. Because of enrichment, juvenile beriberi has become rare in recent years, even in Asia.

RIBOFLAVIN (VITAMIN B$_2$)[1,3,4,9]

Riboflavin is essential for maintenance of the skin, the mucous membranes, the cornea of the eye, and nervous system structures such as the myelin sheaths that surround the nerves. In experimental animals, development of the fetus and resistance to infections are impaired by deficiency of this vitamin.

Riboflavin is a key part of two important coenzymes called flavin mononucleotide (FMN) and flavin adenine dinucleotide (FAD). These coenzymes are involved in complex oxidation-reduction conversions in the liver, electron transport mechanisms that release energy within cells, and other important cellular respiratory functions.

Discovery of Riboflavin[4,9]

The first description of what later was identified as a case of riboflavin deficiency was by Stannus in 1912 in a British journal on tropical medicine. In 1938, the Americans Sebrell and Butler published the first definitive report of riboflavin deficiency in humans which became known as "ariboflavinosis." These and subsequent reports picture victims as suffering from inflammations of the eyes, lips, mouth and tongue, as well as scaly, greasy skin eruptions (seborrheic dermatitis). Much further understanding of riboflavin's role in human nutrition was contributed in 1949 by a research group led by M. K. Horwitt.[10]

Preparing pure riboflavin seemed at first to be an impossible job. Water extracts of vegetable or grain sources turned out to be mixtures of three water-soluble B-vitamins, thiamin, riboflavin and small amounts of niacin. The fact that some symptoms of riboflavin deficiency are similar to those of pellagra created additional confusion. Finally, the research team of Kuhn, Gyorgy and Wagner-Jauregg in 1933 isolated pure riboflavin from milk and proved it was different from thiamin and niacin. Determination of riboflavin's exact chemical structure and its synthesis in pure form were achieved in 1935 by two independent groups, a German group led by Richard Kuhn and a Swiss group headed by Paul Karrer. Dr. Karrer received a Nobel Prize in 1937, and Dr. Kuhn was awarded one the following year. However, because Kuhn was Jewish and had just been placed in a Nazi concentration camp, Hitler refused to let him accept. Surviving the war and the Nazis, Dr. Kuhn finally was formally honored by the Nobel Prize Committee.

How Much Riboflavin Do People Need?

The Recommended Dietary Allowance is 1.3 mg for young women and 1.7 mg for young men. When 2 to 3 times this amount is ingested, the excess is rapidly excreted in the urine, giving it a bright yellow color. In the United States, riboflavin deficiency requiring therapy occurs mainly in severe malnutrition such as is found in alcoholics.

Food Sources of Riboflavin

The richest sources of riboflavin are milk and other dairy products; the organ meats (liver and kidney) of cows, pigs and chickens; and also yeast. As with thiamin, moderate amounts of riboflavin are found in most fruits, grains, vegetables, lean meats and poultry. According to Professor George Briggs, milk supplies nearly 40 percent of the riboflavin in the American diet. Important amounts are also supplied by enriched bread and cereals.

No Toxicity Reported in Humans[3,9]

Riboflavin has always been considered safe for humans or animals at any oral dosage—and no cases of toxicity have been reported. According to Horwitt,[9] 1,000 mg orally per pound of body weight has produced no ill effects in animals.

T. K. Basu[11] reported on animal studies in which high dosages of riboflavin could retard some malignant tumors but increased the growth of others (see Chapter 16).

NIACIN (NICOTINIC ACID)[1,3,4,12]

Niacin is a generic term used by nutritionists to denote either nicotinic acid or its amide derivative, nicotinamide (which is often called niacinamide). "Niacin activity" of a food also can denote nicotinic acid formed by the body from tryptophan, an essential amino acid found in high-quality protein. (Note: nicotinic acid should not be confused with poisonous nicotine.) Obsolete names for nicotinic acid are vitamin B_3, vitamin B_4, and P-P Factor (Pellagra-Preventative Factor).

What Does Niacin Do for You?

Niacin is needed to provide energy to many tissues by promoting biochemical conversions of carbohydrates, fats and proteins. It does this by acting as either of two key coenzymes, nicotinamide adenine dinucleotide (NAD) or its phosphate derivative, NADP. Niacin is essential for growth and aids in the synthesis of hormones. Thus niacin catalyzes several essential oxidation-reduction and electron-transport reactions in many kinds of tissue cells.

Discovery of Niacin[4,12]

Pellagra, the niacin deficiency diseases, first appeared in Europe during the early 1700s when corn became a major source of protein. Peasants unable to afford meat had previously depended upon wheat to provide sufficient tryptophan for conversion by the body into niacin to supplement the tiny amounts in vegetables. But zein, the protein in corn, is almost devoid of tryptophan. Italian peasants of that period called the condition "pellagra," the Italian word for rough skin—one of the first signs of the disease. The first recorded description was published in 1735 by Casals, a Spanish physician who was also the first to cure it by adding milk to a victim's diet. However, the medical diagnosis of pellagra as a specific human disease was not clear-cut until about 1908.

In 1911, Casimir Funk isolated pure nicotinic acid from rice polishings and showed that it had the exact chemical structure as that synthesized by German chemists as early as 1867. A year later Funk published his famous paper, "The Etiology of Deficiency Diseases," in which he coined the term "vitamine." He concluded that the anti-beriberi vitamine was in rice polishings, that the anti-scurvy vitamine was in lime juice, and that pellagra seemed to be a nutritional deficiency (although nobody had proof). If he had tested the nicotinic acid he had prepared the year before on pellagra victims, he might have been awarded a Nobel Prize!

Oddly, as early as 1913, a British physician named Sandwich, working in Egypt, published the suggestion in a little-read journal that pellagra was probably caused by the lack of tryptophan in corn. In 1921, a British physiologist in Cairo, Egypt, proposed that pellagra among the poor people of Egypt and India was due to the "poor biological quality" of the protein in their diet.

Pellagra became epidemic in the southern United States between 1900 and 1920. In 1913, the U.S. Public Service sent bacteriologist Dr. Joseph Goldberger, one of the nation's best researchers, to investigate. Goldberger published his results in 1922. After first proving that pellagra is not an infection, he demonstrated that it is a nutritional deficiency by curing victims by improved diet or supplements of dried yeast added to their usual corn diet. Goldberger concluded that an essential pellagra-preventive factor was present in those foods which would cure the disease.

The understanding of pellagra was further advanced in 1937 when the research group led by Professor Elvehjem of the University of Wisconsin published their findings that nicotinic acid or its amide could cure black tongue in dogs—the equivalent of human pellagra. With Elvehjem's findings pointing the way, it was quickly shown in human cases that the anti-pellagra factor in yeast was also niacin.

Symptoms of Pellagra

The early symptoms of pellagra are usually lassitude, decreased appetite, and indigestion. These are followed by the classical "three D's," dermatitis, diarrhea and dementia. The dermatitis strikes mainly parts of the body exposed to sunlight, heat or mild injury: the face, neck, hands and feet. Inflammation of the mouth is sometimes so severe that the victim refuses to eat. In advanced cases, the whole digestive tract becomes inflamed.

Diarrhea is common in pellagra, but is not present in all cases. If a pellagra victim goes untreated for a considerable time, mental symptoms develop such as irritability, headaches, loss of memory, insomnia and emotional instability. In advanced cases, psychosis, acute delirium and stupor may follow; and then can come coma and death.

How Much Niacin Do Humans Need?

The 1980 Recommended Dietary Allowance is 14 Niacin Equivalents (NE) for young women, and 19 NE for young men. One NE equals 1 mg of niacin or 60 mg of tryptophan from dietary protein. It takes 60 mg of tryptophan for the human body to make 1 mg of niacin.

The human body easily converts nicotinic acid into its biologically active form, niacinamide. This form is preferred for large-dose therapy because it does not cause the unpleasant flushing produced by high-dose nicotinic acid.

Food Sources of Niacin

Each 60 mg of the amino acid, tryptophan, provided by digestion of high-quality protein, can be converted in the body to 1 mg of niacin. The richest sources of ready-made niacin are organ meats (liver and kidney) of beef, pork and chicken. Niacin content is also high in the meat of chicken and turkey, and in halibut and tuna. Moderate to low amounts are found in grains, fruits and vegetables. Milk and eggs contain smaller amounts of preformed niacin, but due to their high tryptophan content are good sources of niacin equivalents.

Very High Doses of Niacinamide May Harm[3,7,12]

In recent years, more than one person discussing vitamins with me has exclaimed, "But the B-vitamins are water-soluble and safe in any amount, aren't they?" No! Excessive amounts of niacin, vitamin B_6 and folic acid can cause trouble. The evidence now shows that nicotinic acid above 500 mg can be harmful, whereas the biologically active form, niacinamide may be reasonably safe (though needlessly high) up to 4,000 mg.[3]

Larry's Liver Flare-Ups[13]

Larry at age 34 had been under medical treatment for schizophrenia for several years but was otherwise healthy. Then his doctor prescribed 3 grams (3,000 mg) of niacinamide daily as part of his "orthomolecular" treatment. He felt well for another year, but then was hospitalized four times for severe nausea and vomiting. During the fourth hospital stay, liver function tests showed impairment, so a tentative diagnosis of infectious hepatitis was made. However, blood tests for hepatitis antibodies were negative. He was taken off all medication except the daily 2 to 3 grams of niacinamide, and within a few weeks, his liver function was back to normal.

Three months later, Larry was hospitalized again because of severe nausea, vomiting, chills, fever, skin rash and joint pain. This time his liver tests were strongly indicative of liver damage. He was then completely taken off his daily niacinamide vitamin dosage. A liver biopsy revealed tissue damage of an inflammatory and fibrotic type. After three weeks without any niacinamide or other medication, Larry's liver function tests returned to normal.

During this period, when Larry's doctor questioned him closely, he revealed that several days before each previous attack of nausea and vomiting he had increased the dose of niacinamide to a whopping 9 grams because it made him "feel better." He said he didn't connect his nausea with the vitamin dosage. To nail down the diagnosis of niacinamide poisoning, the doctors suggested an experiment. Larry agreed and was given gradually increasing doses of niacinamide, starting with 3 grams on the first day and increasing up to 9 grams on the fourth and following days. Liver function tests remained normal during the first 8 days. However, on the 8th day, diarrhea occurred. On the 10th day, Larry awoke with nausea, vomiting, loss of appetite, and extreme fatigue—and his liver tests showed impairment. His huge daily niacinamide intake was stopped, and his liver function tests returned to normal within three weeks and were still normal when tested six months later.

Carl's Cancer Scare[14]

In 1951, when he was 32, Carl developed yellowish plaque-like lesions in the skin of his elbows and knees. Six years later he finally had a hospital checkup which showed his blood cholesterol level to be 590 mg%, more than double the upper limit of normal. His total blood lipids (fats) were also very high. During the next four years, Carl took various prescribed drugs and also used safflower oil products in the hope of lowering his cholesterol level—but it remained elevated. Toward the end of this period, he began taking 100 mg of niacin per day and increased this dosage to 4,000 mg daily.

In 1961, after four months of high-dosage niacin intake, Carl entered a large U.S. military hospital because of the sudden apearance of dark brown wart-like spots on the skin of his armpits and elbows, and the back of his knees. The hospital doctors rightly decided that Carl's skin lesions resembled "acanthosis nigricans," a dangerous warning sign of internal cancer. Skin biopsies revealed slightly increased melanin (dark pigment) content, strengthening the suspicion of cancer. However, no signs of internal cancer could be found. The doctors had heard of rare cases of pseudo-acanthosis nigricans caused by endocrine gland disturbance or some drugs. So they stopped Carl's daily niacin but kept him on the safflower oil products. Two months later, Carl's skin lesion had almost disappeared. To test whether niacin had caused his pseudo-acanthosis nigricans, the doctors put him back on niacin—and the condition soon reappeared.

The medical report on Carl does not follow him much further, but we can assume that niacin was never again advised for his high blood lipid and cholesterol condition.

Niacin Can Harm[3,15]

Niacin, as nicotinic acid, is toxic in much lower dosages than as niacinamide. At doses as low as 300 mg it can cause transient flushing of the skin, headaches, cramps and nausea. After a week or two on this dosage, most patients adapt and can tolerate higher dosages. Yet Belle and Halpern[16] reported that 16 out of 48 patients treated for high levels of cholesterol stopped niacin treatment because of these symptoms. Evidence is strong that daily doses of 2,000 to 6,000 mg of niacin can cause serious liver damage with obstruction of normal flow of bile from the liver into the small intestine. Megadose niacin also can cause high blood sugar, high blood uric acid, widespread itching, skin peeling and irregular heartbeats. Hayes and Hegsted[7] claim that injections of as little as 100 mg of niacin counteract vitamin B_6. People taking the antituberculosis drug isoniazid (chemically a close cousin of niacin) need extra vitamin B_6.

Risk to Some Heart Patients from High-Dose Niacin

A warning of possible harm to heart patients appeared in a review of many medical reports by Dr. William J. Darby[17] and associates. These authorities referred to a report by the Coronary Drug Project Research Group of a cooperative research study in 53 clinical centers. In this study, niacin (nicotinic acid) was given to 1,119 men, all of whom had acquired heart muscle damage from a heart attack. An equal number of men with the same heart condition were given a placebo instead of niacin. The amount of niacin given was 3,000 mg daily for an average of about 6 years.

There was no difference in death rates between the two groups. The niacin group had somewhat fewer new non-fatal heart attacks, but its members also experienced more disturbances of heart rate and rhythm, gastrointestinal distress, and abnormal blood levels of enzymes, sugar and uric acid.

Len's Liver Damage[18]

About 20 years ago, 58-year-old Leonard underwent surgery to relieve impaired circulation to his kidney which had resulted in high blood pressure. Although his pressure fell, he later developed severe leg pains and was found to have narrowing of the arteries to several parts of his body including his legs. Noting that his blood cholesterol was high, and thinking this was probably a factor in causing his circulatory problems, Len's doctors placed him on 3,000 mg of nicotinic acid daily. During the next 6 months, Len's blood cholesterol level dropped to a very low normal of 100 mg percent.

After several more months on high-dosage niacin, Len developed swelling (edema) of the ankles and then of his hands and face. Hospital tests showed that a very low blood albumin (protein) level was responsible for the swelling and that his liver tests were abnormal. Niacin was suspected as the likely cause of the liver damage and was stopped. Within one month, Len's swelling was completely gone, and after three months his blood albumin and liver function tests were near normal.

High doses of niacin are rarely used to lower blood cholesterol because they are too toxic for most patients (see Chapter 17). Neither nicotinic acid nor nicotinamide (niacinamide) are considered safe or effective against schizophrenia by the majority of psychiatrists. Only a few mavericks who call their practice "orthomolecular" continue niacinamide use (see Chapter 15).

VITAMIN B$_6$[1,3,4,19]

Vitamin B$_6$ is found in three forms: pyridoxine, pyridoxal phosphate and pyridoxamine. Supplement pills almost always provide vitamin B$_6$ as pyridoxine hydrochloride. Vitamin B$_6$ is found largely as pyridoxal and pyridoxamine in animal products and occurs predominantly as pyridoxine in vegetables and grains. Rich sources are liver, herring, salmon, nuts, wheat germ, brown rice, yeast and blackstrap molasses. Moderate content of vitamin B$_6$ is found in most vegetables and in a few fruits such as bananas, grapes, pears and avocados; also in lean meats, fish, butter and eggs. Lower levels are available from cheese, milk and most other fruits. The 1980 Recommended Dietary Allowance is 2 mg of vitamin B_6 for young women and 2.2 mg for young men.

Vitamin B_6 is needed for more than 60 enzyme reactions, several of which involve enzymes called transaminases. It also forms a part of a vital coenzyme called co-decarboxylase which is involved in several reactions in the liver and one conversion in muscle tissue cells. Vitamin B_6 is needed for the following: conversion of the amino acid, tryptophan, into the vitamin niacin; manufacture by the body of such hormones as norepinephrine and serotonin; formation of the critical nerve controller, acetylcholine; stimulation (aided by vitamin C) of the production of bile acids from cholesterol; promotion of the health of the adrenal cortex (the production center for hormones of the cortisone type); maintenance of proper growth in the young; preservation of normal functioning of the brain and entire nervous system for which vitamin B_6 works together with thiamin. See Chapter 21 for special pyridoxine supplement needs and warnings about drug interactions with pyridoxine.

Discovery of Vitamin B_6[4,19]

Dr. Paul Gyorgy proved in 1934 that there was an essential food factor, not previously recognized, which he and his co-workers named vitamin B_6. Working with several different nearly pure fractions separated from yeast extracts, Gyorgy and co-workers found one yeast fraction that cured a skin disorder in rats fed a restricted diet. Gyorgy's group also proved that this fraction was neither thiamin nor riboflavin.

Pure crystalline pyridoxine was first isolated in 1938 by four different research teams, one led by Dr. Gyorgy, one led by the famous German chemist, Richard Kuhn, and two others. Dr. Kuhn's team obtained pure pyridoxine by extracting with solvents 14,000 gallons of skimmed milk, then concentrating and separating the extract into many fractions. Dr. Kuhn went further as he determined the exact molecular structure of the pure vitamin and named it "pyridoxine."

Soon evidence that pyridoxine or pyridoxal is essential to humans was provided by a group led by Dr. Thomas Spies,[20] an American pioneer in the medical treatment of vitamin deficiencies. In 1939, his team described vitamin B_6 deficiency in humans and reported that it cannot be cured with vitamins B_1 or B_2, but clears up in 24 hours when pyridoxine is added to the diet. The vitamin B_6 discovery picture was not complete, however, until 1945-48 when Snell and co-workers isolated two active forms of B_6 from vegetable and grain sources, namely pyridoxal and pyridoxamine.

Vitamin B₆ Deficiency

The symptoms of B_6 deficiency are weakness, irritability, nervousness, insomnia, difficulty in walking, and skin problems around the eyes, nose, mouth, forehead and sometimes in the crotch. Symptoms similar to niacin deficiency can also appear, including inflammations of the lips, tongue and mouth lining. A type of anemia called hypochromic anemia can also be caused by deficiency of B_6.

Infants fed heat-sterilized commercial liquid milk have developed irritability and convulsions that improved only when vitamin B_6 was added to their formulas. Some 300 cases were cured with pyridoxine treatment, as summarized in 1955 by Hawkins.

Prevention of Kidney Stones

In 1967, Drs. S. Gershoff and E. Prien[21] at Harvard University reported that a combination of 200 mg of magnesium oxide and 10 mg of pyridoxine daily for 5 years prevented recurrence of calcium oxalate kidney stones in 30 out of 36 patients. All 36 had had two or more stones yearly for two years before the experiment began.

No Help in Arthritis

A few years ago, when it was discovered that a majority of patients with rheumatoid arthritis have low blood levels of pyridoxal, vitamin enthusiasts recommended vitamin B_6 supplements for arthritics. But a study reported in 1975 by H. R. Schumacher and colleagues[22] found no benefit in 22 patients, all but one of whom had very low B_6 blood levels. Three months of daily treatment with 50 to 150 mg of pyridoxine raised the B_6 blood levels of 15 of them, but it did not help their arthritis.

Can B₆ Be Harmful?[3,7,19]

Hayes and Hegsted[7] noted in a 1973 review: "Daily oral doses of 100 to 300 mg of pyridoxine have been administered for the alleviation of drug-induced neuritis without side effects." But for what length of time is it safe? In 1970, after treating 58 women with 50 mg daily of pyridoxine, Baumblatt and Winston[23] reported that one woman complained of "lethargy," and a second woman who raised her dosage to 100 mg without consulting her doctor suffered from restlessness and insomnia. With extremely high doses of pyridoxine, human patients may show evidence of liver damage.[24]

In 1963, Dr. J. E. Canham and colleagues[25] reported treating 8 normal adult male volunteers with 200 mg of pyridoxine daily for 33 days. Three of the men developed abnormal brain wave patterns one week after stopping this high dosage. This may be evidence that adults can become "addicted" to high-dosage B_6.

The action of L-dopa, a drug used to treat Parkinson's disease, can be blocked by as little as 5 mg of pyridoxine daily (the RDA is 2 mg). In 1978, Drs. Jean Mayer and Johanna Dwyer[26] stated that very large doses of pyridoxine interfere with the body's utilization of riboflavin.

In 1980, Dr. G. Krinke and colleagues[27] demonstrated that oral doses of 3,000 to 4,000 mg (300 mg per kg of body weight) of pyridoxine for 8 to 9 days can cause widespread sensory nerve damage in dogs. Not long afterwards, two cases came to light of permanent numbness of the legs and hands which followed high doses of pyridoxine.[28] One was a 25-year-old man who took 3,000 mg daily for three months before symptoms appeared. The other was a 37-year-old woman who took gradually increasing daily doses up to 2,000 mg. These cases do not prove beyond a doubt that huge doses of vitamin B_6 can cause nerve damage in humans, but their difficulty appears to be similar to those of the dogs in Dr. Krinke's experiment.

VITAMIN B_{12} (COBALAMIN)[1,3,4,29]

The chemical name for vitamin B_{12} is cobalamin. "Cobal" is derived from cobalt, the mineral which is bound as an essential feature into vitamin B_{12}'s complicated organic structure. Cobalamin occurs in foods in linkage with small protein-like peptides, but this linkage is split in the stomach by enzymes. The freed cobalamin then joins with a special protein called intrinsic factor (IF) that is secreted by the stomach lining. Vitamin B_{12} cannot be absorbed into the body until hooked onto IF. Free cobalamin is unstable outside the body, so several more stable derivatives have been made such as hydroxycobalamin and cyanocobalamin. Of these, cyanocobalamin is most often used in supplements because it is the most stable.

Vitamin B_{12} Discovery[4,29]

Cases of pernicious anemia were described in the medical journals as early as Combe's report in England in 1822. But it was not until 1926 that Minot and Murphy cured a case using liver extracts. For this achievement, they received the Nobel Prize for Medicine in 1934. However, Minot and Murphy did not know the nature of the curative factor in the liver extracts. Now we know it was vitamin B_{12}. In 1929, Dr. William Castle and co-workers proved that there was an "extrinsic factor" (from outside the body) in the diet and an "intrinsic factor" (within the body) needed to permit absorption of the extrinsic factor during digestion. This extrinsic factor, then called "anti-pernicious anemia principle," is now called vitamin B_{12}.

B_{12} was not isolated in pure crystalline form until 1948, when this was accomplished independently by Rickes, Folkers and co-workers in the United States and by the team of Smith and Parker in England who named it vitamin B_{12}. Castle's "intrinsic factor" turned out to be a glycoprotein (protein attached to a complex sugar) secreted by the stomach lining and proved, indeed, to be essential for the absorption of vitamin B_{12}. The earliest therapeutic use of pure vitamin B_{12} was reported by West and Reisner[30] in 1949; and in 1965, Drs. Herbert and Sullivan[31] showed that as little as 0.1 microgram (μg) of B_{12} was a therapeutic dose—making B_{12} by far the most potent vitamin, molecule-for-molecule.

What B_{12} Does

The 1980 Recommended Dietary Allowance of B_{12} is 3 μg for adults and 4 μg for pregnant and lactating women. (A microgram is 1/1000 of a milligram or 1/millionth of a gram.) Though needed in only tiny amounts daily, cobalamin is a crucial component of coenzymes in three different enzyme systems that carry out 11 key conversions in the liver and several others in many body tissues. These reactions accomplish the following essential jobs: synthesis of RNA and DNA (the hereditary basic nucleic acids that control the life processes of all tissue cells); maintenance of the myelin sheath around nerve structures; maintenance of normal bone marrow (a red blood cell production center); help in the synthesis of porphyrin which, after iron is locked into it, becomes a key constituent of the hemoglobin portion of red blood cells. B_{12} is also required to maintain normal growth in children.

Vitamin B_{12} works together with folic acid in the synthesis of the red and white blood cells. Despite its popular reputation as a "blood builder," it needs folic acid to perform this function.

Pernicious Anemia[3,4,29]

Deficiency of vitamin B_{12} prevents optimum red blood cell development and leads to anemia. Typically, the early signs are weakness, shortness of breath, occasional faintness, headaches and inflammation of the mouth and tongue. Lack of vitamin B_{12} also results in nerve damage, especially to the myelin sheath that protects nerve fibers, causing loss of muscular coordination. It also results in enlargement of the spleen and high levels of unusable iron in the blood. Later stages bring impairment of mental ability and often paranoic disturbance because of the devastating degeneration of nervous structures—especially the spinal cord. Pernicious anemia is the name given to B_{12} deficiency due to inadequate or absent secretion of intrinsic factor. Without treatment with vitamin B_{12}, victims of this condition will die.

Vegetarians May Be At Risk

B_{12} is found in foods of animal origin. It is abundant in organ meats such as liver and kidney. Medium-rich sources are egg yolk, crabs, clams, oysters, salmon and herring. Lower levels of B_{12} are found in most other fish, lean meats, eggs, cheese and milk. There is essentially no vitamin B_{12} in fruits, vegetables or grains. Strict vegetarians who eat no meat, eggs, milk or cheese, may need to take B_{12} supplements by mouth or eat special yeasts. This is discussed in Chapter 21. If cobalt is present in the diet, intestinal bacteria may produce some vitamin B_{12}, but not enough to meet the minimum daily requirement. Cobalt supplements are dangerous (see Chapter 20).

Who Needs B_{12} Injections?

A good supply of vitamin B_{12} from the daily diet, even if supplemented with vitamin B_{12} pills, will not save a person from the tragic fate of pernicious anemia if intrinsic factor is lacking. Without its presence in the digestive juices, vitamin B_{12} cannot be absorbed into the body. When intrinsic factor is absent, the potential victim must receive injections of vitamin B_{12} on a regular basis—usually once a month.

It is important to note, however, that B_{12} shots are being given to many people who do not have pernicious anemia. Most doctors consider this poor medical practice. According to Dr. Philip Alper,[32] Associate Clinical Professor of Medicine, University of California Medical Center (San Francisco):

> Vitamin B_{12} shots are frequently used as placebos. B_{12} does have a lifesaving use—the treatment of pernicious anemia,[12] a *rare* disorder . . . But other uses of B_{12} are unscientific. The doctor who tells you that B_{12} or "liver" shots "will really fix you up" when you feel "run down" is using them as placebos. The use of B_{12} to treat iron deficiency is fuzzy thinking. Surveys of doctors' practices have shown that *frequent* use of B_{12} injections is often associated with poor standards of care in other areas.

Very Low Toxicity[3,7,29]

Vitamin B_{12} is virtually non-toxic in humans, even in doses 10,000 times the RDA.[29] However, a 1968 British medical review article by G. Hovding cites seven cases of adverse reactions to vitamin B_{12} injections reported in the world's medical journals between 1950 and 1967. In 1971, an Italian physician, C. Nava, reported that over a period of many years he had observed three cases of adverse reactions from vitamin B_{12}.

In 1981, Dr. Victor Herbert[33] reported evidence that B_{12} in multivitamin tablets can break down into warped molecules, some of which may have anti-B_{12} activity that can contribute to deficiency. His laboratory found such breakdown products in 10 out of 10 popular vitamin products tested. It also appears that the presence of warped molecules can make the diagnosis of pernicious anemia more difficult because standard methods of measuring B_{12} blood levels may give "normal" results even when no functional B_{12} is present.[34] More work needs to be done to determine the significance of these findings to multivitamin users.

FOLACIN (FOLIC ACID)[1,3,4,29]

Folacin is a generic term covering several complex micronutrients that intestinal bacteria split to form folic acid. Folic acid's full chemical name is pteroylmonoglutamic acid, usually called just pteroylglutamic acid (PGA). Obsolete names are vitamin M, vitamin Bc, anti-anemia factor, or Wills Factor.

Folic acid is a required coenzyme for five different enzyme systems. It is essential for: normal production of red and white blood cells; proper development of the fetus and infants; maintenance of a healthy adult nervous system; normal functioning of the gastrointestinal tract; key reactions for the manufacture of basic cell nucleic acids, DNA and RNA; and other physiologic functions.

The 1980 Recommended Dietary Allowance of folic acid is 400 micrograms (μg) for adults. This amount more than meets the needs of normal adults. Even in cases of medically diagnosed folic acid deficiency, only 50 to 250 μg of synthetic folic acid is enough to correct the condition. Dr. Herbert[29] in 1980 stated that 100 μg (0.1 mg) of folic acid will usually suffice, although 1,000 μg (1 mg) may be used in complicated cases of proven deficiency. The RDA for infants is 30 μg from dietary sources.

Discovery of Folacin[1,3,29]

Illnesses that must have been folic acid deficiencies were described as early as 1851 and were associated mainly with anemia and malnutrition in pregnancy. In 1937, a British scientist, Dr. L. Wills, cured the anemia of pregnant women in India with a yeast preparation. The missing nutrient was called "Wills Factor" and for several years was incorrectly thought to be the anti-pernicious anemia vitamin.

Dr. Wills then fed monkeys a carefully designed diet on which they developed anemia similar to the anemia of pregnant women, and which she could cure with either yeast or crude liver extracts. But purified liver extracts that could cure pernicious anemia failed to cure the anemic monkeys. Later it was shown that the purification process destroyed folic acid but not the vitamin B_{12} in liver.

In 1941, a research team led by Mitchell found "Wills Factor" in spinach. Since the Latin word for "leafy" is folate, he suggested folate as the name of neutral salts of folic acid.

Food Sources of Folic Acid

The richest sources of folic acid are liver, wheat bran, spinach, asparagus and many beans such as navy, lentil, lima. Medium-rich sources include most grains such as oats, wheat, rye and barley; certain vegetables such as corn, snap beans, beet and turnip greens and broccoli; and some nuts. Lower levels of folic acid are found in lean meats, cheese, milk, most fruits, most other vegetables and some nuts.

Folacin Deficiency

Folic acid has been called the anti-anemia vitamin. Lack of folic acid produces an anemia (macrocytic, megaloblastic type) in which the red blood cells are abnormally large and reduced in number.

Some of the symptoms of folacin deficiency mimic those of B_{12} deficiency. Other folic acid deficiency symptoms, unrelated to vitamin B_{12}, are diarrhea, sore tongue and severe weight loss. *If an anemia is due only to a lack of B_{12}, self-treatment with folic acid will improve red blood cells but not prevent continuing disintegration of the nervous system, especially the spinal cord.*

Dorothy's Preventable Decline[35]

When Mrs. Dorothy W. was 72, her acquaintances marveled at her pep and liveliness. She played nine holes of golf three times a week and did volunteer work three mornings a week at the local hospital. She was very fortunate to have such abundant health, and also because she had had a wise family physician for many years. Ten years earlier, Dorothy had been in sad shape. Gradually, after her 61st birthday, she began to notice difficulty in coordinating her muscular movements, mostly in walking or just moving about at home. Later she developed a sore tongue. Finally, she went to her long-time family physician; and fortunately for her, he correctly diagnosed her condition as pernicious anemia.

Dorothy's doctor knew that victims of pernicious anemia cannot absorb vitamin B_{12} from their intestinal tract because they lack "intrinsic factor." Therefore she was given weekly injections of vitamin B_{12} and liver extracts. Within a few months, her anemia and muscle coordination problems had all disappeared, and she felt like her "old" vigorous self again. Faithfully she got her weekly vitamin B_{12} injections for the next 10 years. At age 72, Dorothy had a complete physical examination and was pronounced in excellent condition for her age.

A year later, she moved to another city and, under the care of a new doctor, she went for vitamin B_{12} injections only occasionally during the next five years. Then, for some reason not mentioned in the published case report, she stopped getting the vitamin B_{12} injections altogether and for two years relied only on daily multivitamin pills containing either 0.1 mg or 0.25 mg of folic acid plus vitamin B_{12}.

At age 80, Dorothy was taken to the hospital so badly crippled that she could not walk at all. As a pernicious anemia patient, she could get absolutely no vitamin B_{12} benefit from her diet or the multivitamin supplement. To prove this, the hospital doctors gave her a tiny amount of radioactive vitamin B_{12} by mouth and traced its course through her body. Absolutely none was absorbed from her intestines, clearly confirming her former doctor's diagnosis of pernicious anemia.

Poor Dorothy W., so healthy and vigorous at age 73, and whose pernicious anemia had been completely controlled for 11 years by the regular injections of vitamin B_{12}, was now permanently crippled. While folic acid in the multivitamin pill prevented her from becoming anemic and thus developing early warning signs, her long-time lack of B_{12} had caused irreversible damage to her spinal cord.

The same thing happened to Major J., a retired U.S. Army officer, who became increasingly tired over a year's time during the early 1950s.[35] When he visited the outpatient clinic of a university hospital, he was advised to take a daily multivitamin capsule containing folic acid. Within a few weeks he felt much better, but a year later, he returned to the hospital because of difficulty in walking and occasional inability to control urination (incontinence).

After examination by the medical staff revealed spinal cord disease, further testing was done which led to the diagnosis of pernicious anemia. He was immediately started on weekly injections of vitamin B_{12}. Sad to say, Major J.'s spinal cord damage was permanent and irreversible. Although his vitamin B_{12} weekly injections could prevent further damage, they could not reverse what had already been done.

The army doctors who wrote the case report had this conclusion: "The patient had pernicious anemia . . . The folic acid in the multivitamin capsules improved his symptoms but permitted the disease of his spinal cord to progress until he had difficulty in walking and holding his water. Had he not been given folic acid the symptoms would have persisted and the development of obvious anemia would have led to earlier diagnosis."

The message should be clear to those tempted to cure "tiredness" by self-medication with vitamins, or to follow the advice of quack nutritionists to use folacin for what ails you!

Hoping to limit self-medication with folic acid, the Food and Drug Administration (FDA) requires a doctor's prescription for doses higher than 0.8 mg. This is one of the few vitamin regulations that Congress did not overturn in 1976.

Direct Toxicity[3,7,29]

Direct toxicity from folic acid has not been reported. In adults, doses of folic acid up to 400 mg per day (1,000 times the RDA) for 5 months have been shown to cause no ill effects, provided a person does not have pernicious anemia, according to Hayes and Hegsted.[7] They also stated that 10 mg of folic acid per day has been tolerated for five years without noticeable ill effect.

Diphenylhydantoin (Dilantin) is a drug commonly used by people with epilepsy. According to Dr. Victor Herbert,[29] it is risky for epileptics using this drug to take daily doses of folic acid above the RDA because it can interfere with the drug's protective action against convulsions.

BIOTIN[1,3,4,36]

Biotin is an essential coenzyme for a key enzyme system called Acetyl Coenzyme A Carboxylase, as well as for eight other important enzymes that carry out vital interconversion of amino acids to blood sugar and to needed unsaturated fats (and often the reverse). Biotin is critically involved in these important roles: normal growth of the young; maintenance of normal nervous tissue, skin, hair, blood cells and sex organs. Obsolete names for biotin include vitamin H, anti-egg-white-injury factor, Bios I and Bios II.

In 1940, pioneer nutrition scientist Paul Gyorgy showed that the various growth stimulant factors observed as early as 1924 in yeast, egg yolk, legumes and bacteria, were all biotin equivalents. According to Drs. Appel and Briggs,[36] in order to test whether biotin was really essential in human nutrition, Sydenstricker and co-workers in 1942 produced a specific deficiency illness in human volunteers. Because biotin is so widely distributed in foodstuffs, the volunteers' diet was planned around foods low in biotin and rich in egg white. (Raw egg white prevents the absorption of biotin.) Five weeks later, all volunteers had skin rash, grayish skin, muscular aches, lethargy, depression, extreme sensitivity to touch or pain, loss of appetite, nausea and anemia, high blood cholesterol and electrocardiogram changes. Injections of pure biotin cured all of them within five days.

Amounts Needed

Biotin occurs widely in foods and is plentiful in egg yolk, liver, kidney and in some vegetables, especially peas and soybeans. Moderate to poor sources of biotin include meat, cereal grains (except wheat where it is found in a complex and is not absorbable), fruits and most vegetables.

The Food and Nutrition Board's 1980 estimated safe and adequate intake is 100 to 200 micrograms (μg) a day for adults. Much of the daily requirement is provided by intestinal bacteria. Usually the combined urinary and fecal excretion of biotin exceeds the dietary intake,[1] indicating that extra is made by intestinal micro-organisms.

Reviews of medical journals by Appel and Briggs[36] and by Hayes and Hegsted[7] do not mention any toxicity or adverse effects from biotin taken by mouth, nor did the FDA Advisory Panel[3] in 1979. An earlier review by Drs. Paul Gyorgy and B. W. Langer, Jr.[37] states that in mice, a single dose of the human equivalent of 70 grams (70,000 mg) of biotin had no toxic effects. However, they do point out that biotin appears to depress the secretion of hydrochloric acid by the glands of the stomach lining. Thus daily dosing with biotin might affect elderly individuals whose secretion of stomach acid is already subnormal.

PANTOTHENIC ACID[1,3,4,38]

Pantothenic acid gets its name from the Greek word meaning "from everywhere" because it occurs so widely in foods. Its obsolete names are vitamin B_3, Bios IIA and the Anti-gray-hair factor. Pantothenic acid is an essential part of coenzyme-A which is part of the energy regulating system.

In 1933, Dr. Roger Williams and co-workers observed that pantothenic acid is an essential nutrient for the growth of yeasts, and in 1933-34, they isolated the pure vitamin and synthesized it. In 1939, Dr. Thomas Jukes showed that pantothenic acid was the anti-dermatitis factor necessary for chickens. Soon it was proven essential for rats, mice, dogs, pigs, fish and monkeys. Deficiency in humans is rare because of its widespread distribution in foodstuffs. The Food and Nutrition Board's 1980 estimated safe and adequate intake is 4 to 7 mg daily for adults.

The richest sources of pantothenic acid are eggs, liver, kidneys, wheat bran and peanuts. Medium-rich sources are lean meats, peas, beans, rice, oats, carrots, kale and spinach. Lower levels are found in most fruits, most other vegetables, nuts and seafood.

Deficiency in Humans

Pantothenic vitamin deficiency usually develops as part of a multiple deficiency of all the B-vitamins in severe malnutrition and chronic alcoholism.[38] However, human volunteers given a precisely prepared diet containing all nutrients except pantothenic acid have been studied.[39] After several days, these subjects began to experience the following symptoms: malaise, abdominal cramps, vomiting, leg cramps, nausea, impairment of defenses (antibodies) against infection. Later, fatigue, insomnia develop along with the sensations of prickling, numbness or burning of the hands. The volunteers were restored to normal within a few days by the administration of large doses of pantothenic acid, after which RDA amounts sufficed for health.

No Toxicity Reported

In humans there seems to be a wide margin of safety for the ingestion of pantothenic acid. The Hayes and Hegsted[7] review of the medical journals stated that a dosage as high as 7 grams for a 140-pound man did not cause ill effects; but diarrhea with such intakes has been reported elsewhere. Injections of the human equivalent dose of 70 grams (70,000 mg) has caused death in rats and mice. Unna and Greslin in 1940 showed that rats will tolerate 14 grams of pantothenic acid daily for four months but are killed by one injection of 55 grams. They also found that dogs could tolerate 3,500 mg daily for 100 days.

Even though no human toxicity has been reported, supplementing with pantothenic acid *makes no sense*. People who eat a variety of foods will not develop a deficiency of this nutrient; and malnourished individuals who do so need other B-vitamins as well.

References

1. Food and Nutrition Board: Recommended Dietary Allowances, 9th Ed. National Academy of Sciences, Washington, DC, 1980.
2. Neal, R. A. and Sauberlich, H. E.: *In* Modern Nutrition in Health and Disease, 6th Ed. (R. S. Goodhart and M. E. Shils, Eds.) Philadelphia, Lea and Febiger, 1980, pp. 191-197.
3. FDA Advisory Review Panel: Federal Register 44:16126-16201, March 16, 1979.
4. Kutsky, R. J.: Handbook of Vitamins and Hormones. New York, Van Nostrand Reinhold Co., 1973.
5. Takaki: Lancet 2:189, 1887.
6. Funk, C.: Journal of State Medicine 20:341-368, 1912; reprinted in Nutrition Reviews 33:176, June 1975.
7. Hayes, K. C. and Hegsted, D. M.: Toxicity of Vitamins, *in* Toxicants

Occurring Naturally in Foods, 2nd Ed. Food and Nutrition Board, National Academy of Sciences, Washington, DC, 1973.

8. Ostwald, R. and Briggs, G.: Toxicity of Vitamins, *in* Toxicants Occurring Naturally in Foods, 1st Ed., 1966, *op. cit.*, p. 204.

9. Horwitt, M. K.: *In* Modern Nutrition in Health and Disease, *op. cit.*, pp. 197-203.

10. Horwitt, M. K. et al.: Journal of Nutrition 39:357, 1949.

11. Basu, T. K.: Oncology 33:183, 1976.

12. Horwitt, M. K.: *In* Modern Nutrition in Health and Disease, *op. cit.*, pp. 204-208. .

13. New England Journal of Medicine 289:1180, 1973.

14. Archives of Dermatology 89:222, 1964.

15. Medical Letter 15:7, 1973.

16. Belle, M. and Halpern, M.: American Journal of Cardiology 12:449, 1958.

17. Darby, W., McNutt, K. and Todhunter, E.: Nutrition Reviews 33:289, 1975.

18. JAMA 175:161, 1961.

19. Sauberlich, H. E. and Canham, J. E.: *In* Modern Nutrition in Health and Disease, *op cit.*, pp. 216-229.

20. Spies, T. et al.: JAMA 112:2414, 1939.

21. Gershoff, S. W. and Prien, E. L.: *Ibid.* 20:393, 1967.

22. Schumacher, H. F. et al.: American Journal of Clinical Nutrition 28:1200, 1975.

23. Baumblatt, M. and Winston, F.: Lancet 2:832, April 18, 1970.

24. Gaull, G. E. et al.: Neuropaedriatrie (Stuttgart) 1:199, 1969.

25. Canham, J. E. et al.: Proceedings of the 6th International Congress of Nutrition (1963). E. & S. Livingstone Ltd., London, 1964, p. 537.

26. Mayer, J. and Dwyer, J.: Chicago Tribune, Sec. G, May 4, 1978, p. 26.

27. Krinke, G. et al.: Neurotoxicology 2:13-24, 1980.

28. Schaumberg, H. et al.: Abstract submitted to Annals of Neurology, 1982.

29. Herbert, V. et al.: *In* Modern Nutrition in Health and Disease, *op. cit.*, pp. 229-259.

30. West, R. and Reisner, H.: American Journal of Medicine 6:643, 1949.

31. Sullivan, L. W. and Herbert, V.: New England Journal of Medicine 272:340, 1965.

32. Alper, P.: Avoiding the Marginal Medic. *In* The Health Robbers, 2nd Ed. (S. Barrett, Ed.), Philadelphia, George F. Stickley Co., 1980.

33. Herbert, V. et al.: Clinical Research 29(3):673A, 1981.

34. Medical World News, Sept. 28, 1981, pp. 12-13.

35. Military Medicine 125:233, 1960.

36. Appel, J. A. and Briggs, G. M.: *In* Modern Nutrition in Health and Disease, *op. cit.*, pp. 274-279.

37. Gyorgy, P. and Langer, B.: Pharmacology of Biotin, *in* The Vitamins, Vol. II, 2nd Ed. (W. Sebrell and R. Harris, Eds.), 1968.

38. Sauberlich, H. E.: *In* Modern Nutrition in Health and Disease, *op cit.*, pp. 209-216.

39. Hodges, R. E. et al.: American Journal of Clinical Nutrition 11:45, 1962.

12

Vitamin C Can Help or Harm

Scurvy, the deficiency disease caused by lack of vitamin C in the human diet, was known for at least 3,000 years before its cause was linked to a food factor. A disease that was undoubtedly scurvy is described in the medical writings of the ancient Egyptians of about 1500 B.C. Writings of the ancient Greeks and Romans tell of a sporadic but widespread illness that also sounds like scurvy. Explorers of the 16th, 17th and 18th centuries wrote about the disastrous plague of scurvy that often rendered 90 percent of a ship's crew unable to work and caused the death of half or more of the crews after several months of voyaging. Today, of course, scurvy is quite rare in civilized countries.

Signs of Scurvy[1,2]

The early signs of scurvy in adults include: weakness; pinpoint-size bleeding spots (petechial hemorrhages) under the skin due to leakage of blood from the capillaries; bruises which develop as bleeding increases; and horny overgrowth of skin around the hair follicles of the arms, legs and abdomen. After about two months, victims develop swollen and bleeding gums, loosened teeth, bleeding into the membranes covering the eyeballs, anemia, extreme dryness of the mouth and eyes, dry itchy skin, loss of hair, extreme weakness, aching legs, and severe joint pains. In the final stages (75 to 90 days), the gums may rot, mental aberrations appear, and death can occur suddenly.

In infants, scurvy can be difficult to diagnose. Its early signs are loss of appetite, listlessness and irritability. Bleeding and gum problems similar to those of the adult develop later, as do tenderness of the arms and legs caused by bleeding under the membranes covering the bones.

Discovery of Vitamin C[2]

Credit for first linking scurvy to something lacking in the diet is usually given to James Lind, a British naval doctor who published his famous

Treatise on Scurvy in 1753, telling how he cured and prevented scurvy in English sailors by using lime juice. (They were consequently called "limeys" by the rest of the world.) However, much earlier but little publicized writings tell how the Indians of eastern Canada showed explorer Jacques Cartier a cure for scurvy during the mid-1500s with extracts of needles from the white cedar tree. In 1593, explorer Sir Richard Hawkins reported that he had successfully treated British sailors for scurvy with oranges and lemons—as also did James Lancaster, a British sea captain. But the world ignored these early reports, and even the British Admiralty ignored Dr. Lind's advice for nearly 100 years before providing citrus fruit for voyaging sailors.

The anti-scurvy factor had been recognized as a vitamin and called vitamin C as early as 1920, but full identification of vitamin C as a pure chemical compound required the combined discoveries of Albert Szent-Gyorgyi in 1928 and Professor Charles Glen King in 1932. In the mid-1920s, Dr. Szent-Gyorgyi, a Hungarian biochemist, was looking for biologically important antioxidants in foodstuffs, working in the Cambridge University laboratory of Sir Frederick Hopkins. In 1928, Szent-Gyorgyi[3] reported the isolation of a pure substance he called "hexuronic acid" from oranges, cabbage leaves and the adrenal glands of cattle. It proved to be a potent antioxidant, but he did not realize he had vitamin C in hand.

Meanwhile, at the University of Pittsburgh, Dr. King was searching specifically for the anti-scurvy food factor in lemon juice concentrates. By 1931 he had obtained potent concentrates that protected guinea pigs from scurvy. Finally, in 1932 King[4,5] and his student, W. A. Waugh, isolated pure, crystalline vitamin C and proved it identical to Szent-Gyorgyi's hexuronic acid and able to cure scurvy in guinea pigs. During the same month, Szent-Gyorgyi,[6] having been helped by a former associate of King, reported the curing of scurvy with hexuronic acid. Most nutrition scientists consider King and Szent-Gyorgyi to be co-discoverers of vitamin C.

In 1933, Szent-Gyorgyi and the great English sugar chemist, Walter Haworth, suggested that vitamin C be given the common chemical name of "ascorbic acid"—*a*- meaning without and *scorbic* referring to the scorbutic (scurvy) condition. During the following year, three separate research teams led by future Nobel Prize winners were able to synthesize the pure substance.

What Does Vitamin C Do for You?[2,7-9]

Vitamin C can act as an essential co-factor (similar to a co-enzyme) as part of an enzyme system, but usually functions as a so-called "redox couple." (In the redox couple, ascorbic acid is regenerated, shuttling back and forth between its oxidized and reduced chemical states.) This versa-

tile power of vitamin C gives it the ability to carry out at least ten key
biochemical functions:

1) helps maintain and repair all connective tissues, especially the
   collagen component
2) helps maintain healthy bone, teeth and cartilage
3) promotes the synthesis in the adrenal glands of the anti-inflammatory steroid hormones of the hydrocortisone type
4) aids in the synthesis of the hormones serotonin (involved in nervous system functioning) and norepinephrine (for blood pressure
   control)
5) promotes the healing of wounds and recovery from traumatic stress
6) aids in the control of bleeding by helping to maintain the capillaries
7) maintains healthy adrenal glands and ovaries
8) promotes the absorption of iron from the stomach and small intestines into the blood stream
9) maintains the efficiency of the white blood cells, especially their
   ability to engulf bacteria and viruses
10) helps maintain cholesterol balance.

Food Sources of Vitamin C

Contrary to what many people believe, the richest sources of vitamin C
are not citrus fruits but black currants, sweet peppers, broccoli, turnip
greens, kale and Brussels sprouts. Oranges, lemons, strawberries and pa-
payas are medium-rich, as are cabbage, spinach, watercress, cauliflower
and beet greens. Lower but still significant levels of vitamin C are found in
tomatoes, potatoes, peas, onions and most other vegetables and fruits.
Tomatoes are the number one source of vitamin C in the American diet
because of their high consumption (70 pounds per person per year).

Vitamin C is easily destroyed by oxidation, but its perishability has been
somewhat exaggerated. Exposure to heat, air and a few chemicals hasten
the process, but many foods rich in vitamin C contain antioxidants that
help to preserve the vitamin C they contain. It is a good idea, of course, to
include at least one portion of a fresh or fresh-frozen source of vitamin C
in your daily diet.

How Much Vitamin C Do You Need?

The Recommended Dietary Allowance for vitamin C is 60 mg for adults,
with more needed during pregnancy and lactation. These amounts are
based on the amount needed to prevent scurvy, the amount metabolized
by the body daily, and the amount needed to maintain adequate reserves.
It is known that only 10 mg is necessary to prevent scurvy,[10] but this

amount does not provide for adequate reserves. The use of cigarettes and of oral contraceptives has been observed to lower blood levels of vitamin C somewhat,[11] but RDA-level intake is still adequate to cope with this situation.[12]

In his book, *Vitamin C and the Common Cold,*[13] Linus Pauling estimates the optimum daily intake of vitamin C at a minimum of 2,300 mg, based upon the vitamin C content of over 100 raw plant foods available to (presumably ape-like) ancestors of modern humans. Noting that most animals make vitamin C within their bodies, Pauling claims that the fact that humans do not is an unfortunate evolutionary mistake. But Professor Thomas Jukes, a vitamin pioneer who is Professor of Medical Physics at the University of California (Berkeley), strongly disagrees. In journal articles[14,15] in 1975 and 1976, he argues that primitive humans actually ate animal foods as well as plant foods such as wild raw fruits, grains, nuts and seeds. Meat, nuts and seeds contain practically no vitamin C.

Pauling and Jukes agree that the primitive ancestor of humans lost the ability to make vitamin C at a time and place where vitamin C was plentiful in the food supply. Pauling[16] claims that most animals retained the ability to make vitamin C because they couldn't afford to give it up—and that modern humans therefore have the same requirement. But Jukes believes that humans lost the ability to manufacture vitamin C because they obtained enough from their diet. As he reasons,[14] this loss would be extremely unlikely to occur unless the need for vitamin C was very small— for if it were large and the ability to make it were suddenly lost—human mobility would have been sharply curtailed. He adds: "The evolutionary loss . . . is perhaps the most powerful argument for a low requirement in human beings."[15]

I believe that Dr. Jukes presents by far the better argument. Moreover, Pauling's suggestion that humans need over 2,000 mg daily seems illogical when one looks at what happens when large doses of vitamin C are consumed—or the fact that only 10 mg per day will prevent and cure scurvy.

Maximum Body Storage

Many experiments, starting with Dr. Robert Hodges and co-workers[17] in 1969 and including some with radioactive vitamin C,[10,18] have shown that normal human adults have an average body pool of approximately 1,500 mg of vitamin C. The term "body pool," as used by these researchers, refers to the amount in blood serum plus that which is stored in the white blood cells and blood platelets but which is readily available from them. An adult deprived of dietary vitamin C normally uses up about 3 percent of this 1,500 mg pool—about 45 mg per day.[10] Oral intake of 60 mg is sufficient to replace this loss in most people.[1] Scurvy develops when the body pool falls below 300 mg, which occurs after 55 to 60 days on extremely low or zero vitamin C daily intakes.

The maximum amount of vitamin C which can be held in all body tissues, including the brain, liver, kidneys and adrenal glands as well as the body pool reserves described above, has been estimated by some as being as high as 5,000 mg, but according to Dr. Terence W. Anderson,[19] it is about 4,000 mg. Assuming that 3 percent is used up daily, he reasons that 120 mg per day will maintain "tissue saturation." Kallner et al,[18] using radioactive vitamin C, showed that only 100 mg are needed to maintain an active body pool of 1,400 to 1,500 mg.

Is tissue saturation desirable? Dr. Robert E. Hodges, an international authority on vitamin C and Chief of the Clinical Nutrition Division at the University of Nebraska Medical Center, is skeptical. He states:

> No one pretends that mere avoidance of deficiency disease represents an optimal nutrient intake for humans. But the term *tissue saturation,* when referring to vitamin C allowances, suggests that there is something healthful about "full saturation" with this nutrient. This same philosophy has never been used with regard to any other nutrient, with the possible exception of protein. For example, we make no effort to try to attain the highest possible tissue concentration of thiamin, riboflavin, pantothenic acid or, indeed, even of iron.[2]

The concept of tissue saturation may have some usefulness in evaluating Linus Pauling's suggestion that everyone should take thousands of milligrams of vitamin C daily. Imagine for a moment that you have a bathtub that is plugged at the bottom and has a large overflow valve near the top. When the bathtub is filled (saturated), the water level is just up to the overflow valve. If no water is added (the equivalent of having no vitamin C in your diet), evaporation will gradually lower the water level to a point where there is not enough to take a bath (scurvy). If water is added at the rate it evaporates, saturation will be maintained. If water is added at a slightly faster rate, the level may temporarily rise slightly above the overflow valve, but the extra water will be rapidly drained (just as a small excess of vitamin C is excreted in the urine). If water is added at an extremely fast rate, it will pour over the top and cause a flood (just as excessive vitamin C passes through the intestines unabsorbed and may cause diarrhea). Assuming that the water in the bathtub never needs changing, your most economical course of action is obviously to add just enough water (the Recommended Daily Allowance) to keep it at a comfortable level for your bath.

Limits of Vitamin C Absorption from the Gut

In 1975, Dr. J. Angel and co-workers[20] at the University of British

Columbia tested 5 healthy young men who all had vitamin C dietary intakes of less than 150 mg and were found to have "normal" saturation with a "ready" body pool of about 1,500 mg. On daily supplements of 180 mg of vitamin C, 100 percent was absorbed. When the daily dosage was increased, here is what happened:

Amount of Vitamin C Supplement Given	Amount Absorbed	Amount Lost in Feces*	Amount Found in Urine**
1st week: 1,000 mg/day	500 mg	500 mg	500 mg
2nd week: 2,000 mg/day	1,000 mg	1,000 mg	1,000 mg
3rd week: 3,000 mg/day	1,500 mg	1,500 mg	1,500 mg
4th week: 5,000 mg/day	1,500 mg	3,500 mg	1,500 mg

*(Or destroyed by bacterial action within the intestines)
**Amounts are approximate

As you can see, when vitamin C is given in amounts of 1,000 mg (1 gram) or more, the higher the daily dosage, the smaller the percentage absorbed and the higher the amount excreted unchanged in your feces. This study found the absorbable limit to be 1,500 mg. Another study[21] found that only 1,900 mg out of a single 12,000 mg dose was absorbed. Spacing the daily dosage throughout the day can raise the percentage absorbed,[18,22] but huge amounts are unlikely to do more for you than moderate amounts. Moreover, the more vitamin C you take in, the greater your chances of having trouble from it.

What can happen? For one thing, there is good evidence[23-25] that the human body copes with unnaturally high amounts of vitamin C by developing biochemical methods to destroy it more quickly. As a result, people who take 1,000 mg or more daily for a sufficiently long period of time can become "addicted." If they stop taking it abruptly, their vitamin C reserve drops sharply below normal and they can develop "rebound scurvy." Let's look at two case reports.

Skeptical Professor Scuttled[24]

Professor S. had been reading about what happened when guinea pigs given massive dosages of vitamin C were suddenly withdrawn from them. He had also been astonished to note the vast number of fellow Americans taking 1 to 10 grams (1,000 to 10,000 milligrams) daily in response to Pauling's book. He wondered what would happen to such persons if, after taking such doses of vitamin C for several weeks or months, they suddenly stopped the supplement but continued a normal diet furnishing 60 to 100 mg of vitamin C per day. So he experimented on himself, starting with 10 grams of vitamin C per day for the first few days and continuing with 10 to 15 grams daily for 2 weeks. Then he abruptly stopped and ate only his usual diet which he calculated would furnish about 100 mg of vitamin C daily.

A few days later, he began to notice mild symptoms and soon his condition worsened. On the 20th day, Professor S. awoke with swollen gums that bled slowly. Two days later, his arm and leg joints became painful. His skin erupted with many tiny hard bumps leaving it very rough and uncomfortable. A few days later, he discovered that his teeth were so loose that he could actually wiggle them in their sockets. Without doubt, he had developed rebound scurvy. So he started to treat himself with moderate daily doses of vitamin C. His symptoms slowly cleared up over a 2-week period, and he then gradually reduced his vitamin C supplementation to zero.

This case reflects my belief that the greatest risk of vitamin C megadosage is rebound scurvy. The lesson to be learned, as the experts and even Professor Pauling point out, is not to stop abruptly but to gradually reduce the daily dose over several weeks. But what if you suddenly become severely ill, have a serious injury or undergo emergency surgery? Will your attending doctors know that you are dependent on daily megadose C? What if you are unconscious or forget to tell them? You may become vitamin C-deficient during the first few critical days—just when you need extra —and your recovery may be jeopardized!

How common is rebound scurvy? There are not many medical journal reports of this condition—probably for two reasons. First, many people who take vitamin C supplements do not take enough to become "addicted." Second, many who do take enough to become dependent either keep on taking it or gradually reduce their dosage when they stop. Below, however, is a case of a totally innocent victim.

Paul's Painful Joints[26]

Paul M., born healthy in 1960, was fed an infant formula plus 60 mg of vitamin C daily. He thrived for a few weeks before problems began to develop. Then he became irritable and would cry out in pain when picked up. His breath became bad and he developed tenderness of the arms, legs and ribs. When Paul's mother noticed reddish-purple bleeding spots in his skin, she became alarmed and finally took him to a hospital.

There the doctors quickly diagnosed the problem as scurvy. It is known that as little as 10 mg of vitamin C per day prevents scurvy in adults. Young Paul had been getting 60 mg of vitamin C every day since birth.

Why then did he develop scurvy? One of the doctors had read about experiments reported a few years earlier by Czech medical researchers[27,28] in which guinea pigs and human volunteers put on high-dose vitamin C for several weeks develop high levels of vitamin C in their main storage depots, the white blood cells, and in the blood. Then, if suddenly given only normally adequate amounts of vitamin C, their vitamin C level in blood and white cells dropped well below normal within two days.

It occurred to Paul's doctors that Paul may have become conditioned to high levels of vitamin C during his fetal development if his mother took excessive vitamin C during pregnancy. Questioned, she revealed that indeed she had been taking extra vitamin C, but would admit to taking only about 400 mg daily. Thus Paul had become dependent upon abnormally high daily vitamin C intake. Fortunately, this problem is temporary because the body has marvelous powers of adjustment.

The doctors placed Paul on extra high vitamin C, giving some by injection the first ten days, and then instructing the mother to gradually reduce the dosage over a period of six weeks. Paul responded quickly to the injections and, within two weeks, most of his bones became much less tender. After one month, he seemed happy and healthy. When checked at age 6 months and again at 9 months, Paul was thriving on a daily intake of just 60 mg of vitamin C.

Other Adverse Reactions

Encouraged by promotional efforts of Pauling and others, millions of Americans have been taking large doses of vitamin C with little concern about possible risks. Fortunately, adverse reactions do not seem to be common, even in the range of 1,000 to 2,000 mg per day. There is considerable individual variability, however, and for some people even 1,000 mg of vitamin C can be harmful. Thus, if you are taking vitamin C or thinking of doing so, you should be aware of its potential hazards:

Diarrhea. Instances have been reported of nausea, abdominal cramps and diarrhea in individuals ingesting 1,000 mg or more daily.[29,30]

Interference with pregnancy. Human equivalent dosages of 1,250 mg or more given to guinea pigs caused a high percentage of interruption of pregnancy and deaths among the fetuses.[31] Russian studies[32,33] of pregnant women indicate that daily dosages of 6,000 mg can cause menstrual-like bleeding. An Australian study[34] found several women in which daily dosages ranging from as low as 200 mg to as high as 4,000 mg appeared to prevent conception from taking place. Dr. Abraham Hoffer,[35] an extremely enthusiastic prescriber of megavitamins, has reported treating over 3,000 women with daily intakes ranging from 2 to 20 grams without one case of "lowered fertility." But it is not clear that he actually looked for such cases.

Interference with copper absorption. It is known that large intakes of vitamin C can hinder the absorption of copper from the intestinal tract of animals. This could conceivably cause copper deficiency in individuals whose dietary intake of copper is low. Animal experiments[36,37] suggest the possibility that decreased copper absorption can elevate blood cholesterol and thus increase the risk of coronary heart disease.

Increased iron absorption. While the ability of vitamin C to increase iron absorption is likely to benefit people whose dietary iron intake is marginal, there are some rare individuals whose ability to limit iron absorption is impaired. Such persons may increase their risk of iron poisoning by taking vitamin C supplements.[38]

Increased uric acid excretion. Daily doses of 4,000 mg or more can cause some persons to decrease the uric acid level in their blood and increase the amount in their urine. Such individuals would be at increased risk for acute gout and the urate type of kidney stones.[39]

Decreased tolerance to low oxygen levels. One study[40] has reported that human volunteers taking 3,000 mg of vitamin C for 6 days suffered an appreciable loss of ability to endure low oxygen at high altitudes. This could be of significance to high-flying aviators.

Interference with urine tests for sugar. Excessive daily doses of vitamin C are known to cause false test results for sugar in the urine. One type of test ("Clinitest") can give falsely high results, while another ("Test-tape") can give falsely low results.[41]

Interference with stool tests for blood. Excretion of as little as 55 mg of vitamin C daily in the stool can obscure the presence of blood in human feces.[42] This can be extremely serious in cases where individuals are bleeding into their digestive tract from a cancer which would be curable if diagnosed early. Individuals undergoing laboratory tests of their urine or stool should therefore avoid vitamin C supplements for at least a week before such tests.

Decreased resistance to bacterial infections and tumors. Evidence of this possible risk is presented in Chapters 13 and 16.

Damage to tooth enamel. Ascorbic acid is apparently strong enough to dissolve tooth enamel under certain circumstances. A Philadelphia dentist[43] recently reported that persons who *chewed* many vitamin C tablets rather than swallowing them whole have damaged their teeth.

To illustrate other potential problems, let's look at a few more cases.

Ronald's Rocky Road to Recruitment[44]

Ronald M. was a candidate for an officer's commission in the U.S. Army. Shortly before he was to undergo the final physical examination, he was struck with a severe throbbing pain in the left side below his ribs.

Within half an hour. the pain subsided to off-and-on-again dull stabs. On the following day, at 15-minute intervals, he had attacks of painful spasms lasting one-half to two minutes. He managed to see a urologist on the third day who diagnosed the problem as a kidney stone and arranged for a special x-ray examination of the kidneys and bladder. The pains turned out to be due to a kidney stone being squeezed through the ureter tube toward the bladder. Ron was told to watch for possible passage of a kidney stone and to recover it if possible. Fortunately, he succeeded in doing so. The stone turned out to be made of calcium oxalate.

X-ray examination of Ron's urinary tract revealed that its structure was normal. His blood level of calcium was normal, but his 24-hour urine sample was found to contain three times the normal amount of oxalate. Questioning Ron, the doctor discovered that he had been taking 1,000 mg of vitamin C daily for many months "to prevent colds." He was asked to stop the vitamin C supplements, at least long enough for more tests. After 18 days, Ron's urine oxalate level was reduced to almost normal.

Calcium oxalate stones occur when the levels of calcium and oxalate are high enough in the urine to chemically combine with each other. Perhaps 2 or 3 percent of persons taking high doses of vitamin C can increase their urinary oxalate concentration to a dangerous level. Most published reports[45-48] refer to people who took at least 4,000 mg of vitamin C, but Ron apparently ran into trouble with only 1,000 mg.

Connie's Clotting Crisis[49]

Connie D. was a 52-year-old nurse who developed a severe pain in the calf of her right leg. She struggled through the next week hoping it would clear up, but then was rushed to the hospital because of chest pains and shortness of breath which came on with every brief exertion. Tests showed inflammation (phlebitis) of the veins in her right calf. An x-ray film of the chest and an electrocardiogram were both normal. But the suspicious doctors took a closer look at her lungs with a rather new (at that time) examination technique called a lung scan. This revealed evidence of a lung clot (pulmonary embolism).

A blood clot in one of the larger blood vessels carrying blood to the lungs for purification is a potentially death-dealing situation. The doctors put Connie on heparin, an anti-clotting drug, for 9 days in an effort to dissolve the lung clot. For the next two days the heparin dose was tapered down while a second anti-clotting drug, warfarin, was started. On the 17th hospital day, much improved, Connie was sent home on a daily dosage of warfarin.

Following her doctor's instructions, Connie reported back for tests once a week to show the blood's quickness or slowness in clotting. Each week, for four weeks, the tests showed that she was effectively anticoagulated. Then, for no apparent reason, her prothrombin time shortened—which meant that her blood clotted too easily. Her dosage of warfarin was increased a little, but the next week her prothrombin time was still too short. The doctors asked whether she had been eating unusually large amounts of food high in vitamin K which promotes clotting, but she hadn't. Asked if she had been taking any medication other than warfarin, she again said no. The next week, her prothrombin time was even shorter, so they questioned her more carefully. Finally, she admitted that every morning, starting a few weeks previously, she had taken a vitamin C supplement along with her warfarin pills. She hadn't mentioned this before because she hadn't considered vitamins a medication!

The doctors persuaded Connie to stop the vitamin C supplement because high-dose vitamin C blocks warfarin. Two days later, her prothrombin time test returned to the therapeutic range where she was protected from potentially fatal blood clots.

Sickle Cells Sickened by "C"[50,51]

In December of 1970, 40-year-old Sylvia was back in the hospital with chest pains, shortness of breath, severe bone pains and a fever of 101°F. This was her fifth time that year for the same trouble. The diagnosis remained the same: sickle cell crisis. She had experienced minor crises in previous years but none that required hospitalization.

Examinations revealed that the chest pains and respiratory distress were due to blockage of the blood flow to some parts of the lungs by clogging of the ends of small arteries—a potentially fatal condition called pulmonary infarction. Sylvia's bone pains were related to a similar process taking place in the blood vessels serving her bones. After intensive care for several days, Sylvia's lungs were much improved, her fever was gone, and she was sent home.

It is known that people with sickle cell disorder will suffer a crisis similar to Sylvia's if provoked by unusual stress such as respiratory infection, but seldom do such crises become as severe as the five attacks Sylvia had in 1970. Between 1967 and 1969, she had not had a single serious attack. Why the sudden upsurge?

A clue to this puzzle was discovered when Sylvia called the same doctor a few months later in early 1971 and fearfully reported the beginning symptoms of a cold. She was scared because her five bad attacks in 1970 had all started that way, not with a full-blown cold, but just with what she thought were "beginning symptoms." The doctor discussed her worries over the telephone, and to his consternation learned that all during 1970, whenever she had felt the first signs of a cold, she had taken from 1 to 10 grams of vitamin C for several days.

Sylvia didn't know that high-dose vitamin C can cause gradual destruction of red blood cells with sludging of the debris in sickle cell anemia and several other types of hereditary anemias; but fortunately, her doctor did. He advised her strongly not to take high-dose vitamin C at any time; and she obeyed. In 1971 and 1972, Sylvia had only two minor crises per year, with some bone pain but none of the death-threatening clots of 1970.

An experiment performed by Mengel and Greene[52] in 1976 suggests that even normal individuals taking more than 5,000 mg of vitamin C may be at risk for abnormal breakdown of their red blood cells.

Fred's Flirtation with Anemia[53,54]

Fred K. was 58 years old when he read a newspaper report that high-dose vitamin C, if taken with meals, might lead to pernicious anemia in some persons by destroying most of their vitamin B_{12}. The newspaper referred interested readers to the Metropolitan County Hospital where a special program was underway to test persons for vitamin B_{12} sufficiency. So Fred went there to be tested. He had been taking three grams daily of vitamin C, one gram with each of three meals, for more than three years. According to his doctor's report, Fred complained of lassitude and mental irritability. Tests showed that he was not anemic, but found two types of abnormal blood cells that are early warning signs of vitamin B_{12} deficiency.

Vitamin B_{12} is used and destroyed by the body at a very much slower rate than other vitamins. On a diet lacking vitamin B_{12}, it requires approximately one year for half of the body stores of B_{12} to disappear. When Fred's blood serum was analyzed for B_{12}, it showed only 65 picograms per milliliter (pg per ml), normal being 200 to 900.

Pernicious anemia occurs whenever the human body lacks either vitamin B_{12} in the diet or a substance needed to absorb it secreted by the stomach lining (see Chapter 11). Fred had been eating a varied, balanced diet with enough meat and dairy products to provide an adequate daily supply of vitamin B_{12}, and tests showed that his B_{12} absorption mechanism was intact.

Three months after stopping his daily vitamin C supplements, Fred's B_{12} blood level had risen from 65 to 180 pg per ml. "Fred" was one of 90 persons who requested checkups because they had been taking daily doses of vitamin C between 500 and 3,000 mg per day. None had symptoms of anemia, but all 90 had below normal B_{12} levels in their blood, ranging from 65 to 110 pg per ml. In the reporting doctor's opinion: "Possibily 2 to 3 per cent of subjects on megadose regimens of ascorbic acid may well be at risk for ultimate development of vitamin B_{12} deficiency." This conclusion is supported by a study by Dr. Victor Herbert and co-workers[55] who found that 4 of 18 patients taking 2,000 mg of vitamin C daily developed low vitamin B_{12} levels in their blood.

Conclusion

Most authorities believe that healthy people need no more than the RDA of vitamin C, an amount which is easy to obtain from food. The evidence is also clear that for healthy people there is no benefit from obtaining from all sources more than 200 mg of vitamin C—twice the amount known to produce tissue saturation in almost all people. Daily doses in the range of 250 to 500 mg are quite unlikely to cause difficulty, and amounts up to 2,000 mg daily are still fairly safe for most individuals. But anyone wishing to supplement with vitamin C should weigh the possible risks against the doubtful benefits. Even if the risk is small, there is no reason to supplement if the potential benefit is even smaller! The issue of supposed benefits is discussed further in Chapters 13 and 16 as we evaluate Linus Pauling's claims that large daily dosages are effective against infections and cancer.

References

1. Food and Nutrition Board: Recommended Dietary Allowances, 9th Ed. Washington, D.C., National Academy of Sciences, 1980.
2. Hodges, R. E.: *In* Modern Nutrition in Health and Disease, 6th Ed. (R. Goodhart and M. Shils, Eds.) Philadelphia, Lea and Febiger, 1980.
3. Szent-Gyorgyi, A.: Biochemical Journal 22:1387, 1928.
4. King, C. G. and Waugh, W. A.: Science 75:357, April 1, 1932.
5. Waugh, W. A. and King, C. G.: Journal of Biological Chemistry 97:325, May, 1932.
6. Svirbely, J. L. and Szent-Gyorgyi, A.: Biochemical Journal 26:865, April 25, 1932.
7. FDA Advisory Review Panel: Vitamin and Mineral Drug Products for Over-the-Counter Human Use, Federal Register 44:16126-16201, March 16, 1979.
8. Kutsky, R. J.: Handbook of Vitamins and Hormones. New York, Van Nostrand Reinhold Co., 1973.
9. Hodges, R. E.: *In* Human Nutrition, Vol. 3B. New York, Plenum Press, 1980, p. 78.
10. Baker, E. M., Hodges, R. E., et al.: American Journal of Clinical Nutrition 24:444, 1971.
11. Nutrition Reviews: 34:15, 1976.
12. Herbert V. and Barrett, S.: Vitamins and "Health" Foods: The Great American Hustle, Philadelphia, George F. Stickley Co., 1981.
13. Pauling, L.: Vitamin C and the Common Cold. San Francisco, W. H. Freeman & Co., 1970.
14. Jukes, T. H.: Proceedings of the National Academy of Sciences 71:1949, 1974.
15. Jukes, T. H.: *Ibid.* 72:4151, 1975.
16. Pauling, L.: *Ibid.* 71:4442, 1974.

17. Hodges, R. E., Baker, E. M. et al.: American Journal of Clinical Nutrition 22:535, 1969.
18. Kallner, A., Hartmann, E. and Hornig, D.: *Ibid.* 32:530, 1979.
19. Anderson, T. W.: Nutrition Today 12:6-13, 1977.
20. Angel, J., Alfred, B. et al.: International Journal of Vitamin and Nutrition Research 45:237, 1975.
21. Kubler, W. and Gehler, J.: *Ibid.* 40:442, 1970. Note that in 1970 this journal was: International Zeitschrift fur Vitamin Forschung.
22. Mayersohn, M.: European Journal of Pharmacology 12:140, 1972.
23. Masek, J. and Hruba, F.: International Zeitschrift fur Vitamin Forschung 34:39, 1964.
24. Schrauzer, G. N. and Rhead, W. J.: International Journal of Vitamin and Nutrition Research 43:201, 1972.
25. Spero, L. M. and Anderson, T. W.: British Medical Journal 4:354, 1973.
26. Canadian Medical Association Journal 93:893, 1965.
27. Masek and Hruba: Ernahrungforschung (Nutrition Research) 3:425-445, 1958.
28. Gordonoff, T. von: Schweizerische Medizinische Wochenschrift (Basel) 90: 726, 1960.
29. Hume, R. and Weyers, E.: Scottish Medical Journal 18:3, 1973.
30. Goldsmith, G.: JAMA 216:337, 1971.
31. Mouriquand, G. and Edel, V.: Comptes Rendus des Seances de la Societe Biologie et de Ses Filiales (Paris) 147:1432, 1953.
32. Samborskaya, E. P. and Ferdman, T. D.: Biulletin (or Bjulleten) Eksperimental Biologii i Meditsiny (Moscow) 62:96, 1966.
33. Samborskaya, E. P. and Ferdman, T. D.: Bulletin of Experimental Biology and Medicine (Moscow) pp. 934-935, 1967; official English translation of the 1966 Samborskaya and Ferdman report.
34. Briggs, M. H.: Lancet 2:1083, Nov. 10, 1973.
35. Hoffer, A.: *Ibid.* 2:1146, Nov. 17, 1973.
36. Klevay, L.: American Journal of Clinical Nutrition 26:1060, 1973.
37. Klevay, L.: Proceedings of the Society for Experimental Biology and Medicine 151:579, 1976.
38. Cook, J. and Monsen, E.: American Journal of Clinical Nutrition 30:235, 1977.
39. Stein, H., Hasan, A. and Fox, I.: Annals of Internal Medicine 84:385, 1976.
40. Schrauzer, G., Ishmael, D. and Kiefer, G.: Annals of the New York Academy of Science 258:377, 1975.
41. Herbert, V.: Proceedings of the Western Hemisphere Nutrition Congress IV, 1974, pp. 84-91. Acton, Mass., Publishing Science Group, 1975.
42. Annals of Internal Medicine 83:824, 1975.
43. Dannenberg, J. L.: Journal of the American Dental Association 105:172, 1982.
44. JAMA 237:768, 1977.
45. Lamden, M. and Chrystowski, G.: Proceedings of the Society for Experimental Biology and Medicine 85:190, 1954.

46. Briggs, M. H.: Lancet 2:48, July 7, 1973.
47. Briggs, M. H.: *Ibid.* 1:154, Jan. 17, 1976.
48. Smith, L. H.: New England Journal of Medicine 298:856, 1978.
49. JAMA 215:1671, 1971.
50. *Ibid.* 216:332, 1971.
51. Patient's physician: Personal communication, April 6, 1978.
52. Mengel, C. and Greene, H.: Annals of Internal Medicine 84:490, 1976.
53. JAMA 234:24, 1975.
54. Physician for the patient: Personal communication, March 19, 1976.
55. Herbert, V., Jacob, E. et al.: American Journal of Clinical Nutrition 31: 253, 1978.

13

Can Megavitamin C Help Against Colds or Other Infections?

Whatever the mind seizes and dwells upon with peculiar satisfaction is to be held in suspicion.
—Sir Francis Bacon[1]

Few things have ever stirred the imagination and hopes of the public in matters of nutrition or vexed nutrition scientists as much as Linus Pauling's 1970 book, *Vitamin C and the Common Cold.*[2] The book's main claim is that taking 1 gram (1,000 mg) of vitamin C daily will reduce the incidence of colds by 45 percent for most people, but that some persons might need much larger amounts. It recommends that if symptoms of a cold do start, you should take 500 to 1,000 mg every hour for several hours—or 4 to 10 grams daily if symptoms don't disappear with smaller amounts. The book also suggests that most people need a daily vitamin C intake of 2,300 or more for "optimum" health and to meet stresses, including infections. Without question, publication of this book, combined with Pauling's reputation as a Nobel Prize-winning scientist, has made vitamin C a best seller. When his theory was announced, millions of Americans rushed to try it for themselves.

The second edition of the book, issued in 1976 as *Vitamin C, the Common Cold and the Flu,*[3] suggests even higher dosages:

> It is wise to carry some 1,000-mg tablets of ascorbic acid with you at all times. At the first sign that a cold is developing, the first feeling of scratchiness of the throat, or presence of mucus in the nose, or muscle pain or general malaise, begin the treatment by swallowing one or two 1,000-mg tablets. Continue the treatment for several hours by taking an additional tablet or two tablets every hour.

122

Many concerned persons have wondered if Pauling's advice is prudent, and millions have been experimenting upon themselves to see if they can tell. Pauling himself reportedly[4] takes 12,000 mg daily and raises it to 40,000 mg when symptoms of a cold appear! However, the vast majority of reputable medical and nutritional scientists strongly disagree with him.[5-7] Before looking at the experimental evidence, let's discuss how scientists form their opinions.

How Scientific Facts Are Determined

The "scientific community" consists of millions of scientists throughout the world who operate under a strict set of rules known as the scientific method. Simply stated, this is a system of logical steps designed to separate cause-and-effect from coincidence. This method is used to answer such questions as: "If you do a particular thing, will something else take place?" and "If two things follow one another, are they related?"

A scientific "fact" is determined by analyzing the results of all the experiments that bear on that particular fact. In the case of vitamin C, there are two key questions. First, does vitamin C prevent colds? And second, does it reduce their severity? Before discussing experiments on these questions, however, we should note that not all experiments are "created equal." *To be valid, an experiment must be well designed, and its data must be honestly collected and interpreted with good techniques of statistical analysis.* One hallmark of a good experiment is that others can repeat it and get the same results.

Experimental studies of the possible value of vitamin C in the prevention of infections have been conducted by medical investigators ever since preparations of the pure crystalline vitamin became commercially available during the 1930s. On the basis of experiments performed through 1982, the majority of medical scientists conclude that supplementation with vitamin C does not prevent colds and, at best, may slightly reduce the symptoms of a cold. Linus Pauling disagrees, basing his ideas on the same experiments but interpreting their results differently. Moreover, Pauling suggests that you can easily determine what your vitamin C dosage should be: "If you are taking 1 gram per day, and find that you have developed two or three colds during the winter season, it would be wise to try taking a larger daily quantity." Presumably, if you have fewer colds than expected, you should believe that vitamin C has been responsible for the decrease.

Unfortunately, in the real world, scientific facts cannot be determined that simply. Consider the following questions:

1. Is it possible that you actually had a different number of colds than you recall? This would be *faulty data collection.*

2. Is it possible that you would have had only one cold this year anyway? If so, what happened to you would be a mere *coincidence*.
3. Is it possible that you had a very mild cold but wish so strongly for a favorable result that you didn't count it? If so, this would be an effect of *bias*.

Scientific experiments must be designed to overcome these possible sources of error. The problem of faulty memory can be overcome by keeping close track of the individuals involved in an experiment. The problem of coincidence can be overcome by using large numbers of people and following them for significant lengths of time. The problem of bias, however, is far more complicated. Use of the double-blind method is critical, but as you will see, experiments with vitamin C have encountered some very curious results when subjects were able to figure out whether they were getting the vitamin or the placebo during experiments intended to be "double-blind."

Does Vitamin C Prevent Colds?

There have been at least 30 experiments done to test the effects of vitamin C against colds in humans. Most biomedical scientists[5-7] who have analyzed the results of these trials have found Pauling's claims mainly unsupported in 15 of those trials which were the best designed, as shown in the following examples.

One way to test whether high-dosage vitamin C prevents colds is to inoculate the throats of volunteers with cold viruses. Two studies of this type found that everyone got colds whether they took vitamin C or not. Walker and co-workers[8] in 1967 and Schwartz, Hornick and associates[9,10] in 1972-73 gave half of their volunteers a placebo and the rest 3,000 mg of vitamin C daily for several days before inserting live cold viruses directly into their noses; and then continued 3,000 mg of vitamin C (or placebo) for 7 more days. All of the volunteers got colds—of equal severity.

Another way to test vitamin C is to see what happens to matched groups over a period of time. Two teams of investigators have done this more than once, one team led by Dr. John L. Coulehan and the other by Dr. Terence Anderson.

Dr. Coulehan's first study[11] was done on 641 Navajo Indian children, half of whom received a placebo while the rest received 1,000 mg of vitamin C daily. A complicated system of judging the severity of head, throat and chest symptoms was used. The Coulehan team reported in 1974 that the vitamin C group had less severe colds, but other scientists who reviewed the study criticized the method of judging the severity of symptoms.

So in 1976 the Coulehan team[12] repeated their study with 868 Navajo children but used a better system of scoring severity. The children receiv-

ing vitamin C averaged .38 colds per person while the placebo group averaged .37. The average duration of the colds was 5.5 days in the vitamin
group and 5.8 in the placebo group. Thus, in this test, vitamin C neither
prevented colds nor shortened their duration.

In 1979, Dr. Coulehan[13] published his analysis of vitamin C versus the
common cold and concluded that extra vitamin C is not worth taking.

The Anderson Trials

In their first trial in 1972, Dr. Terence Anderson and colleagues[14] at
the University of Toronto instituted a 3-month double-blind study of 818
volunteers aged 10 to 65. Half received 1,000 mg of vitamin C daily before
colds and 4,000 mg per day during the first 3 days of a cold, while the
other half received "equivalent" placebos. This study was designed to test
Pauling's claims that ingestion of 1,000 mg of vitamin C daily would reduce the frequency of colds by 45 percent and the total days of illness by
60 percent. These claims were certainly not supported by the study's outcome. In the vitamin group, 74 percent had one or more colds during the
study period while 82 percent of the placebo group had one or more colds.
The difference, which amounted to "one-tenth of a cold per person," was
judged by Dr. Anderson to be "of no practical importance." The severity,
as measured by days confined indoors, averaged 1.30 days for the vitamin
group and 1.87 days for the placebo group—a 30 percent difference which
Anderson decided to explore further.

At the end of this trial, before the double-blind code was opened, all
volunteers were asked whether they had experienced any unusual feelings
of well-being during the trial. Nineteen percent of *both* groups said yes—
an interesting example of the placebo effect.

In 1974, the Anderson team[15,16] organized a larger trial to see what results would be obtained with different amounts of vitamin C. Some 3,500
volunteers were divided into 8 groups, six of which received various daily
dosages of vitamin C while the others received placebos for 3 months. No
difference in the incidence of colds were found among the groups taking
no vitamin C, 250 mg, 1,000 mg or 2,000 mg daily. A possible slight reduction in severity of symptoms was found in the vitamin C groups, but
volunteers taking dosages of 4,000 or 8,000 per day when a cold began
did no better than those taking only 250 mg per day.

The third Anderson trial,[17] reported in 1975, covered 16 weeks and used
488 volunteers (ages 14-67), with one-third receiving a pill of vitamin C
as its sodium and calcium salts, and one-third given vitamin C in slow-
release capsules, and one-third getting a placebo. The vitamin C dosage
was 500 mg once a week (equivalent to about 70 mg daily) before colds,
but 1,500 mg the first day of a cold followed by 1,000 mg on the second

and third days. No reduction in the incidence of colds was observed, but those taking vitamin C averaged less time at home (1.62 vs. 1.12 days indoors). Do you think that a half-day's less confinement is of practical significance?

Taken together, the Anderson studies suggest that extra vitamin C may slightly reduce the severity of colds, but that it is not necessary to take the high dosages suggested by Pauling to achieve this result. Nor is there anything to be gained by taking vitamin supplements year-round in the hope of preventing colds.

Other Studies

Pauling cites as important a study by Ritzel[18] who ran two separate 1-week trials in 1961 using vacationers at a ski lodge in Switzerland. Half were given a placebo and half took 1,000 mg of vitamin C daily for 7 days. Ritzel claimed that the severity of colds was less in the vitamin group, and Pauling judges the difference to be significant. However, critics of Ritzel's study judge its results to be unreliable because one week is too short a time for a valid study of the incidence or duration of colds.

Carson and co-workers[19] in 1975 told of treating company employees with 1,000 mg of vitamin C or a placebo daily during colds. The number of colds per person, the duration of colds and their severity were the same in both vitamin and placebo groups.

In 1975, Karlowski and associates[20] at the National Institutes of Health reported treating volunteers as follows: 25 percent received placebos; 25 percent took 3,000 mg of vitamin C daily before colds but placebos during colds; 25 percent were given placebos daily before colds and 3,000 mg of vitamin C daily during colds; and 25 percent got 3,000 mg daily before colds and 6,000 mg daily during colds.

The experiment was supposed to be double-blind, but the doctors had failed to make the placebo taste the same as the vitamin C pills as is done in most trials. As a result, half of the volunteers correctly guessed which pill they were getting and therefore became "unblinded." When the results were tabulated with all volunteers lumped together, the average number of colds per person was 1.27 colds for the vitamin group and 1.41 for the placebo group. But among those who remained "blinded," no differences in the incidence or severity were found. This fascinating result shows how many people who think they are taking a positive step (such as taking a vitamin) may report a favorable result even when none really exists!

In 1977, Miller and colleagues[21] treated 44 pairs of identical twins for 5 months as follows: One twin in each pair received a vitamin C capsule while the other got a placebo. The daily vitamin C dosages before and during colds ranged from 500 for younger children to 1,500 mg for older ones. The investigators noted "no significant overall benefit on cold symptoms" as reported by the children's mothers, but the responses varied among the subgroups when the children were divided according to sex and age. After the data were analyzed, four mothers admitted tasting the capsules in an attempt to figure out which twin was getting the vitamin C! Thus it is possible that the ratings of these mothers and possibly others were influenced by guessing which twin was getting the vitamin C.

A double-blind Australian trial with 95 pairs of identical twins was reported in 1981.[22] One of each pair took 1,000 mg of vitamin C for 100 days while the other received a placebo. The vitamin C group had slightly more colds but a shorter duration of colds (5 days instead of 6).

Tyrell and co-workers[23] in 1977 reported treating 743 men and 758 women for 5 months as follows. Half received placebo pills daily. The others took vitamin C but only during colds at these dosages: 4,000 mg on the first and second days of a cold and 200 mg on the third day. There was no benefit from taking vitamin C. The incidence and duration of colds were the same for both men and women in the vitamin and placebo groups. Men in both groups missed an average of half a day's work while women missed about a day.

Possible husband and wife differences were checked in a 6-month trial in South Wales in 1977 by Dr. Elwood and associates.[24] No differences were found between vitamin and placebo groups except that men in the vitamin group had worse chest colds. Overall, those taking vitamin C had slightly more colds than those taking the placebo.

An 8-week trial with 764 Marine recruits carried out by Pitt and Costrini[25] was reported in 1979. Half of the recruits received 2,000 mg of vitamin C daily, while the others took placebo pills on the same schedule. No benefit from vitamin C was found. Ninety percent of both groups got colds, and no difference in severity or duration of colds was found.

Some studies have tested vitamin C in other infections besides colds. For example, a Russian study reported benefit from vitamin C against bacterial pneumonia, but an American study[26] showed no benefit of vitamin C against viral or bacterial meningitis in infants.

Do Added Bioflavonoids Help?

Dr. I. M. Baird and co-workers[27] reported in 1979 a 10-week experiment with 350 volunteers (ages 17 to 25) who were divided into 3 groups. One-third of them, as the placebo group, received a daily "supplement" of a synthetic orange drink containing no vitamin C. A second group got a synthetic orange drink containing 80 mg of synthetic vitamin C. The third group was given enough pure orange juice daily to provide 80 mg of natural vitamin C plus bioflavonoids.

The incidence of colds was the same for all three groups. Both vitamin

C groups had slightly less severe colds than the placebo group. Thus the synthetic vitamin C was as effective as the natural vitamin C and the presence of bioflavonoids had no apparent effect.

Laboratory Experiments

Vitamin C has been tested not only against cold viruses in people, but also against bacteria and viruses in the laboratory. This can be done by growing bacteria with nutrients without the presence of live tissues, and by growing viruses with live tissue cells ("tissue cultures"). Although such experimental conditions do not furnish all of the chemicals and enzymes available to live animals or humans, their results may yield clues about the mechanism of action of vitamin C or possible ideas for further human studies. However, experimental results have been contradictory. Here are some examples:

In one laboratory experiment,[28] extra vitamin C was found to interfere with the ability of white blood cells to kill bacteria; but in another,[29] white cells from C-deficient guinea pigs had weaker antibacterial activity. In two others,[30,31] vitamin C increased destruction of viruses or virus-like particles called bacteriophages. Another[8] experiment demonstrated no effect of vitamin C on viruses. And another[32] showed that the ability of white blood cells to fight bacteria was decreased in healthy young men after they had taken 2,000 mg of vitamin C daily for two weeks.

In an experiment on guinea pigs,[33] vitamin C appeared to offer a protective effect against rabies virus. Another experiment with monkeys found some protective effect against influenza virus.[34,35] In others, mice given extra vitamin C appeared to increase their general immunity to viruses[36]; and rabbits given vitamin C showed decreased ability to fight bacteria.[37] In another experiment,[38] vitamin C demonstrated increased ability to counter infection with pseudomonas bacteria in tissue culture, mice and children if taken along with antibiotics.

If vitamin C does give some protection to humans from bacterial or viral infections, it is probably caused by increasing the fighting capacity of white blood cells, as well as by raising general health and the ability to overcome stress. It has also been thought that if vitamin C can increase the body's immune response to bacteria and viruses, it might raise defenses against "foreign substances" like cancers. Experiments with vitamin C against tumors are discussed in Chapter 16.

Interferon and Vitamin C

Interferon was discovered in 1957 by Isaacs and Lindenmann[39] who described it as a specialized protein whose production is stimulated by viruses that invade human or animal cells. Interferon migrates out of dying cells and then helps protect other cells by "interfering" with attempts by the virus to penetrate their walls. In his 1976 book, Pauling[3] points out that in 1970 he proposed the idea that vitamin C somehow had a role in the body's synthesis of interferon and possibly also acted jointly with interferon in preventing viruses from penetrating human tissue cells. He also admitted there was no evidence to support this hypothesis in 1970, but claimed than an experiment by Schwerdt and Schwerdt[40] does offer support.

In 1975, the Schwerdts cultured a common cold virus (Rhinovirus RV20) with human tissue cells for several generations. The "control" cultures had no vitamin C added, while the test dishes contained vitamin C plus glutathione, a vitamin C stabilizer. After about 48 hours, there was considerably less viral reproduction in the vitamin C dish than in the control dish. The authors suggest that the presence of vitamin C increased the amount of interferon released from the infected cells.

In 1975, B. V. Siegel[41] demonstrated in mice that vitamin C increased interferon production during stimulation with infective agents. Also, mouse cells in tissue culture, stimulated with simulated viral nucleic acid as the attacker, produced more interferon in the presence than in the absence of vitamin C.

In 1975, Geber and co-workers[42] injected mice with vitamin C and later stimulated their white blood cells with a virus-like chemical. The vitamin C mice produced more interferon in their white cells than did the control mice. However, injection of mice with an aspirin-like drug produced an even greater production of interferon. Obviously, a great deal more work has to be done to clarify the relationship between vitamin C and interferon.

Antihistamine Effect of Vitamin C

Histamine in varying amounts is almost always released in the tissues of the respiratory tract by an allergic-type response to the stress of common cold infections. Perhaps the first clue that animals and humans might use vitamin C to combat stress that involves histamine release came in 1940 from the research team led by the co-discoverer of vitamin C, Professor Charles Glen King of Columbia University.

His group[43] showed that stressing rats with certain drugs stimulated their bodies to synthesize extra vitamin C. Later, evidence was presented to support the belief that animals, such as the rat, who can make their own supply of vitamin C, react to histamine by producing extra vitamin C. D. A. Long[44] provided further evidence that vitamin C plays a part in the prevention or moderation of allergy reactions involving histamine in man and animals.

In 1973, Zuskin and co-workers[45] reported that vitamin C could relax the guinea pig windpipe and increase airflow after trachea swelling caused by prior treatment with histamine.

In 1974, two other research teams[46,47] found that rats given vitamin C along with histamine-releasing drugs had decreased amounts of histamine in their urine. These researchers concluded that vitamin C detoxifies histamine. Rats and guinea pigs were stressed, some with and some without vitamin C supplements, by a variety of stressing challenges. The stressing conditions included injections with vaccines, toxoids, and certain physical stresses. In all cases, large doses of vitamin C reduced the stress symptoms and reduced the amount of histamine in the urine.

These experiments support the idea that vitamin C acts somewhat like an antihistamine in reducing the symptoms of a cold. But whether this is of practical value is a matter of dispute.

Overview

Does it make sense to supplement with vitamin C? If so, should it be done daily or only at the first sign of a cold or other infection? And what dosage should be used?

In my opinion, vitamin C has not been shown to prevent colds, and therefore there is no reason to supplement on days when you don't have a cold. Vitamin C may offer a slight reduction in the *symptoms* of a cold. Dr. Thomas Chalmers[5] concluded in 1975: "I, who have colds as often and as severe as those of any man, do not consider the very minor potential benefit that might result from taking vitamin C three times a day for life worth either the effort or the risk, no matter how slight the latter might be."

If you choose to supplement when a cold strikes, there is no reason to take more than 250 mg per day (an amount easily obtained from the age-old "remedy," fruit juices). Supplementation with larger amounts of vitamin C has not been shown to be more effective, and it may cause diarrhea or have other adverse effects.

What about other infections? It is known that the body's ready-pool of vitamin C in the blood serum and white cells declines rapidly the first day or two in the presence of stresses such as severe infections, burns or surgery. Some doctors believe that under these circumstances, a supplement of 250 mg—but never more than 500 mg per day for a few days—may aid in recovery.

References

1. Bacon, Francis (1561-1626): Quoted in the Great Quotations (G. Seldes, Ed.) Secaucus, N.J., Castle Books, 1968.

2. Pauling, L.: Vitamin C and the Common Cold. San Francisco, W. H. Freeman, 1970.
3. Pauling, L.: Vitamin C, the Common Cold and the Flu. San Francisco, W. H. Freeman, 1976.
4. Pauling, L.: Speech at Natural Foods Exposition, March 29, 1982, reported in Natural Foods Merchandiser, June 1982, p. 65.
5. Chalmers, T. C.: American Journal of Medicine 58:532, 1975.
6. Dykes, M. H. M. and Meier, P.: JAMA 231:1053, 1975.
7. Taft, G. and Fieldhouse, P.: Public Health (London) 92:19, 1978.
8. Walker, G. H. et al.: British Medical Journal 1:603, 1967.
9. Schwartz, A. R., Hornick, R. B. et al.: Journal of Infectious Diseases 128: 500, 1973.
10. Hornick, R. B.: Medical Counterpoint, Feb. 1972, p. 15.
11. Coulehan, J. L. et al.: New England Journal of Medicine 290:6, 1974.
12. Coulehan, J. L. et al.: *Ibid.* 295:973, 1976.
13. Coulehan, J. L.: Postgraduate Medicine 66:153, 1979.
14. Anderson, T. W. et al.: Canadian Medical Association Journal 107:503, 1972.
15. Anderson, T. W. et al.: *Ibid.* 111:31, 1974.
16. Anderson, T. W.: Annals of the New York Academy of Sciences 258:498, 1975.
17. Anderson, T. W. et al.: Canadian Medical Association Journal 112:823, 1975.
18. Ritzel, G.: Helvetica Medica Acta 28:63, cited in Chalmers, T. C., *loc cit.*
19. Carson, M. et al.: Journal of the Society of Occupational Medicine 25:99, 1975.
20. Karlowski, T. R., Chalmers, T. C. et al.: JAMA 231:1038, 1975.
21. Miller, J. D. et al.: JAMA 237:248, 1977.
22. Carr, A. B. et al.: Medical Journal of Australia 2:411, Oct. 17, 1981.
23. Tyrell, D. A. J. et al.: British Journal of Preventative and Social Medicine 31:189, 1977.
24. Elwood, P. C. et al.: The Practitioner 218:133, 1977.
25. Pitt, H. A. and Costrini, A. M.: JAMA 241:908, 1979.
26. Destro, R. L. and Sharma, V.: Clinical Pediatrics 16:936, 1977.
27. Baird, I. M., Hughes, R. E. et al.: American Journal of Clinical Nutrition 32:1686, 1979.
28. McCall, C. E. et al.: Journal of Infectious Diseases 124:194, 1971.
29. Shilotri, P. G.: Journal of Nutrition 107:1513, 1977.
30. Murata and Kitagawa: Agricultural and Biological Chemistry 37:1145, 1973.
31. Murata, A.: Proceedings of the First Intersectional Congress of the International Association of Microbiological Societies; Science Council of Japan (Tokyo, Sept. 1974) 3:432, 1975.
32. Shilotri, P. G. and Bhat, K. S.: American Journal of Clinical Nutrition 30:1077, 1977.
33. Banic, S.: Nature 258:153, 1975.
34. Thomas, W. R. and Holt, P.G.: A Review: Vitamin C and Immunity, *in* Clinical and Experimental Immunology 32:370-379, 1978.

132

35. Murphy, B. L. et al.: Laboratory Animal Science 24:229, 1974.
36. Siegel, B. V. and Morton, J. I.: Experientia 33:393, 1977.
37. Pletsityl, D. F. and Fomina, V. G.: Bulletin of Experimental Biology and Medicine (Moscow) 77:653, 1974. (Official English translation.)
38. Rawal, B. D. et al.: Medical Journal of Australia 1:169, 1974.
39. Isaacs, C. and Lindenmann, J.: Proceedings of the Royal Society of London B147:258, 1957; *cited in* Pauling, 1976, *loc. cit.**
40. Schwerdt, P. R. and Schwerdt, C. E.: Proceedings of the Society for Experimental Biology and Medicine 148:1287, 1975.
41. Siegel, B. V.: Nature 254:531, 1975.
42. Geber, W. F. et al.: Pharmacology 13:228, 1975.
43. Longnecker, H. E., Fricke, H. H. and King, C. G.: Journal of Biological Chemistry 135:497, 1940.
44. Long, D. A.: British Journal of Experimental Pathology 31:183, 1950.
45. Zuskin, E. et al.: Journal of Allergy and Clinical Immunology 51:218, 1973.
46. Subramanian, N. et al.: Biochemical Pharmacology 23:637, 1974.
47. Nandi, B. K. et al.: *Ibid.* p. 643.

Loc. cit., for *loco citato* (in the place cited), refers to an author's name whose publication is listed above.

14

Can Megavitamin E Help the Heart, Prolong Life, Increase Sexuality or Do Anything Else For You?

Dr. William T. Jarvis, Professor of Health Education at Loma Linda University and a noted authority on quackery, points out that since ancient times, humans have sought at least four different "magic potions"—the love potion, the fountain of youth, the cure-all and the athletic superpill. Claims made for vitamin E fit into all of these categories!

Megadoses of vitamin E are being recommended by vitamin hucksters and ill-informed physicians for the treatment of acne, atherosclerosis, cancer, coronary heart disease, diabetes, sexual frigidity, infertility, habitual abortion, high blood cholesterol, muscular dystrophy, peptic ulcer, rheumatic fever, and blood clots. Vitamin E is being claimed to increase stamina, prolong life and protect against the effects of atmospheric pollution. It is also being added to after-shave lotions, soaps, underarm deodorants and so-called skin conditioners!

Let's look at the scientific facts.

Help for Heart Disease?

Does extra vitamin E protect a healthy heart or strengthen a heart that's been weakened? The evidence does not encourage this kind of hope. The Shute brothers, Drs. Evan V. and Wilfrid, together with another Canadian, Dr. Albert Vogelsang, published several reports of their vitamin E treatments between 1946 and 1970 (see Chapter 9). Dr. Wilfrid Shute also co-authored a book in 1969 recommending 200 to 600 units daily and claiming favorable results with hundreds of heart patients. Does that prove extra E is needed for the heart? It certainly does not!

133

Let's look at the record of scientifically acceptable evidence. Three respected reviewers, Drs. Robert E. Olson,[1] Robert Hodges[2,3] and Terence Anderson,[4,5] found no benefit from vitamin E therapy for angina pectoris in well-designed studies published between 1946 and 1972. (Angina is a condition where severe chest pain occurs when the blood supply to the heart is temporarily insufficient.) Summarizing the results of 15 trials, including the poorly-designed studies from the Shute Clinic, Dr. Olsen concluded: "All . . . have been negative except those from the Shute clinic."

The 1973 review by Dr. Hodges[2] entitled *Vitamin E and Coronary Heart Disease* indicates clearly why world medical opinion disbelieves the Shute brothers' claims: although Wilfrid Shute has had vast experience using vitamin E, apparently he has never conducted controlled studies, but has relied only on his "clinical impression." Dr. Hodges, an internationally renowned nutrition scientist, concluded that "massive doses of vitamin E are useless in the prevention or treatment of coronary heart disease."[3]

Dr. Anderson's work also includes a double-blind, controlled trial in which 18 patients taking 3,200 units of vitamin E daily for 9 weeks did no better than 18 others who took a placebo (dummy pill). Four of the original 24 who received the vitamin E were forced to drop out due to undesirable side effects.

A Canadian Veterans Hospital was the site of a well controlled double-blind study of 22 angina patients conducted by Dr. W. M. Toone.[6] Half of the patients received 1,600 units of vitamin E while the other half received a placebo for two years. Dr. Toone found some benefit as shown by reduction in the need for nitroglycerin tablets in the vitamin E group, with 7 or the 11 needing much less of the drug to relieve chest pain.

In 1976, the National Institutes of Health's vitamin E research team of Bieri and Farrell[7] stated: "There is abundant evidence against the claim that vitamin E is effective for ischemic heart disease." During the following year, an NIH team led by Dr. R. E. Gillilan[8] reported another well-controlled trial. Each of the 48 patients (average age 57) had been judged by two cardiologists to have typical, stable, effort-related angina, and all had been proven by electrocardiogram or special x-ray testing to have significant heart disease. The trial was double-blind and "crossover." Half of the patients took 1,600 IU of vitamin E daily for 6 months while half got a placebo capsule; then for crossover the next 6 months the groups were switched. Once a month, a cardiologist interviewed each patient and recorded the number of anginal pain attacks and how many nitroglycerin tablets were used for pain relief. The results:

1. *Number of angina pains per week*: About the same, averaging 7.3 per week in the vitamin E group and 6.7 per week for the placebo group.

2. *Need for nitroglycerin tablets to relieve pain*: Same for both groups. The vitamin E group averaged 7.6 tablets per week while the placebo group 7.7 tablets.

3. *Treadmill tests*: This is a test in which pulse rate, blood pressure, electrocardiogram are monitored as the patient walks faster and harder. Each patient in the study had six tests. No difference was found between the vitamin E and placebo groups during either 6-month period.

4. *Systolic time interval*: This test indicates the strength of heart contractions. Each patient was tested six times in this manner, but again, no improvement was found during the vitamin E treatment period.

5. *Overall benefit* from the vitamin E during the 1-year trial: *None!*

This study is far more significant than previous studies because it is the first performed with technical methods that make possible a high degree of diagnostic accuracy in selecting patients as well as provide improved means of measuring any treatment response. As a result, the concept of "extra vitamin E protecting the heart" has probably been dealt a final defeat in the eyes of medical scientists.

Effect on Lipoproteins

Since 1979 there have been several reports on the effects of vitamin E supplements on blood cholesterol. Many experts now believe that there is a higher risk of atherosclerosis (and therefore heart disease) if cholesterol bound to high density lipoprotein (HDL) is low. One team of researchers[9-11] who gave vitamin E supplements to a small number of experimental subjects found possible benefit, while two other teams[12,13] found none. This subject is discussed further in Chapter 17.

Blood Clot Prevention?

The idea that extra vitamin E might prevent blood clots probably began with the anti-vitamin K mechanism proposed to explain the results of the 1945 experiments of D. W. Wooley[14] who fed large doses of vitamin E quinone (oxidized vitamin E) to pregnant mice daily with no effect until the third week when vaginal bleeding began. The bleeding could only be stopped by giving a generous dose of Vitamin K_1. Also, it is recognized that the molecular spatial structure of vitamin E quinone is very similar to vitamin K_1. According to the vitamin E expert, M. K. Horwitt,[15] it is well known that vitamin E is readily oxidized outside or inside the body to its quinone derivative. Rao and Mason in 1975 reported that large doses of vitamin E-quinone could block vitamin K's clotting property in rats. That same year, however, the prestigious journal, *Nutrition Reviews*[16] warned that interference with vitamin K activity by high-dosage vitamin E is hazardous in humans because of the risks of blood clotting.

Inhibition of platelet clumping is a second mechanism proposed for a possible anti-clotting effect of vitamin E. Platelet clumping is part of the complex sequence of steps in clot formation. Most of the support for this mechanism is based on the findings that blood platelets have a relatively high vitamin E content and that vitamin E-deficient rats have increased platelet counts and a tendency to clump. However, in 1976, the research group of Dr. J. A. C. Gomes[17] provided evidence that 1,000 IU of vitamin E daily had little influence on preventing platelet clumping in healthy men or men with heart disease.

One of the most influential promoters of vitamin E supplements was the late Dr. Alton Ochsner, the renowned New Orleans surgeon. In 1950, Dr. Ochsner and co-workers published details of their use of vitamin E as a possible clot preventive. In 1964, Dr. Ochsner[18] stated that he gave all his surgical patients 100 units of vitamin E three times a day to prevent clots in their veins. The Ochsner reports have been criticized by Dr. Gomes[17] and Dr. Robert Olson[1] for several reasons including a lack of adequate scientific double-blind controls.

In 1974, a Swedish research group led by Dr. K. Korsan-Bengsten[19] reported that vitamin E slowed clotting time, but this required 18 weeks of daily treatments. Furthermore, their study involved not average persons but post-myocardial infarction (heart-muscle-damaged) patients who are known to have dangerously short clotting times. Commenting on this study in 1976, the vitamin E authority, Dr. M. K. Horwitt[15] concluded that it at least gives "some credence" to investigators who claim that supplementation with vitamin E affects blood clotting.

Two important negative studies have been published. In 1954, R. M. Paul[20] and co-workers administered 660 units of vitamin E for a week to 11 individuals and found no effect on clotting. In 1978, H. J. Roberts[21] observed an *increased* clotting effect in 46 patients taking daily dosages of 400 to 800 units of vitamin E without medical advice. Some of these patients had life-threatening lung clots. Two who stopped and then resumed vitamin E supplements suffered recurrent leg vein clots (see Chapter 9). By 1981, Roberts[22] reported having seen a total of 80 vitamin E self-medicators who experienced blood clots.

In 1976, Steiner and Anastasi[23] reported that when vitamin E was added to human blood in laboratory dishes, it prevented platelet aggregation; but they did not study what would happen inside the human body. A more recent study done on rats by Dr. R. V. Panganamala[24] and co-workers led him to propose a mechanism by which vitamin E might decrease clotting tendencies. However, this study was done by comparing E-deficient rats with others given high dosage of vitamin E. But, as Dr. Roberts[25] has pointed out, there are "extraordinary differences" between species so that studies of vitamin E in rats may have little application to humans. Moreover, in the studies of Dr. M. K. Horwitt discussed in Chapter 9, men kept on a near-zero vitamin E diet for four years showed no signs of leg clots.

Clearly, the bulk of the evidence so far shows that vitamin E has little or no practical value in clot prevention and that its use increases the risk of dangerous clotting in some individuals (see Chapter 9). Vitamin E as an anti-clotting agent thus has very few advocates in the scientific community.

Better Products?

In recent years, many doctors have begun to prescribe small amounts of aspirin to certain patients, particularly males who are believed prone to strokes. The rationale for this is the discovery of H. J. Weiss and Aledont[26,27] in 1967 that low-dosage (300 mg) aspirin is a "potent inhibitor" of platelet clumping, a phase of clotting.

More potent than aspirin as an anti-clotting agent is the hormone-like prostacyclin, discovered by Dr. John Vane's research team[28] in 1976. This is an anti-clot substance secreted by the walls of arteries. In 1979 and 1980, there appeared many reports about prostacyclin and possible benefits provided by eicosapentenoic acid ("EPA"), a special highly unsaturated fatty acid which converts to prostacyclin (see Chapter 23). According to Dr. S. Moncada (a member of Dr. Vane's team), high-dosage aspirin also inhibits prostacyclin and should be avoided by clot-prone people. More research on these complicated matters is of course under way.

Can Extra Vitamin E Benefit Sickle Cell Anemia?

In 1980, Dr. C. L. Natta[29] and co-workers reported treating 6 patients with sickle cell anemia with 450 IU of vitamin E daily for 6 to 35 weeks and observed an average reduction of the sickled red blood cells from 25 percent to 11 percent of the total red blood cells. This preliminary finding is interesting and certainly warrants additional studies.

Intermittent Claudication

Intermittent claudication is a condition in which decreased circulation of blood to lower leg muscles leads to severe pain when walking. This condition seems to be the only cardiovascular disorder of adults for which vitamin E supplements may prove to be of use. Up to 1974, there were about as many negative as positive reports, but most of them are not based on well-designed studies. Then in 1974 a controlled study by K. Haeger[30] showed that 400 IU of the d-alpha-tocopherol acetate form of vitamin E daily required at least 4 months of treatment before any benefit appeared. Of the 32 patients in the vitamin E group, most continued treatment for 5 years, all for at least 2 years. After 6 months, 54 percent of the vitamin E group were able to reach the walking test limit of about 1,000 yards. In the control group of 14 patients who had been getting only anti-clot drugs such as dicoumarin or a blood vessel dilator drug to increase circulation, only 23 percent could walk the 1,000 yards. After 20 months, the blood flow to the impaired leg muscle of the entire vitamin E group had increased by an average of 34 percent; whereas there was no improvement of blood flow in the control group.

Despite Haeger's favorable report, Bieri and Farrell[7] point out in their lengthy review article on vitamin E that all trials of vitamin E for this affliction of less than 7 months' duration have been negative; and they conclude: "Although these studies favor the use of large doses of vitamin E in intermittent claudication, further clinical studies are needed."

Vitamin E for Benign Breast Cysts

As early as 1965, Dr. Archie Abrams of Boston University School of Medicine used vitamin E supplements to provide moderate relief for 16 women with fibrocystic breast disease, reducing pain and tenderness as well as the size of the cysts. Though they seldom became cancerous, these so-called "lumpy cysts" of the breasts afflict several million American women and can cause discomfort and anxiety. In 1978, Dr. Robert London[31] and co-workers at Johns Hopkins University School of Medicine reported that vitamin E supplements caused breast cysts to shrink and relieved tenderness in 20 women.

More recently, Dr. London's group[32-35] recorded a detailed study of 26 women with fibrocystic breast disease plus 8 normal women in a double-blind test utilizing 600 IU of vitamin E daily for 8 weeks. Treatment with vitamin E appeared to produce complete or near-complete disappearance of cysts in 10 patients; fair to moderate improvements in 12 patients; and no change in 4 patients. All of the treated women had significant but probably harmless changes in their levels of sex hormones and blood cholesterol. Dr. London[32] concluded that: "If clinicians can get symptomatic relief in patients with something as benign as vitamin E, I think it's a reasonable therapy." But he added:

> Right now you can go to the drugstore and buy thousands of grams of vitamin E and take as much as you want, not knowing that it may affect you profoundly . . . At the dosage levels we prescribed (600 IU for 8 weeks), which weren't all that high, vitamin E is not a benign vitamin . . . It is—and we need to stress this—a pharmacologic agent.

More research needs to be done to see whether Dr. London's findings can be confirmed and put to practical use. Meanwhile, women thinking of self-treatment of breast cysts with megadose vitamin E should first seek medical supervision.

Does Vitamin E Help Sexual Functioning?

The idea that vitamin E might increase sexual ability, as noted in Chapter 9, is based primarily upon faulty interpretation of animal experiments which showed that E-deficient animals had reduced fertility but normal sexual ability. In 1944, Dr. E. V. Shute claimed that vitamin E treatments increased sperm counts and aided recovery from infertility in men. Shute's claim was reviewed in 1972 by two vitamin E experts, Mason and Horwitt[36] who concluded there was insufficient evidence to support it. One noteworthy study is that of Farris who in 1949 tried vitamin E on infertile men and found no beneficial effect on the sperm count, sperm mobility or sperm structure.

In 1979, Dr. Edward Herold[37] and co-workers studied the effects on volunteers of 1,000 IU of vitamin E daily for 28 days. The study was done double-blind, with 17 volunteers receiving vitamin E while 18 others got a placebo. No differences in sexual arousal or behavior were found between the two groups.

Medical and biological journals of the 1940s and 1950s contain hundreds of reports on the use of vitamin E therapy to prevent miscarriages. Most of these reports were favorable because other factors governing the outcome of pregnancies were not taken into account. Professor John Marks,[38] who presented a detailed analysis at the 1962 International Symposium on Vitamin E held in Switzerland, concluded that "sound evidence supporting such treatment is lacking."

A well designed study was done in 1955 by a team led by Professor William Darby.[39] Surveying 1,611 pregnant women, they found that those who had previous miscarriages had vitamin E blood levels as normal as those who had not had miscarriages.

In 1977, an Institute of Food Technologists' panel of experts[40] pointed out how difficult it is to measure sexual performance in humans: "So much of human sexuality is psychological that the placebo effects are strong, as are unpredictable variations from time to time and place to place." The panel's conclusion, based on a study of reports of the previous 35 years, was that supplements of vitamin E have no value in preventing male impotence or sterility, or in altering the outcome of pregnancy.

Because large numbers of obstetricians and gynecologists in the United States, Great Britain and Europe were experimenting with vitamin E, some trials were conducted with the hope of relieving severe menopausal symptoms such as drenching sweats, hot flashes and loss of sleep. Although many published reports were favorable, none of these trials used adequate double-blind techniques.[38]

Effect on Athletic Ability

Vitamin E is one of several substances which many athletes believe can improve their stamina and endurance. Some athletes consume large amounts of wheat germ oil for this reason. The belief in vitamin E, which has been promoted by several very prominent coaches, is based primarily on faulty interpretation of experiments done with animals and humans. It is well known that deficiency of vitamin E in animals causes abnormal muscle functioning associated with weakening. But this does *not* mean that extra vitamin E causes muscles to be stronger—either in animals or humans. It is also known that E-deficient animals are less able to tolerate periods of low oxygen supply (hypoxia) to body organs. But again, this does not mean that greater than normal amounts of vitamin E will increase tolerance to low oxygen states in animals or humans.

Such benefits, if they exist, would have to be demonstrated by well de-signed experiments in humans. Positive results were claimed for experiments conducted prior to 1970 by such individuals as T. K. Cureton, L. Percival and L. Prokop; but according to Dr. I. M. Sharman,[41] these experiments were not well designed. In contrast, several recent double-blind tests have shown *no* benefit from vitamin E supplementation:

• In 1971, Dr. Sharman[41] published a double-blind trial with 26 boarding school boys, half receiving 400 IU of vitamin E for 6 weeks while the other half received a placebo. No differences in swimming performance, heart-lung endurance or muscular coordination were found between the two groups.

• In 1974, R. J. Shepherd[42] and co-workers at the University of Toronto tested 1,200 IU of vitamin E against a placebo in two groups of 10 swimmers undergoing 85 days of intensive training. Performance improved equally in both groups to the degree expected from training alone.

• In 1975, J. D. Lawrence[43] and co-workers at Tulane University compared the effect of 900 IU of vitamin E with a placebo in two groups of swimmers undergoing training. One group was highly trained to begin with while the other was less trained. Again, vitamin E was found to have no effect upon swimming endurance.

Does Extra Vitamin E Slow Aging?

Interest in the possible effect of vitamin E upon the aging process was probably stimulated by the development of atomic weapons and the wish to find ways to protect people from the terrible effects of atomic radiation. Studies after World War II revealed similarities between dead "clinker" cells found in animals exposed to radiation and age-pigment cells which develop naturally as people get older. Then it was found in animals that deficiency of vitamin E leads to increased numbers of such cells, and also that the antioxidant property of vitamin E appears to exert a protective effect against certain effects of radiation. But here are at least two reasons why these facts do not mean that supplementation with vitamin E can retard aging.

First, as noted by the pioneer vitamin E researcher, Dr. A. L. Tappel,[44] both animals and humans have several kinds of antioxidant "protectors" that are as good or perhaps better than vitamin E. Second, although it is clear that vitamin E is needed, there is evidence that *extra* vitamin E (above the RDA) is not beneficial. In 1973, for example, Dr. Tappel[45] reported that mice fed the human equivalent of 2,000 IU of vitamin E aged at the same rate as similar mice that did not get the supplement. It has also been found that adding vitamin E to cultures of human tissues does not prolong their survival.[46,47]

Protection from Pollution?

It has been shown[48,49] that animals made deficient in vitamin E suffer from many serious disorders including increased susceptibility to lung damage from air pollutants such as ozone and nitrogen dioxide. It has also been shown[48,50] that increasing vitamin E intake above normal exerts a *slight* protective effect in rats, but the significance of this to humans is doubtful.[45,51] Dr. Tappel[45] states that 20 to 30 IU "could be recommended" for adults exposed to photochemical smog (ozone), but that megadoses are certainly not needed.

Vitamin E Ointment for Wound Healing?

Many health food publications suggest that vitamin E liquid or ointment placed directly onto burned areas or other skin wounds can speed healing. However, scientific studies have found that it actually *delays* healing.[52]

Overview

Consumer Reports magazine provided a good summary of reliable information about vitamin E in its January 1973 issue. After listing 68 conditions for which vitamin E was being improperly promoted, the article concluded: "During the 19th century, patent medicine manufacturers vied with one another in compiling long lists of diseases for which their panaceas were alleged to be effective . . . Products that contain vitamin E are currently touted in the same tradition."

I must agree! A few claims for vitamin E (for the treatment of fibrocystic breast disease and perhaps of intermittent claudication or sickle cell anemia) deserve further scientific study, but I suggest that you ignore the rest.

References

1. Olson, R. E.: Circulation 48:179, 1973.
2. Hodges, R. E.: Journal of the American Dietetic Association 62:638, 1973.
3. Hodges, R. E.: Drug Therapy 3:103, 1973.
4. Anderson, T. W.: Canadian Medical Association Journal 101:401, 1974.
5. Anderson, T. W.: American Journal of Clinical Nutrition 27:1174, 1974.
6. Toone, W. M.: New England Journal of Medicine 289:979, 1973.
7. Bieri, J. G. and Farrell, P. M.: In Vitamins and Hormones 34:31-75, 1976.
8. Gillilan, R. E. et al.: American Heart Journal 93:444, 1977.
9. Hermann, W. J., Jr., et al.: American Journal of Clinical Pathology 72: 848, 1979.
10. Hermann, W. J., Jr.: Ibid., p. 124.
11. Hermann, W. J., Jr.: Ibid., p. 844.
12. Hatam, L. J. and Kayden, H. J.: Ibid., p. 122.
13. Schwartz, P. and Rutherford, I.: Ibid., p. 843.
14. Wooley, D. W.: Journal of Biological Chemistry 159:59, 1945.
15. Horwitt, M. K.: American Journal of Clinical Nutrition 29:569, 1976.
16. Nutrition Reviews 33:269, 1975.
17. Gomes, J. A. C. et al.: American Heart Journal 91:425, 1976.
18. Ochsner, A.: New England Journal of Medicine 271:211, 1964.
19. Korsan-Bengsten, K.: Thrombosis et Diathesis Haemorrhagica (Stuttgart) 31:505, 1974.
20. Paul, R. M. et al.: Canadian Journal of Biochemistry and Biophysics 32: 347, 1954.
21. Roberts, H. J.: Lancet 1:49, January 7, 1978.
22. Roberts, H. J.: JAMA 246:129, 1981.
23. Steiner, M. and Anastasi, J.: Journal of Clinical Investigation 57:732, 1976.
24. Karpen, C. W., Panganamala, R. V. et al.: Prostaglandins 22:651-661, 1981.
25. Roberts, H. J.: Personal communication, August 16, 1982.
26. Weiss, H. J. and Aledont, L. M.: Lancet 2:495, 1967.
27. Barnett, H. J. M. et al.: Stroke 9:295, 1978.
28. Moncada, S., Vane, J. et al.: Nature 263:663, 1976.
29. Natta, C. L. et al.: American Journal of Clinical Nutrition 33:968, 1980.
30. Haeger, K.: American Journal of Clinical Nutrition 27:1179, 1974.
31. London, R. S., Solomon, D. M. et al.: Breast 4:19, 1978.
32. London, R. S., Sundaram, G. S. et al.: A Report to the 1980 Meeting of the Endocrine Society; reviewed by E. R. Gonzalez, in JAMA 244:1077, 1980.
33. London, R. S., Sundaram, G. S. et al.: Cancer Research 41:3811, 1981.
34. Sundaram, G. S., London, R. et al.: Ibid. 41:3814, 1981.

35. Sundaram, G. S., London, R. S. et al.: Lipids 16:223, 1981.
36. Mason, K. D. and Horwitt, M. K.: *In* The Vitamins, Vol. V, 2nd Ed., 1972, pp. 293-309.
37. Herold, E. et al.: Archives of Sexual Behavior 8:397, 1979.
38. Marks, J.: *In* Vitamins and Hormones 20:573-597, 1962.
39. Ferguson, M. E. et al.: Journal of Nutrition 55:305, 1955.
40. Institute of Food Technologists' Expert Panel on Food and Nutrition: Nutrition Reviews 35:57-62, 1977.
41. Sharman, I. M. et al.: British Journal of Nutrition 26:265, 1971.
42. Shephard, R. J. et al.: European Journal of Applied Physiology 33:119, 1974.
43. Lawrence, J. D. et al.: American Journal of Clinical Nutrition 28:205, 1975.
44. Tappel, A. L.: Geriatrics 23:97, 1968.
45. Tappel, A. L.: Nutrition Today 8:4-12, 1973.
46. Packer, L. and Smith, J. R.: Proceedings of the National Academy of Sciences, 74:1640, 1977.
47. Balin, A. K. et al.: Journal of Cell Biology 74:58, 1977.
48. Menzel, D. B. et al.: Journal of Agricultural and Food Chemistry 20:481, 1972.
49. Chow, C. K. and Tappel, A. L.: Lipids 7:518, 1972.
50. Mustafa, M. G.: Nutrition Reports International 11:473, 1975.
51. Bieri, J. G.: Nutrition Reviews 33:161-7, 1975.
52. Ehrlich, H. P. et al.: Annals of Surgery 175:235, 1972.

15

Can Megavitamins Help Mental Health?

"Orthomolecular psychiatry is the achievement and preservation of mental health by varying the concentration in the human body of substances that are normally present, such as vitamins."

Thus, Nobel Prize-winning chemist Professor Linus Pauling coined the term "orthomolecular" (meaning "right molecule") and joined the megavitamin psychiatrists who were very few in 1968. By means of his brilliant talent for chemical theorizing, Pauling provided the megavitamin advocates with some semblance of theoretical justification for treating severely mentally ill (schizophrenic) patients with mega (huge) doses of vitamins daily. Niacin/nicotinic acid (vitamin B_3) or its amide was the earliest vitamin used. Later, combinations of two or more of these vitamins were and still are used: niacin, pyridoxine (vitamin B_6), vitamin C, folic acid and vitamin E. However, it should be emphasized that the diagnosis of schizophrenia by "orthomolecular" psychiatrists is unconventional and their treatment frequently includes the use of conventional psychiatric therapy with psychoactive drugs, electroconvulsive shock or both. The reported treatments have so many variable parts that scientists find it impossible to measure which parts, if any, are effective.

The megavitamin concept of treating mental illness got its start back in 1957 when two Canadian psychiatrists, Abram Hoffer and Humphry Osmond reported, in a now defunct journal, that large daily doses of niacin seemed to improve the condition of several schizophrenic patients. In 1962, Osmond and Hoffer[1] described their "nine years of study" of niacin for schizophrenia in the British journal, *Lancet*. During this period, several other proponents of megavitamin therapy for schizophrenia and other mental illnesses began to publish their observations but none conducted scientifically controlled double-blind studies. Among these were, Dr. Alan Cott in 1967-71, Dr. David R. Hawkins during 1967-70, and Dr. Carl C. Pfeiffer. Hawkins and Pauling[2] edited the book, *Orthomolecular Psychiatry: Treatment of Schizophrenia,* published in 1973.

By 1975, the "orthomolecular" psychiatrists had grown in number, though they were still a tiny minority. They were, in the words of *Medical World News* writer David Leff,[3] "not a dissenting faction within American and Canadian medicine but a self-contained medical counter-culture." Some 78 practitioners of orthomolecular psychiatry in 28 states—MD's, Ph.D.'s osteopaths, chiropractors and lay workers (including indoctrinated ex-patients)—were on the referral list published by the American Schizophrenia Association. (Today the list numbers about 150 medical and osteopathic physicians.) In Leff's excellent article, the judgment of the overwhelming majority of the medical and psychiatric practitioners was stated succinctly by Dr. Seymour Kety, Professor of Psychiatry at Harvard Medical School who then was also Chief of Psychiatric Research at Massachusetts General Hospital: "If it hadn't been for Linus Pauling, that outfit (the orthomolecular psychiatrists) would have died of its own fallacy."

Who Is Right?

Make no mistake, Dr. Kety was not making an unwarranted "snap" judgment. In July 1973, the American Psychiatric Association (APA)'s *Task Force Report 7: Megavitamin and Orthomolecular Therapy in Psychiatry*[4] was published in which six distinguished experts evaluated all the available reports of megadose niacin therapy for schizophrenic patients. They concluded that the trials reported by megavitamin enthusiasts demonstrated no benefit because they had not been performed with acceptable scientific controls. Nor did megadose niacin appear of value in the scientifically controlled studies conducted by other psychiatrists.

When Linus Pauling protested vigorously against the APA report, he was invited to write a rebuttal which was published in 1974 in the prestigious and widely respected *American Journal of Psychiatry*. In the same issue, three distinguished psychiatrists[5-7] offered critical comments about Pauling's rebuttal. Here is a summary of these arguments and counterarguments.

Criticism of Megavitamin Therapy

The APA's Task Force Report is a 54-page booklet which evaluates the results of megavitamin treatment for mental illnesses, particularly niacin for schizophrenia, and cites 105 references reviewed. Of these, no less than 26 reports were from the team of Hoffer and Osmond published jointly or singly. What did the APA Task Force conclude? Their chief criticisms were that 1) none of the megavitamin psychiatrists had ever conducted studies that were adequately controlled scientifically; and 2) several conventional psychiatrists *had* performed well-controlled studies with megadose niacin for schizophrenia and had found no benefit. The report's devastating conclusion is perhaps the most strongly-toned comment ever issued by a prestigious medical review body:

> Socially desirable outcomes have sometimes been derived from myths or fervently held beliefs. To this extent the orthomolecular movement in psychiatry may be socially useful. But if psychiatry is to become and remain scientific, it must meet the test of scientific validity. Nicotinic acid (niacin) therapy does not do so at this time. Their credibility (the orthomolecular psychiatrists) is further diminished by a constant refusal over the past decade to perform controlled experiments and to report their new results in a scientifically acceptable fashion. Under these circumstances this Task Force considers the massive publicity which they promulgate via radio, the lay press and popular books, using catch phrases which are really misnomers like "megavitamin therapy" and "orthomolecular treatment," to be deplorable.

Pauling's Rebuttal

In seven pages of rebuttal, Pauling[8] complains that the APA Task Force did not adequately recognize the possible and perhaps likely existence of genetically determined biochemical abnormalities in certain schizophrenic patients which could result in an extraordinarily high requirement for niacin or vitamin C or pyridoxine (vitamin B_6). He also interprets as positive some of the experiments judged negative by the APA Task Force.

Then he presents an argument that puzzles and distresses most scientists because it runs counter to the "rules" of the scientific community:

> I have talked with the leading orthomolecular psychiatrists and have found that they feel the principles of medical ethics prevent them from carrying out controlled clinical tests . . . It is the duty of the physician to give to every one of his patients the treatment that in his best judgment will be of the greatest value. Some psychiatrists, including Hoffer and Osmond, carried out controlled trials 20 years ago. They became convinced that orthomolecular therapy, along with conventional treatment, was beneficial to almost every patient. From that time on their ethical principles have required that they give this treatment and not withhold it from half of their patients . . . It is the critics, who doubt the value of orthomolecular methods, who are at fault in not having carried out well-designed clinical tests.

Pauling's rebuttal concludes: "There is evidence that an increased intake of some vitamins, including ascorbic acid (vitamin C), niacin, pyridoxine, and cyanocobalamin (vitamin B_{12}), is useful in treating schizophrenia, and this treatment has a sound theoretical basis."

Counter-Argument by Dr. Donald Klein[5]

Dr. Klein is now Director of Research at New York State Psychiatric Institute and Professor of Psychiatry at Columbia University's medical school. He notes that Pauling reveals his basic recognition of the value of good scientific controls by discussing at some length the study of Dr. B. Milner. Milner[9] conducted a well-controlled trial with 40 chronic psychotic patients with megadose vitamin C with beneficial results. However, before the trial started, most of the patients were deficient in vitamin C, and 12 patients were so depleted of vitamin C they actually showed symptoms of scurvy. Dr. Klein correctly reasons: "Unless it is demonstrated that vitamin C deficiency is characteristic of schizophrenia itself and not of malnourished patients in general, there is no reason to believe that Milner's study demonstrates the value of giving ascorbic acid to well-nourished schizophrenics."

In 1971, Pitt and Pollitt[10] reported a well-controlled vitamin C trial that compared 32 schizophrenic patients with 24 non-schizophrenic patients— with both groups on the same diet in the same hospital. The object was to see if schizophrenics tended to be deficient in vitamin C. Both groups were tested for the vitamin C content of the white blood cells and blood platelets, the chief "ready reserve" storage site for vitamin C. The schizophrenic group actually had significantly higher vitamin C levels than the control group. Twelve patients from each group were then given 1,000 mg of vitamin C daily for 14 days while the vitamin C content of their white cells and platelets was measured before, during and after the vitamin C treatment. No difference was found between the schizophrenics and the other patients.

Dr. Klein was also troubled by Pauling's "incomprehensible acceptance of very minimal differences that lack statistical significance as solid evidence of therapeutic efficiency."

In regard to Pauling's defense of the orthomolecular psychiatrists' refusal to run double-blind scientifically controlled trials with vitamins plus conventional treatment (wherein half the patients would get only the conventional treatment as a control group for comparison), Dr. Klein comments:

> I agree that this is an ethical, not a scientific question. My ethical stand is that scientific honesty comes first because it yields the best long-term clinical care. The scientific clinician, as opposed to the cultist, has the responsibility to use the scientific tools available for proper validation before making sweeping claims.
>
> History provides countless examples of worthless and dangerous medical treatments that have been promulgated with zeal, and have achieved widespread acceptance. Since the trials referred to by Pauling have not won the assent of the scientific community as well designed, it seems possible that orthomolecular psychiatry is wishful thinking rather than useful fact.

Comments by Dr. Richard J. Wyatt[6]

Dr. Wyatt was Acting Chief and later became Chief of the National Institute of Mental Health's Laboratory of Clinical Psychopharmacology, St.

Elizabeth's Hospital, Washington, D.C. Pauling stated that "the incidences of toxicity and other serious side-effects of doses of vitamins used in orthomolecular medicine are low." But Dr. Wyatt counters by citing a 1965 study by Chinaglia, in which 5 out of 14 acute schizophrenic patients treated with megadose niacinamide had to be taken off the "drug" because of severe adverse reactions. Mindful of the harmful effects of high-dose niacin on some people, as outlined in Chapter 11 of this book, I agree that Dr. Wyatt's warning about daily treatment with 3,000 mg of niacin is justified.

Dr. Wyatt also criticized Pauling and the "orthomolecular" movement, by referring to a 1970 report by Ramsay and co-workers in which the niacin-treated group required more psychiatric drugs and longer stays in the hospital than conventionally treated patients. Dr. Wyatt cited the bad effect of niacin in the study reported in 1969 by Meltzer and co-workers in which chronic schizophrenic patients who received niacinamide in its coenzyme form, NAD, along with antipsychotic drugs, showed "increased anger, negativism, belligerence and irritability." Also, according to Wyatt, in a 1967 study by Dr. Nathan Kline and associates, 6 out of 9 patients given niacinamide as NAD showed "some increase in hostility."

Dr. Wyatt also reviewed the only three "controlled" studies offered by Pauling and the orthomolecular psychiatrists as producing positively beneficial results from adding megavitamins to the treatments. These studies were those of Hoffer, Osmond and colleagues in 1957, Osmond and Hoffer in 1962 and R. Denson in 1962. Dr. Wyatt points out serious flaws in the scientific controls as well as a lack of sufficient data to allow conclusions in these three studies. Then he cites three well-controlled studies which failed to show any significant benefit from adding megavitamins to the conventional treatment of schizophrenic patients. These were Meltzer and co-workers in 1969; Ananth, Ban and Lehmann in 1973; and S. D. McGrath in 1974.

In response to a claim by Pauling that the cost of megavitamin treatment is low, Dr. Wyatt estimates the cost of megadosage of vitamins B_6, C, E and niacin at $205/year. "This cost is in addition to the cost of conventional treatment, which is also used," he points out. "Certainly the additional cost is well worth it if the treatment is successful. If not, it becomes an expensive mistake. Assuming that there are 2,000,00 schizophrenic patients in the United States, the cost is $410 million a year. Treatment of this many patients from the time they are age 20 to the time they become 65 would cost $18 billion."

Dr. Wyatt concludes: "While the concepts of orthomolecular psychiatry are attractive and stimulating, the data supporting them are weak and the therapeutic claims based upon them are unwarranted." Well-designed studies could have been done by comparing patients treated with megavitamins and matched controls of similar patients treated by conventional psychiatric methods, but megavitamin proponents have not done so.

Comments of Dr. Morris Lipton[7]

Dr. Lipton is Professor of Psychiatry and Director, Biological Sciences Research Center of the Child Development Research Institute, University of North Carolina. He was also the Chairman of the APA Task Force. Dr. Lipton challenged Pauling's chief theoretical base that schizophrenics are another example of genetic illness due to mutant apoenzymes (the protein part of a complete enzyme) which are abnormal in requiring vastly larger daily amounts of the vitamin coenzyme to form the complete workable enzyme system. He states:

> Dr. Pauling's theory is attractive but too general. Who could argue against the thesis that optimum vitamin intake is essential for mental health? So is an optimum protein intake, social environment, marriage and income. The question is: What is optimum?

Dr. Lipton proceeds by first agreeing with Pauling that there are known genetic illnesses that require daily megadoses of a certain vitamin, but then notes that they typically occur early in life (in children) and that both the physical and mental symptoms are quickly reversed by large doses of the *single* appropriate vitamin. However, as Dr. Lipton points out, schizophrenia fails to meet both of these criteria.

Dr. Lipton chides the megavitamin psychiatrists for crediting the vitamin part of the treatment for success when the complete orthomolecular therapy also includes psychotropic drugs. Pauling attempts to justify the term "orthomolecular psychiatry" by claiming that these drugs are used only during the periods of psychotic crisis, along with vitamins which are continued indefinitely. But Dr. Lipton argues that many reported "megavitamin" trials continued the drugs for over a year—as did the study reported by Dr. Hawkins[11] in 1973.

Dr. Lipton concludes by warning of the potentially harmful long-range effects of megadose niacin or pyridoxine treatments as follows: First, it is scientifically and economically improper to give huge doses of vitamins when there is no evidence that there is a deficiency in function of any of the enzymes for which they serve as co-enzymes. Second, there is the matter of toxicity.

The Canadian Mental Health Association Study

Answering the challenge of the megavitamin psychiatrists, the Canadian Mental Health Association (CMHA) sponsored a series of 12 trials with niacin for schizophrenic patients in an effort to duplicate the claims of good results from the "orthomolecular" advocates. These trials, conducted under the overall supervision of Drs. T. A. Ban and H. E. Lehmann, of McGill University, involved several mental hospitals, a diverse staff of psychiatrists and a large number of patients. The first results from five of the trials were published during 1970-72 and were summarized in the APA Task Force Report that concluded that a dosage of 3,000 mg/day of nicotinic acid/niacin "has no therapeutic effect and may have a negative effect in unselected groups of schizophrenic patients."

In March, 1975, the CMHA Study's *Progress Report II* was published by Ban and Lehmann.[12] In this report is a summary of the interesting 1973 study directed by Rutgers University psychologist, Dr. Richard Wittenborn.[13] This is a well-controlled double-blind study with 86 schizophrenic patients given niacin or a placebo for 18 to 24 months. It found that: the vitamin group fared worse than the placebo group in 1) total days required to stay in hospital; 2) adjustment to home and community (the niacin group showed less self-confidence, slightly less sense of responsibility and more complaints of not feeling well); and 3) other aspects of community adjustment (the niacin-treated patients adjusted less well compared to the placebo group).

The Wittenborn study also found that the vitamin and placebo groups of patients showed no difference in 1) the amount of tranquilizing drugs needed; 2) the rehospitalization rate; and 3) as determined by psychological testing, the degree of anxiety, manic symptoms, psychotic belligerence, paranoia, retardation or intellectual impairment. Furthermore, many of the niacin-treated patients suffered from hyperkeratosis, a widespread rough and sometimes itchy skin condition that was absent in the placebo group.

Recent Developments

The Research Advisory Committee of the National Institute of Mental Health reviewed pertinent scientific data through 1979 and agreed that orthomolecular therapy is ineffective and may be harmful. After the U.S. Senate Defense Subcommittee looked into this therapy, it was removed as a covered treatment under the CHAMPUS insurance program for military dependents.

In 1976, the California legislature passed a law to make orthomolecular services available through the Medi-Cal program on a trial basis. The pilot program ran from April 1979 through June 1980, a total of 15 months. Recipients of the treatment were all volunteers. The study was set up to evaluate the cost of orthomolecular treatment but not its effectiveness. The Health Department's[14] report to the legislature concluded that there were no significant changes in Medi-Cal costs when orthomolecular services were added, but noted that decisions to expand the schedule of benefits are primarily based upon the medical efficacy of services in question. A bill to add orthomolecular services as a regular Medi-Cal benefit was subsequently introduced; but it was opposed by the Department of Health and the California Medical Association and died in a legislative committee.

None of these developments has, of course, dampened the enthusiasm of megavitamin practitioners. In fact, while most of the controversy has centered about the treatment of schizophrenia, megavitamin proponents do not limit themselves to that condition. They are also treating mentally retarded children—as well as adults with depression and various other emotional disorders—at fees which range as high at $500 for the initial psychiatric evaluation![3]

References

1. Osmond, H. and Hoffer, A.: Lancet 1:316-319, 1962.
2. Hawkins, D. and Pauling, L., Eds.: Orthomolecular Psychiatry: Treatment of Schizophrenia. San Francisco, W. H. Freeman & Co., 1973.
3. Leff, D.: Medical World News, Aug. 11, 1975, pp. 71-82.
4. Lipton, M. A., et al.: Megavitamin and Orthomolecular Therapy in Psychiatry. Washington, D.C., American Psychiatric Association, 1973.
5. Klein, D. F.: American Journal of Psychiatry 131:1258, 1974.
6. Wyatt, R. J., *Ibid.,* p. 1262.
7. Lipton, M. A.: *Ibid.,* p. 1266.
8. Pauling, L.: *Ibid.,* p. 1251.
9. Milner, G.: British Journal of Psychiatry 109:294, 1963.
10. Pitt, B. and Pollitt, N.: British Journal of Psychiatry 118:227, 1971.
11. Hawkins, D.: *In* Hawkins and Pauling, *op. cit.,* 631-673, 1973.
12. Ban, T. A. and Lehmann, H. E.: Canadian Psychiatric Association Journal, 20:103, 1975.
13. Wittenborn, J. R.: Archives of General Psychiatry 28:308, 1973.
14. Berger, K. et al.: Report to the Legislature on the Orthomolecular Demonstration Project Conducted by the California Department of Health Services. Sacramento, Calif., October, 1981.

16

Can Megavitamins Help Against Cancer?

In 1979, 8-year-old Chuckie Peters entered the University of Chicago Wyler Children's Hospital suffering from headaches, extreme sensitivity to bright light, severe bone pain, mental impairment and a 10-pound weight loss. Previously diagnosed as having leukemia, the boy had been receiving effective treatment with chemotherapy. But his mother had been persuaded by promoters of quack methods to give him 120,000 units of vitamin A daily for over a year as part of a so-called "metabolic therapy" program.

According to Mrs. Peters' testimony to the Illinois state legislature's Commission on Cancer Quackery,[1] Chuckie reached a point where "he couldn't walk at all and the touching of his arms and legs brought screams of pain." After thorough examination and testing, the University doctors diagnosed severe vitamin A poisoning and noted brain swelling, near-blindness, and painful abnormalities of the bone coverings.[2] Chuckie stayed in the hospital for 2½ weeks so that the doctors could relieve his severe bone pain with narcotics and check the slow clearing of his brain swelling. Then he returned home, but according to his mother's testimony:

> He was unable to return to school for another 2½ months. Almost half the time we carted him around in a wheel chair. His thinking capabilities and concentration were minimal for a time; his weight loss was almost ten pounds. Our son was a shell of what he was a few months before. The three years on the chemotherapy program never yielded the amount of pain he experienced during that 3½ months of pain from vitamin A toxicity . . . which almost cost him his life!

Fortunately, this story may have a happy ending. Chuckie's cancer drug therapy was continued for a total of three years, at which time he showed no signs of cancer. According to his principal physician, Dr. Robert R. Chilcote, the boy has remained healthy for another 1½ years and may well be cured.[3]

According to *The Medical Letter,* "Physicians are seeing more patients with vitamin A toxicity because of its increasing use, together with other vitamins, by health food faddists."[4] Is there any evidence that vitamins have a role in the prevention or treatment of cancer? Yes, there is some. Deficiency of certain vitamins has been shown to increase the risk of cancer,[5,6] but this does not mean that taking more than the Recommended Dietary Allowance (RDA) is beneficial. Only one vitamin, folic acid, has a major role in the *treatment* of some cancers, but high doses can worsen leukemia. And vitamin E may have a role in reducing the toxicity of certain chemotherapeutic agents.

Let's look at some of the evidence behind these facts.

Vitamin A and Cancer

There are many reports in scientific journals of animal experiments involving vitamin deficiencies and vitamin supplementation in the quest to control cancer. These will be mentioned below only as the interpretations and conclusions of several prominent biomedical scientists who have published review articles since 1976.

Dr. Michael B. Sporn is the Chief of the Lung Cancer Branch, Division of Cancer Cause and Prevention, of the National Cancer Institute. According to Dr. Sporn,[7] vitamin A deficiency has been associated with cancer in the lungs, bladder and colon of the rat. In humans, it has been linked to lung cancer and also to stomach and colon cancer, as shown by a survey of over 8,000 Norwegian men reported by E. Bjelke.[8,9] His 1975 study[9] found that in those getting less than 1 RDA of vitamin A from dietary sources, there were twice as many lung cancer cases as in those getting 1 RDA or slightly higher amounts. This suggests that adequate vitamin A—not an extra amount—is needed to protect against lung cancer.

In 1978, Smith and Jick[10] asked 800 individuals with newly diagnosed lung cancers and 3,433 patients with other diseases whether they took vitamin A supplements. It was found that men who took an average of 1 RDA of supplementary vitamin A had only half as many cancers as those not taking supplements. Among women patients, no difference was found. The investigators did not try to determine how much vitamin A these patients had been getting in their diet. This study supports the idea that getting at least 1 RDA of vitamin A is helpful. But since total vitamin A intakes were not measured, it was not possible to tell whether getting more than the RDA was helpful.

In 1980, Dr. Nicholas Wald[11] and colleagues in Oxford, England, published a study comparing the blood levels of vitamin A of 86 men who developed cancer and 172 men who did not. The blood samples had been collected as part of a government health screening program one to three years before the cancers were discovered. Men with lower vitamin A blood levels had a slightly higher incidence of cancer than did those with higher blood levels (many of whom were still within the normal range), but the difference did not appear great enough to be of practical importance.

Thus there is good reason to believe that adequate vitamin A in the daily diet plays some role in preventing cancer. But no need for more than the RDA of 5,000 IU daily to guard against cancer has been demonstrated by any acceptable scientific evidence as of 1982.[7]

Anyone thinking of taking large daily doses of vitamin A as a lung cancer preventive should heed the warning of Dr. Paul Newberne,[12] a prominent researcher at the Massachusetts Institute of Technology: "Deficiency of vitamin A increases susceptibility to lung cancer, but large excess of vitamin A also increases lung tumors in animals." He and a colleague[13] found that with some cancer-causing chemicals there were *fewer* tumors in A-deficient animals than in animals getting normal intakes of vitamin A. According to Professor J. R. Bertino[14] of Yale University Medical School, "The possibility exists that large doses of vitamins may be harmful and can actually accelerate tumor growth." Moreover, as explained by Drs. J. R. DiPalma and R .McMichael,[15] even if it were effective against cancer, vitamin A cannot be used in large enough doses for a sufficient period of time without causing toxicity.

In 1979, Drs. Vernon Young and D. P. Richardson[16] published a lengthy review article entitled, "Nutrients, Vitamins and Minerals in Cancer Prevention—Facts and Fallacies." In it they indignantly attack the flood of dangerous advice in recent paperback books about cancer prevention. They referred to one especially questionable book by naturopath Paavo Airola which advocates daily dosing with up to 150,000 IU of vitamin A.

Carotenes as Cancer Preventives?

"Carrots May Cut Lung Cancer Risk, Doctor Says" was a headline in the February 7, 1981 issue of the *Los Angeles Times*. Does this mean you should start taking 5 times the RDA of vitamin A?

In recent years many studies have shown that low blood levels of cholesterol, vitamin A and carotene are associated with a higher risk of cancer, especially lung cancer.[17] Two such studies were those of Dr. J. D. Kark[18] and co-workers and the Framingham study reported by R. R. Williams[19] and colleagues. However, a few studies, most notably the Western Electric Study reported by Dyer, Stamler and co-workers,[20] found that low cholesterol was not associated with a greater risk of cancer.

Carotenes from vegetable sources are converted to vitamin A in the intestinal wall. However, higher intakes of carotenes are only partly converted, and unchanged carotenes are absorbed into the blood with some stored in the liver. The British research team led by the U.N. prizewinning cancer researcher, Dr. Richard Doll, recently suggested that increasing blood levels of carotenes may help reduce the risk of cancers.[21,22] To test this theory, more than 25,000 American physician volunteers are now participating in a 5-year double-blind study. Directed by Dr. Charles H. Hennekens of Harvard Medical School, the study is designed to see whether beta-carotene supplements can prevent cancer and also whether small dosages of aspirin can prevent heart disease. Meanwhile, don't go overboard on carrots, because eating too many of them causes carotenemia, a condition in which the skin turns yellow.

Dr. William Darby[23] points out that diets high in carotene are also high in fiber and usually differ from low-carotene diets in protein and fat content as well as other food constituents. Thus the possibly reduced incidence of colon cancer in people whose diets are high in fiber may be related to the carotene content or any of several other aspects of such diets. Cancer and diet are discussed further in Chapter 23.

Are Retinoids Useful against Cancer?

Synthetic retinoids are structurally modified vitamin A and are no longer vitamins. Considerable research in recent years has revealed that these compounds, acting as drugs, are effective for the prevention or cure of certain cancers in animals. One used commonly is retinoic acid (sometimes referred to as "vitamin A acid" although it is not a complete vitamin). It has the growth effects of vitamin A, but lacks its function in vision and in reproduction. Dr. Sporn[7] states that "Vitamin A and its synthetic analogs (retinoids) have been successfully used to prevent cancer of the skin, lung, bladder and breast in experimental animals—synthetic retinoids are definitely superior to vitamin A for this purpose." He claims that 13-cis-retinoic acid is one of the most effective anti-cancer agents in animals.

Few reports of treatment of humans with retinoids are available. One such report is that of the Swiss researcher, Dr. H. Mayer in 1976. As cited in *Medical World News,*[24] he used retinoic acid to treat 60 patients with actinic keratosis (a precancerous skin lesion), producing complete regression in 24 and partial regression in 27 of them. In 16 patients with basal cell carcinoma of the skin, 5 had complete regression and 10 had partial regression.

Self-medication with retinoic acid should be avoided. Retinoic acid can sensitize the skin to sunlight and make it more susceptible to future skin cancer. Moreover, when a skin cancer is treated, expert follow-up care is needed to determine whether it has been completely eradicated.

B-Vitamins and Cancer

According to Dr. J. A. Bertino,[14] cancer patients have been shown to suffer from vitamin deficiencies, especially of folic acid, vitamin C and pyridoxine. But Dr. Bertino answers the question of "How much is enough?" by stating: "With the exception of folic acid . . . the generally accepted view is that further increase in vitamin intake (above the RDA) has no appreciable effect on growth of human cancers."

Professor C. E. Butterworth[25,26] and colleagues have reported on treatment of 52 young women with mild to moderate cervical dysplasia (abnormal growth). In a scientifically controlled double-blind experiment, the Butterworth team gave half the patients 10 mg (10 times the RDA) of folic acid daily for three months while the other half were given a placebo. The results were:

	Improved	No Change	Worsened	Developed Cancer
Folic Acid Group	7	18	1	0
Placebo Group	0	12	9	5

Some investigators[14,15] are using vitamin E along with anti-cancer drugs because its antioxidant capability can reduce their toxicity.

Does Extra Vitamin C Prevent Cancer?

As with vitamin A, there is good evidence that deficiency of vitamin C increases the risk of cancer; but how much is needed daily? It has been known for a long time that vitamin C is required by the body to make collagen which is essential for the health and repair of connective tissue. However, most authorities[14,27] do not believe that a daily intake of vitamin C above the RDA level helps to prevent cancer.

In October 1976, many newspapers coined headlines such as: "Pauling Study Suggests Vitamin C Prolongs Lives of Cancer Patients." These were based on a report published in 1976 by Dr. Ewan Cameron, a Scottish physician, and Professor Linus Pauling. The report claimed that the majority of 100 terminal cancer patients treated with 10 grams of vitamin C daily survived 3 to 4 times longer than similar patients without vitamin C supplements. However, scientific reviewers believe that this study was poorly designed. Moreover, Alcantara and Speckman[28] warned in 1977 that "although large doses of ascorbic acid may be associated with favorable clinical response in some cancer patients, others may not respond at all or even may be affected adversely."

Who is Right?

Several publications of Dr. Ewan Cameron and his associates are considered here. In 1966, Dr. Cameron had published a book, *Hyaluronidase and Cancer,* which suggested that the enzyme hyaluronidase weakens the matrix ("cement") between cells and thereby aids the spread of cancer. Pauling and Cameron[29] claim that vitamin C helps to inhibit and restrict this enzyme, and therefore that extra vitamin C improves the body's defense mechanisms. Experiments claiming that vitamin C deficiency leads to a breakdown of the intercellular matrix of body tissues and thereby supposedly facilitates the spread of cancer were published by Cameron, Pauling and Leibovitz[30] in 1979. That same year, Cameron and Pauling[31] published a lengthy book, *Cancer and Vitamin C.*

In 1974, Cameron and Campbell[32] reported at length on 50 patients with "advanced human cancer." The study was expanded to encompass a total of 100 patients and was more briefly reported by Cameron and Pauling[33] in 1976. These patients had been given 10,000 mg of vitamin C daily for 10 days by slow infusion into the veins, followed by 10,000 mg daily by mouth. For comparison, a "control group" of 1,000 patients who supposedly had died of similar cancers was selected from the 10-year historical records of the Vale of Leven Hospital in Scotland.

The average survival time was originally reported as 210 days for the vitamin C group and only 50 days for the selected controls. Later, in response to criticism of the study's design, Cameron's team[28,33] picked a new group of 1,000 controls from the hospital records including about half of the original controls. They also eliminated 10 of the original vitamin C-treated patients who had unusual cancers for which there were no similar control patients available. After making these changes, Cameron and Pauling revised the survival figures to 193 days for the vitamin C group and 38 days for the control patients.

However, the scientific community still raises doubts about the validity and significance of Cameron's results with megadose vitamin C for cancer patients.[14,28,34] The criticism centers around three chief concerns:

1. *Lack of acceptable scientific controls.* As noted by Dr. William DeWys,[34] chief of the clinical investigations at the National Cancer Institute, the patients were not randomly selected:

> The vitamin C patients were cancer patients under the care of Dr. Cameron, while the comparison patients were under the care of other physicians. We are told that patients are assigned "in an essentially random way" to Dr. Cameron and other physicians. However, this was not randomized assignment to treatment as we understand it in the research setting. One can easily envision a slanted assignment, for example, if patients with the most severe pain, or with evidence of spinal cord compression,

were assigned directly to a radiation therapist, rather than to Dr. Cameron . . .

Dr. Cameron's patients were started on vitamin C when they were judged "untreatable," and their subsequent survival was compared to the survival of the control group from the time that *they* were labeled "untreatable." However, the criteria for labeling a patient "untreatable" are not given, and it is likely that different physicians use this label differently.

Analyzing Cameron and Pauling's tables of average survival times, Dr. DeWys then makes two startling observations. If the vitamin C group and the control group were comparable, the average time from entry into the hospital to that of being labeled "untreatable" should be the same for both groups. But it isn't! Cameron's patients were labeled untreatable much earlier in the course of their disease—which means that they should be expected to survive longer than "similar" ones of other doctors. Moreover, while many patients in the control group died within a few days of being labeled untreatable, none of the Cameron patients did so. This is additional evidence that Dr. Cameron's patients had less advanced disease when labeled untreatable.

2. *Possible harm.* Referring to the 1974 Cameron/Campbell[32] report, Alcantara and Speckman[28] have noted that 17 of the 50 advanced cancer patients had *no* response to vitamin C; and in four patients, its administration was followed by widespread tumor hemorrhage and decay with disastrous consequences. Referring to the 1976 Cameron/Pauling[33] report, these critics noted that 19 out of the 100 vitamin C cases had shorter survival times than their counterpart controls.

Mayo Clinic Tests

In 1979, researchers at the Mayo Clinic[35] reported a study covering 123 patients with advanced cancer, all but 9 of whom had previously been treated with drugs and radiation. Sixty of these patients were given vitamin C in the daily dosage recommended by Pauling, 10,000 mg divided into four doses. The 63 patients serving as "controls" received a placebo pill four times a day. The trial was double-blind, with neither the patients nor the observing doctors knowing until the end of the trial which group was receiving the vitamin C capsules. No differences were found between the vitamin C and placebo groups with respect to survival time, appetite, weight loss, severity of pain or amount of nausea and vomiting.

Linus Pauling[36] claims that the Mayo Clinic trial was invalid because nearly all of the American patients had had their "immune competence compromised" by earlier chemotherapy that prevents vitamin C from helping. Cameron and Pauling[33] had stated on pages 3687-88 in their 1976 report: "All patients are treated initially in a perfectly conventional way, by operation, use of radiotherapy, and the administration of hormones and cytotoxic substances (anti-cancer drugs)." Later, however, Pauling stated that only four of the 100 patients had received chemotherapy.[36]

Pauling's assertion that chemotherapy interferes with vitamin C "treatment" makes testing his claims very difficult. Reputable scientists are not willing to deprive cancer patients of effective chemotherapy in order to test their response to vitamin C. However, a controlled study is under way at the Mayo Clinic that will test Pauling's theory in patients with cancer of the colon (large intestine) who were not terminal.[34] The patients being studied had all had spread of the tumor (metastasis) but no symptoms. Patients who develop symptoms will receive chemotherapy, but the study will be able to test whether vitamin C does better than a placebo in slowing down progression of this cancer in patients before they need chemotherapy. The study should be completed early in 1983.

The Amazing Cancer Case

The most spectacular report coming out of the Cameron medical team is that of a 42-year-old truck driver diagnosed in October 1973 as a worsening case of cancer.[37] At that time, x-ray examination of the chest revealed extensive lung involvement, and biopsy of a lymph node in the neck yielded a diagnosis of "reticulum cell sarcoma." The patient was hospitalized at once, but because radiation therapy was not readily available in that hospital, vitamin C therapy of 10 grams daily was begun.

Within 10 days, he was already much improved. X-ray studies of the chest after 22 days showed some reversal of the cancer. After 60 days of treatment, the chest x-ray picture was normal and the patient was back at work! The daily dose of vitamin C was then gradually reduced over the next three months, and finally stopped.

About a month later, the patient returned to the clinic feeling worse. X-ray films of the chest showed that the cancer had again progressed. He was told to take 10,000 mg of vitamin C daily for two weeks and sent home. Two weeks later, x-ray films revealed that the cancer was slowly getting worse. So the truck driver was readmitted to the hospital and given 20,000 mg of vitamin C daily by vein for 14 days, and then 12,500 mg daily by mouth thereafter. A slow improvement ensued, and after six months of continued vitamin C supplementation, the x-ray picture returned to normal.

Dr. Cameron and co-workers concluded their report by emphasizing how rare it would be for a "spontaneous" reversal to occur for such a cancer. They believe the megadose vitamin C contributed substantially, even critically, to strengthening the patient's waning immune system and enabling it to fight off the cancer. Scientifically, it is difficult to decide one way or the other. Very rare cases are known of "spontaneous" regression of human cancers that never received any kind of treatment.

In November 1982, Dr. Cameron informed me that the patient is still alive and well—and still taking his high doses of vitamin C. Curiously, in 1977, despite the supposed protective effect of vitamin C, he was found to have a small thyroid cancer of a different type (papillary adenocarcinoma) which was surgically removed and has not recurred.

Does Vitamin C Combat the Nitrite Hazard?

Nitrite salts in certain processed meats such as bacon, ham and bologna may react with organic amines that occur naturally in many foods to form nitrosamines. Nitrosamines are known to have cancer-causing capability, but there is good evidence that adequate daily intakes of vitamin C will prevent formation of nitrosamines in the stomach or intestines.

Dr. John H. Weisburger is Vice-President for Research of the Naylor Dana Institute for Disease Prevention, American Health Foundation. In 1977, in a brief summary of important research findings, Dr. Weisburger[27] points out that stomach cancer is especially high in Japan where certain fish, plentiful in the diet, are rich in amines that readily form nitrosamines in the presence of nitrites. If vitamin C is added to the fish, no nitrosamines are formed. These findings fit with epidemiological evidence that populations consuming adequate amounts of vitamin C in their diet have a low incidence of stomach cancer.

Nitrites are used in foods, especially processed meats, to prevent the development of botulism bacteria. Since nitrite levels in foods have been reduced in recent years, Dr. Weisburger believes that the current parts-per-billion level of nitrosamines found in such foods "may not be a cause of cancer in man." He supports the policy of adding vitamin C to such processed foods at the time of the nitrite addition, but he does not advocate that people take megadose vitamin C daily as a cancer preventive. He simply suggests a "year-round intake of foods containing adequate supplies of vitamin C." Dr. Vernon Young,[38] Professor of Biochemistry at M.I.T., believes that more research is needed to explore whether higher than RDA level intakes of vitamin C can have practical value in the prevention of cancer caused by diets high in nitrites.

Other Claims for Vitamin C Related to Cancer

It is believed that cancer of the colon and rectum usually arise in polyps. In 1975, Dr. J. J. DeCosse's Milwaukee research group[39] reported a 35 percent reduction in rectal polyps in an uncontrolled trial with nine patients on 3,000 mg of vitamin C daily for two years. Recently, however,

DeCosse and Morson[40] reported a double-blind study of 49 patients. About half of them received 3,000 mg of vitamin C while the rest received a placebo daily for 15 to 24 months. Periodic examination by endoscope revealed no differences between the vitamin and placebo groups. The researchers emphasized that rectal polyps and adenomas tended "to wax and wane during treatment," making evaluation of vitamin C efficiency difficult. Similar but larger trials are planned.

In a preliminary report from the National Cancer Institute in 1976, Dr. Robert Yonemoto[41] and co-workers claimed that when 5,000 mg of vitamin C was administered daily to five healthy volunteers for three days, their immune response (resistance to infections and possibly to cancer), as measured by increased lymphocyte activity, lasted for several days after the last dose of vitamin C. However, in 1977, Dr. J. A. Migliozzi[42] found that megadose vitamin C can cause some kinds of tumors to grow larger in animals. And in 1976, Dr. H. F. Stich's group found that, in the absence of sufficient catalase enzyme, megadose vitamin C may alter nucleic acid chromosomes with a possible mutagenic-cancer effect in tissue cultures of human skin cells[43] and in live mice.[44]

In 1976, Dr. T. K. Basu[45] published a brief review of many research reports entitled "Significance of Vitamins in Cancer." Two references are cited which claim that the majority of cancer patients have low tissue stores of vitamin C; but whether this is caused by poor appetite and thus poor nutrition is not yet clear. Basu concluded: "The relationships between vitamin nutrition and cancer are complex. One vitamin may act as an inducer of one kind of tumor, but an inhibitor for another kind." He pointed to excessive riboflavin as one such vitamin.

What Should You Believe?

In an exchange with Linus Pauling via letters-to-the-editor of the *New England Journal of Medicine* in March 1980, Drs. C. G. Moertel and E. T. Creagan[46] of the Mayo Clinic stated the following:

> On the basis of claims derived from speculation and nonrandomized studies endorsed by the Pauling name, megadoses of vitamin C are being used by thousands of patients with cancer, and such treatment has been embraced by the metabolic-therapy cults. Our randomized double-blind study indicates that for at least one segment of the population of cancer patients, such treatment is of no value . . . The name of Dr. Linus Pauling is one of the most revered in American science, and rightly so. We hope very much that Dr. Pauling will join us in discouraging patients with cancer from using high-dose vitamin C or any other cancer treatment unless it has been proved to be of value by properly designed scientific study.

In my opinion, as of early 1983, the claim that high-dose vitamin C is effective against cancer is not supported by scientific evidence. If there is any validity at all to such a claim, there is at most a slim chance that a tiny percentage of cancer patients (perhaps less than 1 percent) might be helped. Even if such people exist, however, identifying them is a seemingly impossible task.

So far I have focused on the fact that high doses of vitamins have no proven effectiveness against cancer and can cause troublesome side effects. An even worse type of problem can arise when they are used *instead* of effective treatment.

A Case of Second-Degree Murder

In 1961, 8-year-old Linda Epping complained of pain in her left eye, but nothing unusual was noted for some time. When her discomfort became acute, her worried parents took her to their doctor who, together with consultants, confirmed that Linda had cancer of the left eye. The parents were then advised that surgical removal of the eye could result in a complete cure because the tumor did not appear to have spread. So little Linda was scheduled for surgery.

However, shortly before the eye operation could be performed, Linda's parents struck up a conversation with another couple in the hospital waiting room. Upon learning about Linda, the other woman told the Eppings that a chiropractor had cured their son's brain tumor without surgery. Linda's mother was so excited she rushed to the telephone, called the chiropractor and described Linda's diagnosis to him. Without seeing the child, the chiropractor told the mother, "Yes, absolutely," he could help by "chemically balancing her body."[47]

The Eppings were so elated by their hopes that they quickly removed Linda from the hospital and took her to Dr. Phillips for treatment with vitamins and food supplements—up to 124 pills plus 150 drops of iodine solution daily. In addition, the chiropractor "adjusted" Linda's spine and told the parents to manipulate the ball of her foot each day until she cried.

The new "treatment" had only one immediate effect—it padded the chiropractor's income by $739. The tumor grew rapidly, and within three weeks it was tennis-ball size and had pushed Linda's eye out of its socket. At about this time, Linda's frightened parents filed a complaint with District Attorney's office for Los Angeles County. Assistant District Attorney John Miner went to investigate and reported, in part:

> The right side of her face was that of an angel. The left side was covered with a growth so monstrous as to seem beyond nature's capacity to be cruel and grotesque . . . When I walked out of her room, I knew two things: Linda E. would soon die; second, when it happened, I would seek a murder indictment.

At this stage, there was no longer any hope that surgery could save her; and in a few months, little angel-face Linda was dead.

John Miner kept his word. The chiropractor was convicted of second-degree murder and sentenced to prison. In 1964, in a final farewell to Linda, Miner published her story in the *Journal of Forensic Science,*[48] calling it "a new dimension in murder."

References

1. Peters, P.: Testimony to Illinois State Senate Subcommittee on Medical Fraud and Cancer Quackery, Sept. 1, 1982.
2. Chilcote, R. R.: Personal communication to author, Sept. 2, 1982.
3. Chilcote, R. R.: Testimony to Illinois State Senate Subcommittee on Medical Fraud and Cancer Quackery, Sept. 1, 1982.
4. The Medical Letter 22:19, 1980.
5. Young, V. and Newberne, P.: Cancer 47:2125, Suppl. No. 5, 1981.
6. Wynder, E.: Cancer Research 35:3548, 1975.
7. Sporn, M. B.: Nutrition Reviews 35:65, 1977.
8. Bjelke, E.: Scandinavian Journal of Gastroenterology 9:1-235, 1974.
9. Bjelke, E.: International Journal of Cancer, 15:561, 1975.
10. Smith, P. G. and Jick, H.: Cancer 42:808, 1978.
11. Wald, N., Idle, M. et al: Lancet 2:1813, 1980.
12. Newberne, P.: Cancer Detection and Prevention 1:129-173, 1976.
13. Rogers, A. E. and Newberne, P.: Cancer Research 35:3427, 1975.
14. Bertino, J. R.: Cancer 43:2137, 1979.
15. DiPalma, J. R. and McMichael, R.: Cancer—A Journal for Clinicians 29: 281, 1979.
16. Young, V. and Richardson, D.: Cancer 43:2125, 1979.
17. Kark, J. D. et al.: Lancet 1:1371, June 20, 1981.
18. Kark, J. D., Smith, A. H. and Hames, C. G.: Journal of Chronic Diseases, 33:311, 1980.
19. Williams, R. et al.: JAMA 245:247, 1981.
20. Dyer, A. R., Stamler, J. et al.: Preventive Medicine, 8:688, 1979.
21. British Medical Journal: 281:957, 1980.
22. Peto, Doll, Buckley and Sporn: Nature 290:201, 1981.
23. Darby, W.: Personal communication to Dr. Barrett, Dec. 23, 1982.
24. Medical World News, Sept. 6, 1976.
25. Butterworth, C. E. et al.: Clinical Research 26:677A, 1978.
26. Butterworth, C. E. et al.: American Journal of Clinical Nutrition, 33:926, 1980.
27. Weisburger, J. H.: Lancet, 3:607, Sept. 17, 1977.
28. Alcantara, E. N. and Speckman, E. W.: American Journal of Clinical Nutrition 30:662, 1977.
29. Cameron, E. and Pauling, L.: Chemico-Biological Interactions 9:273, 1974.
30. Cameron, E., Pauling, L. and Leibovitz, B.: Cancer Research 39:663, 1979; cited in Creagan, E. T., *loc cit.*

164

31. Cameron, E. and Pauling, L.: Cancer and Vitamin C, New York, W. W. Norton, 1979.
32. Cameron, E. and Campbell, A.: Chemico-Biological Interactions 9:285, 1974.
33. Cameron, E. and Pauling, L.: Proceedings of the National Academy of Sciences 73:3685, 1976.
34. DeWys, W. D.: How to Evaluate a New Treatment for Cancer. *In* Your Patient and Cancer, May 1982, pp. 31-36.
35. Creagan, E. T., Moertel, C. G. et al.: New England Journal of Medicine 301:687, 1979.
36. Medical World News, June 25, 1979, p. 19.
37. Cameron, E., Campbell, A. and Jack, T.: Chemico-Biological Interactions 11:387, 1975.
38. Young, V.: Personal communication, Nov. 22, 1982.
39. DeCosse, J. J., Adams, M. B. et al.: Surgery 78:608, 1975.
40. Medical World News, Nov. 24, 1980, p. 21.
41. Yonemoto, R.: ASCO Abstracts (Abstracts of the Proceedings of the American Society of Clinical Oncology), 1976, p. 288.
42. Migliozzi, J. A.: British Journal of Cancer 35:448, 1977.
43. Stich, H. F., Koropatnich, T. K. et al.: Nature 260:722, 1976.
44. Koropatnich, J.: Personal communication to author, Sept. 6, 1978.
45. Basu, T. K.: Oncology 33:183, 1976.
46. Moertel, C. and Creagan, E. T.: New England Journal of Medicine 302:694, 1980.
47. Smith, R. L.: At Your Own Risk—The Case Against Chiropractic. New York, 1969, Simon and Schuster, p. viii.
48. Miner, J.: Journal of Forensic Science 9:1, 1964.

17

Can Megavitamins Help Reduce Cholesterol and Protect Against Heart Disease?

Atherosclerosis is a gradual process that begins with spot injury to the artery wall followed by cholesterol deposition and then the formation of a plaque or bulge which contains fibrin, calcium and overgrowth of artery muscle cells. Arteries which become narrower as a result have decreased blood flow and can even become completely blocked. "Coronary heart disease" is a term used to describe atherosclerotic narrowing or blockage of the arteries to the heart.

During the late 1930s and 1940s, nutritional scientists and biomedical researchers began to believe that high blood cholesterol and perhaps high blood triglycerides (fats) were a major risk factor for atherosclerosis and therefore coronary heart disease. Since about 1940, when most vitamins became available in good supply, hundreds of studies have been done to see whether supplementary vitamins can lower blood cholesterol or prevent atherosclerotic plaque formation in animals or humans.

Effects of Vitamin C on Cholesterol and Atherosclerosis

"Vitamin C for Cleaner Arteries" is the title of an article in the April 1977 *Prevention* magazine. Similar headlines have appeared in recent years in the *National Enquirer* and other weekly tabloid newspapers with wide circulation. One of the many claims of vitamin enthusiasts is that extra vitamin C can lower blood levels of cholesterol and thereby prevent cholesterol deposits and plaque formation in artery walls. The *Prevention* article suggests that 500 mg per day may not be enough and states that a researcher who tested megavitamin C on guinea pigs now takes 3,000 mg per day himself.

165

Is it realistic to take more than the RDA of 60 mg/day of vitamin C in the hope of preventing heart attacks? Let's look at the evidence.

At the outset, we note that by 1975, experts recognized two opposite effects of vitamin C on cholesterol in humans. First, vitamin C promotes the action of the liver enzyme involved in making about 800 to 1,500 mg of new cholesterol each day. Second, directly or indirectly, vitamin C is involved with the liver enzyme that controls the first step in the conversion of cholesterol to bile acids—the only route the body has for getting rid of excess cholesterol.

Between 1940 and 1960, most of the studies of vitamin C on animals and humans were done by Russian scientists. These were summarized in 1961 by Simonson and Keys[1] in a review article called "Research in Russia on Vitamins and Atherosclerosis." These early trials found that high blood cholesterol levels could be lowered by vitamin C administered only by daily injections (an impractical method) or taken orally by patients with near-scurvy levels of vitamin C deficiency. In 1970, Dr. Carl Shaffer[2] reviewed many reports from Russia and elsewhere and concluded that persons with "normal" intakes of 45 to 100 mg of vitamin C will receive no additional benefit from extra vitamin C with respect to blood cholesterol levels or atherosclerosis.

What about the supposedly favorable results with vitamin C since 1970? An outline of such research reports follows:

1) *Vitamin C can reduce blood cholesterol in C-deficient humans.*

In 1970, Dr. Emil Ginter's Czech research team[3] found moderately high blood cholesterol levels in people severely deficient in vitamin C from poor winter diets, but only 300 mg per day of vitamin C for a few weeks was needed to reduce cholesterol to "normal" levels (below 250 mg%).

2) *Vitamin C does not reduce blood cholesterol in normal humans.*

Many attempts have been made to try to reduce high-normal (200-250 mg%) levels of blood cholesterol with oral megadose vitamin C in humans. I could not locate one report of success. Among the failures were seven trials by five research teams.[4-10] Attempts to reduce high (above 250 mg%) or very-high (above 300 mg%) blood levels of cholesterol by oral megadose vitamin C in humans have also failed in all of the reports I could find.[8,9,11,12]

3) *Results in animals are mixed.*

Success in lowering blood cholesterol levels and reducing the severity of arterial plaques with megadose vitamin C was claimed in three early trials[8,13,14] in rabbits and in one by Verlangieri[15] with guinea pigs. The *Prevention* article emphasizes the Verlangieri experiment. Failures in attempts to lower blood cholesterol levels in rabbits with extra vitamin C were reported by Flexner[16] in 1941, W. R. Pool[17] in 1971, and F. J. Finamore[18] in 1976. Flexner's vitamin C-supplemented rabbits had more cholesterol in their artery deposits, Finamore's had less. The *Prevention* article mentions only Finamore on this and does not mention the many failures in human studies cited above.

The *Prevention* article suggests that Finamore's first trial[18] and Ver-langieri's guinea pig study indicate that megadose vitamin C can "pull" cholesterol out of plaques. However, Finamore,[19] has done another study of the effect of vitamin C injections on atherosclerotic plaques induced in the arteries of rabbits. No difference in the severity of plaques was found between the rabbits injected with vitamin C for 10 weeks and those in-jected with salt water.

    4) *Blood cholesterol can remain low on a diet very low in vitamin C.*

Surprisingly, this is what happens with the nomadic herdsmen of the Masai and Turhana tribes of Kenya, Africa.[20,21] Professor George V. Mann's research group[20] has reported that the diet of the Masai consisted mainly of meat and fermented milk and contained very little vitamin C. Their blood serum levels of vitamin C were only one-tenth the normal range, yet they showed no clinical signs of scurvy. All of them had blood cholesterol levels below 170 mg%, and most were below 150 mg%. Al-though the Masai rarely die of heart attacks, Dr. Mann's team found a considerable amount of arteriosclerosis in the hearts and aortas of Masai males who had died of other causes. Apparently, vigorous daily physical activity over a lifetime (or genetic factors) had caused the diameters of their heart arteries to enlarge gradually and permit good blood flow despite the plaques.

What keeps the Masai's blood cholesterol level low, despite a diet rich in fat and cholesterol? Dr. Mann said in 1980 that nobody yet knows, but attention is being focused on factors in milk, especially in fermented milk such as yogurt (see Chapter 23).

    5) *Vitamin C does not raise the percentage of "good" HDL-cholesterol.*

HDL is the high-density lipoprotein that can bind with cholesterol and supposedly restrict its tendency to deposit in artery wall defects (see Chap-ter 23). Of two 1981 reports, one found no change of HDL-cholesterol percentage in 9 normal males on 1,000 mg of vitamin C daily for 6 weeks,[22] and the other study[23] had the same negative results with 13 healthy young women on the same dosage for several weeks.

Two recent expert reviews are those of Turley, West and Horton[24] and G. Taylor.[25] As of 1982, the bulk of the scientifically acceptable evidence indicates that megavitamin C is good for rabbits (who don't need it), is of slight or doubtful benefit for guinea pigs, but does nothing for humans who are not severely deficient in vitamin C.

Can Extra Vitamin E Increase "Good" HDL-Cholesterol?

Between 1979 and 1981, several research teams administered 600 to 800 units of vitamin E daily to patients or healthy volunteers for 30 to 40 days to see whether this dosage would cause the percentage of "good" HDL to increase. Most of the results have not been encouraging. Dr. William J. Hermann, Jr., who obtained positive results in two trials[26,27] and negative results in one,[28] now believes that only individuals under age 30 with below 15 percent HDL-cholesterol may benefit. Negative results were reported by four other research groups,[29-32] with no appreciable shift of cholesterol even for some persons with below 15 percent of cholesterol as HDL-cholesterol. Mixed results were obtained in two studies, one team[33] finding no benefit for healthy women but moderate benefit for male volunteers. The other group[34] found no beneficial shift of cholesterol in 5 healthy volunteers but achieved a modest beneficial shift in 22 of 26 patients with benign breast cysts (see Chapter 9).

Effects of Other Vitamins on Blood Cholesterol

I can find no reports of studies of the effects of vitamins A, D, thiamin (B_1) or riboflavin (B_2) on blood cholesterol in humans. In animals, vitamin A has shown little or no effect,[1,13,35] and thiamin and riboflavin have shown no effect,[1] but megadoses of vitamin D have caused increased blood cholesterol and artery plaques.[1] According to Dr. F. A. Kummerow,[36] excessive vitamin D is a villain which can injure artery walls, causing thickening and hardening (arteriosclerosis, not atherosclerosis).

In humans, megadosage of niacin (nicotinic acid), 1,000 to 5,000 mg daily, can lower blood cholesterol levels.[37,38] But as a Mayo Clinic report[38] warned, this is accomplished at too high a price of intestinal distress, hot flashes, nervousness and eventual liver damage. Also, among 1,119 men treated for 6 years with megadose niacin, many developed dangerously irregular heartbeats (see Chapter 11).[39] Niacinamide is a little less toxic but does not lower blood levels of cholesterol.

I can find no reports of megadose pyridoxine effects on blood cholesterol in humans or animals. Monkeys made vitamin B_6-deficient show no changes in blood levels of cholesterol but do develop plaque-like lesions in their artery walls. Based on this finding, Dr. Kilmer McCully[40] theorizes that pyridoxine deficiency leads to an accumulation of homocysteine which is injurious to the artery wall. He recommends that 10 mg pyridoxine supplements be taken daily by everyone, but most scientists believe that 1 RDA (2 mg) provides enough protection.

Megadose vitamin E has been found to raise blood cholesterol in humans by 10 to 37 percent by one research group[41,42] and by about 10 percent by several other groups,[32,43,44] all of whom gave 400 to 800 units of vitamin E daily to people. However, several other researchers have found no change in blood cholesterol after several weeks or more on megadose-E.[26,29,30,45,46]

Conclusions

Severe vitamin deficiencies have many adverse effects on human physiology and metabolism and could contribute indirectly to atherosclerosis and thus to heart disease. But severe deficiencies due to diet are quite rare in the United States and are corrected in a few weeks with moderate daily doses (2 to 5 times the RDA). Megadoses of any of the vitamins do not help prevent atherosclerosis and can be harmful (see Chapters 7 through 12).

Niacin, but not niacinamide, is the only vitamin which, when given in high dosage, can lower blood levels of cholesterol. Very high dosages are no longer used because of toxicity (see Chapter 11), but moderate amounts may be used together with other drugs to lower cholesterol in high-risk patients.

Vitamin E in megadosage (above 400 IU/day) may raise blood cholesterol about 10 percent in many people and is unlikely to benefit (increase) the percentage of "good" HDL-cholesterol except in persons under the age of 30 who have below "normal" (under 15 percent) of their total blood cholesterol bound to HDL.

As of 1982, the bulk of the scientifically acceptable evidence offers no hope that extra vitamin C (above the RDA) will help lower blood levels of cholesterol, prevent or cure arterial plaques or protect against atherosclerosis or heart disease. Vitamin C deficiency is another matter. Persons at near scurvy levels of vitamin C deficiency may have elevated levels of cholesterol. However, as Emil Ginter's[3] research has shown, it takes only 300 mg of vitamin C daily for a few weeks to correct the deficiency and lower cholesterol to "normal" in his patients. In the absence of deficiency, more than the RDA (60 mg/day) of vitamin C is not likely to be of any help.

References

1. Simonson, E. and Keys, A.: Research in Russia on Vitamins and Atherosclerosis, *in* Circulation 24:1239-1248, 1961.
2. Shaffer, C. F.: American Journal of Clinical Nutrition 23:27, 1970.
3. Ginter, E. et al.: Nutrition and Metabolism 12:76, 1970.
4. Ginter, E.: New England Journal of Medicine 294:559, 1976.
5. Ginter, E. et al.: International Journal of Vitamin and Nutrition Research 47:123, 1977.
6. Crawford, G. P. M. et al.: Atherosclerosis 21:451, 1975.
7. Anderson, T. W. et al.: Lancet 2:876, Oct. 31, 1972.
8. Sokoloff, B. et al.: Journal of the Geriatrics Society 14:1239, 1966.
9. Sokoloff, B. et al.: Journal of Nutrition 91:107, 1967.
10. Elwood, P. D. et al.: Lancet 2:1197, 1970.
11. Samuel P. and Shalchi, O.: Circulation 29:24, 1964.

12. Peterson, V. et al.: American Journal of Clinical Nutrition 28:584, 1975.
13. Myasnikov, A. L.: Circulation 17:99, 1958.
14. Zaitsev, V. F. et al.: Kardiolgiya 2:30, 1964 (in English).
15. Verlangieri, A. J. et al.: Blood Vessels 14:157, 1977.
16. Flexner, J. et al.: Archives of Pathology 31:82, 1941.
17. Pool, W. R. et al.: Atherosclerosis 14:131, 1971.
18. Finamore, F. J. et al.: International Journal of Vitamin and Nutrition Research 46:275, 1976.
19. Finamore, F. J. et al.: International Journal of Vitamin and Nutrition Research 47:62, 1977.
20. Mann, G. V. et al.: American Journal of Epidemiology 95:26, 1972.
21. Gatenby-Davies, J. D. and Newson, J.: American Journal of Clinical Nutrition 27:1039, 1974.
22. Johnson, G. and Obenshein, S.: Ibid. 34:2088, 1981.
23. Khan, A. and Seedarnee, F.: Atherosclerosis 39:89, 1981.
24. Turley, S. et al.: Ibid. 24:1-18, 1976.
25. Taylor, G.: Lancet 1:247, Jan. 31, 1976.
26. Hermann, W. J., Jr. et al.: American Journal of Clinical Pathology 72:848, 1979.
27. Hermann, W. J., Jr.: Ibid. 76-844, 1981.
28. Hermann, W. J., Jr.: American Journal of Clinical Pathology 76:124, 1981.
29. Hatam, L. and Kayden, H.: Ibid. 76:122, 1981.
30. Schwartz, P. and Rutherford, I.: Ibid. 76:843, 1981.
31. Howard, D. R. et al.: American Journal of Clinical Pathology 77:86, 1982.
32. Kesianiemi, Y. A. and Grundy, S. M.: American Journal of Clinical Nutrition 36:224, 1982.
33. Barboriak, J. et al.: Abstract of Poster-Paper No. P-4, Conference on Vitamin E, New York Academy of Sciences, Nov. 11-13, 1981.
34. Sandaram, G., London, R. et al.: Lipids 16:223, 1981.
35. Brattsand, R.: Atherosclerosis 22:47, 1975.
36. Kummerow, F. A.: American Journal of Clinical Nutrition 32:58-83, 1979.
37. Belle, M. and Halpern, M.: American Journal of Cardiology 2:449, 1958.
38. Berge, K. G. et al.: American Journal of Medicine 31:24, 1961.
39. Coronary Drug Project Group: JAMA 231:360-381, 1975.
40. McCully, K.: American Heart Journal 83:571, 1972.
41. Dahl, S.: Lancet 1:465, March 16, 1974.
42. Dahl, S.: Personal communication, Dec. 20, 1975.
43. Leonhardt, E. T. G.: American Journal of Clinical Nutrition 31:100, 1978.
44. Farrell, P. and Bieri, J.: Ibid. 28:138, 1975.
45. Tsai, A. C. et al.: American Journal of Clinical Nutrition 31:831, 1978.
46. Lewis, J. S. et al.: Ibid. 26-136, 1973.

18

The Macrominerals: Calcium, Phosphorus, Magnesium, Sodium, Potassium, Chloride

Mineral nutrients can be defined as inorganic compounds (usually salts and oxides), as distinguished from the huge class of organic (carbon-containing) nutrients which includes the proteins, fats, carbohydrates and vitamins. At present, the Food and Nutrition Board[1] considers 16 minerals essential for humans.* Of these, the 6 needed in amounts of 100 mg or more daily are called major or macrominerals. They are calcium, phosphorus, magnesium, sodium, potassium and chloride. The other 10 are the microminerals, usually called "trace elements" because they are required only in tiny amounts daily in the human diet, some at far less than even 1 mg (1/28,000 of an ounce) daily. The trace elements are cobalt (usually as part of vitamin B_{12}), iron, zinc, iodine, copper, fluorine, manganese, chromium, selenium and molybdenum. For animals, nickel, silicon, tin and vanadium are probably also essential.

CALCIUM

Calcium, a major component of the bones and teeth, is the most plentiful mineral in the human body. The body of a 150-pound adult contains nearly three pounds of calcium with 99 percent of it in the skeletal bones. The remainder is in the soft tissues and body fluids where it participates in highly important biochemical functions.

Calcium is necessary for blood clotting and for maintenance of cell membranes and structural supports (cements) within cells.[1,2] Together

---

*Sulfur, an essential macromineral not included in this list, is a component of the essential amino acid, methionine. Thus it is automatically obtained by eating adequate protein and is of no separate or practical importance.

171

with activated vitamin D, calcium is essential for proper growth and maintenance of the bones. Like all body tissues, bone matrix is alive and dynamic; and in adults, about 25 percent (700 mg) of its calcium is resorbed into the circulating fluids and redeposited into new matrix every day. Perhaps calcium's most vital role is in controlling nerve impulses and therefore the excitability of peripheral nerves and muscles, including the heart muscle. Since prevention of heart failure is more important than bone strength, nature gives priority to ensuring proper calcium concentration in the fluids bathing the heart muscle. If the blood calcium level falls below normal, parathyroid hormone is secreted and commands the withdrawal of calcium from bone.

How Much Calcium Do We Need?

The Recommended Dietary Allowance for adults is 800 mg, with more needed during pregnancy. In setting these levels, the Food and Nutrition Board[1] stated: "Studies have shown that men adapt in time to lower calcium intakes and maintain calcium balance on intakes as low as 200 to 400 mg/day . . . However, no advantage accrues from such low intakes . . . In view of the high levels of protein and phosphorus provided by the United States diet, an allowance of 800 mg/day is recommended." The reason for this last sentence is that high-protein diets increase urinary and fecal losses of calcium, and high-phosphate foods (meat, dairy products, soft-drinks) cause calcium loss in the feces.

Calcium deficiency can result from any of the following:

1. Extremely low calcium in the diet.

2. Vitamin D deficiency

3. Inability to convert vitamin D to its active 1,25-dihydroxy-vitamin D form, due to diminished strength of the two enzymes involved.

4. Interference with absorption of calcium in the intestines, leading to the formation of calcium salts which are excreted in the feces. In some elderly individuals, high phosphate intake causes calcium to be lost as calcium phosphate. In rare but serious malabsorptive diseases, unabsorbed fatty acids form soapy calcium salts. Of minor concern, unless dietary calcium is very low, are high intakes of oxalic acid from spinach, rhubarb and tea, and phytic acid from whole grains, soybeans and some other vegetables. These substances cause calcium to be excreted (without being absorbed into the body) as insoluble calcium oxalate or calcium phytate in the feces.

Effects of Calcium Deficiency[1,2]

Insufficient calcium absorption from the intestines results in rickets (stunted bone growth) in children and osteoporosis (bone fragility) or osteomalacia (bone softening) in adults. Calcium deficiency severe enough to allow blood calcium levels to fall below the critically required concentration is extremely rare, but if it happens, tetany ensues. Tetany is a state of high irritability of the nervous system, muscle spasms and twitchings, and impairment of heart muscle contraction which can be fatal. Such dangerously low levels of blood calcium can only occur if the body is no longer able to borrow calcium from the bones under the influence of parathyroid hormone. Thus anything that shuts off or impairs the parathyroid gland is life-threatening.

Except for osteoporosis in the elderly, symptomatic calcium deficiency is rare in the United States.[1-3] However, perhaps 10 percent of Americans (25 percent of the elderly women) are at or near the risk level. Serious dietary deficiencies are rare because when dietary calcium is low, the body adapts by increasing the percentage absorbed from food.

Osteoporosis[1-3]

A recent review from the Mayo Clinic[3] begins by declaring: "Osteoporosis, a comon disorder associated with increasing age, usually affects postmenopausal white women." The review also noted that, "Although the osteoporotic bone is normal in quality, its quantity is decreased and it thus is predisposed to fracture." Osteoporosis has enormous socio-economic impact, say the two doctors, affecting one out of four women over the age of 60 and causing, at a cost of $1 billion, 700,000 of the one million fractures that occur annually.

Years ago, this condition was thought to be simply a calcium deficiency disease. Now it is recognized that increasing dietary calcium alone will not prevent or cure osteoporosis, but raising calcium intakes to 1,200 mg daily helps to restore positive calcium balance in most women after menopause. Diminished secretion of female sex hormone (estrogen) after menopause seems definitely related to lowered calcium absorption and lowered conversion of vitamin D to its active form (1,25-dihydroxy-vitamin D). However, estrogen therapy has its risks, so doctors at the Mayo Clinic[4] have used tiny amounts of activated vitamin D added to milk to treat osteoporosis (see Chapter 8).

According to Drs. Seeman and Riggs,[3] bone loss in the elderly may be minimized by the following precautions:

1) Maintain a generous intake of calcium (1,200 to 1,400 mg daily, but no more), because evidence is strong that the ability to absorb calcium declines with age.

2) Avoid deficiency or megadosage of vitamin D. Deficiency, which is rare, has been detected in some housebound elderly people.

3) Avoid very high phosphate or very high-protein diets. *Moderate*

intakes of meat and dairy products are desirable, however, because they contain many nutrients, including calcium in the dairy products.

4) If negative calcium balance persists despite generous calcium and adequate vitamin D intakes, further medical evaluation should be done to detect a possible reduction in the enzyme activity required to convert vitamin D to its fully active 1,25-dihydroxy-vitamin D form. Without this activated vitamin D, very little, if any, calcium is absorbed from the intestines.

Danger of Calcium Excess

According to Dr. D. Mark Hegsted,[2] the eminent Harvard nutrition scientist, there appears to be no adequate evidence that high calcium intakes by themselves are a "primary causal factor" for adverse conditions such as kidney stones and calcium deposits in soft tissues. But, he adds, "It is logical that high intakes may contribute since low intakes are an integral part of therapy."

The RDA for calcium is 800 mg. Dr. Hegsted was probably referring to the most likely level of self-administered supplements of calcium salts, the range of 2 to 5 grams daily. Vitamin-mineral enthusiasts thinking about trying 10 grams or more should consider what can happen with such massive daily dosage.

Cal's Clash With Calcium[5]

Cal was a merchant marine sailor about 50 years old who suffered from stomach and abdominal pains for a year before seeking medical attention. X-ray films then revealed a stomach ulcer for which he was told to take Maalox, a non-absorbable antacid mixture of aluminum hydroxide gel and magnesium oxide. Two years later, because of continuing pain, he went to a large West Coast hospital and agreed to participate in a study of 40 ulcer patients. The study was designed to compare non-absorbable antacids with absorbable antacids such as calcium carbonate.

For 7 days, Cal was placed on a bland diet and was given alternating servings of milk or calcium carbonate antacid every two hours while awake. Each day he received 1½ quarts of milk (which is rich in calcium and phosphorus) and about 10 grams of calcium in the antacid. Thus he received more than 10 times the RDA of calcium.

Cal's epigastric pain was relieved the 1st day, but on the 4th day he began to experience loss of appetite, nausea, vomiting, dizziness, weakness and lethargy. More serious was the finding of kidney impairment which probably caused the rise in his blood pressure from 165/95 on the first day to 190/109 on the 5th. The kidney trouble was shown by the rise, starting on the 4th day, in blood levels of two major body waste products, urea and creatinine, which rose to double the normal levels. The kidneys were also unable to excrete normal amounts of phosphate, and most serious was the rise of blood calcium to 12 mg percent, peaking at 18 mg% (normal is 9 to 10.6 mg%).

After 7 days, Cal's treatment with milk and calcium carbonate was stopped and Maalox was again given as the antacid. All of his symptoms cleared up within two days, and his blood tests returned to normal levels at the end of a week. A large gastric ulcer was still apparent on x-ray films however, so surgery was performed to remove half of Cal's stomach and cut the vagus nerve responsible for excess acid formation. Four weeks after surgery, Cal left the hospital free of symptoms.

Fortunately for Cal, the study period was only 7 days, because abnormally high calcium and phosphate blood levels can lead to calcium deposits in the soft tissues, especially the kidneys, causing permanent damage. Cases of this sort are described in a 1949 report of Dr. Charles H. Burnett[6] and colleagues. Six ulcer patients they treated arrived at the hospital after several months or years of taking massive daily doses of calcium salts and 1 to 3 quarts of milk daily. All six were found to have serious kidney damage, high blood pressure (probably caused by the kidney impairment) and most serious, calcium deposits in many soft tissues including the kidneys and eyes. Four of these patients died within a year after leaving the hospital, presumably from kidney failure.

Bone Meal and Dolomite

Because of the tendency in recent years for "health food" enthusiasts to indulge in generous daily supplements of bone meal as a source of calcium, it is noteworthy that some commercial bone meal (made from animal bones) contains appreciable amounts of lead. Lead poisoning from bone meal ingestion has been reported, and the FDA is now investigating this problem. Significant amounts of lead have also been found in dolomite, a form of limestone also marketed as a calcium supplement.

PHOSPHORUS

Phosphorus in its ionic phosphate form teams up with calcium to participate in the complex mineral matrix that provides bone growth, strength and maintenance. Phosphorus is very versatile and also enters into all of the high-energy transfer systems involving the so-called phosphogens (such as ATP) which possess very high-energy phosphate bonds. These release vital energy in the cells of many tissues, especially those involved in muscle contractions.

Phosphorus is needed in amounts similar to those of calcium except in young infants. Because phosphorus is present in nearly all foods, dietary deficiency is extremely unlikely to occur in humans. As noted in the discussion of calcium, high phosphate ingestion, occurring with high-protein diets (especially high-meat diets), can present risks to the elderly and postmenopausal women by promoting calcium deficiency if the calcium intakes are low.

MAGNESIUM[1,7]

The 150-pound human body contains a total of about 25 grams of magnesium as salts, half stored in the bones and one quarter in muscle. Little magnesium circulates in the blood, normal serum levels being about 2 mg per 100 milliliters, because most magnesium resides inside the body's cells. Like calcium, magnesium salts form part of the bone matrix. The blood level of magnesium is controlled precisely by the human kidney.

Magnesium is necessary for transmission of nerve impulses to muscle by providing proper electrical potential. It is essential for the normal utilization (metabolism) of potassium and calcium. Magnesium acts as a coenzyme, a vital part of such enzyme systems as the phosphokinases required for the utilization, storage and release of the energy in carbohydrates. It is also a coenzyme for the synthesis of body protein and for DNA, the genetic controller of all cell reproduction, replacement and repair.

Magnesium Deficiency

The current RDA for magnesium is 300 mg for women and 350 mg for men, but magnesium occurs so widely in foods and drinking water (except soft water) that dietary deficiency in humans is rare.[1]

Magnesium deficiency is usually seen only in chronic alcoholics and in pathological conditions such as malabsorptive diseases and intestinal disturbances requiring prolonged intravenous feeding. The early signs of magnesium insufficiency may be nausea, apathy and loss of appetite. More severe deficiency leads to nerve-muscle malfunction with hyperexcitability, behavioral disturbances, and sometimes tremors and convulsions similar to the tetany of calcium deficiency.

Magnesium deficiency has been suggested as a factor in sudden death from heart disease. Several reports since 1967 have associated sudden-death heart attacks with areas having soft drinking water or magnesium-poor soil. (When water is "softened," calcium and magnesium are removed.) Dr. Terence Anderson[8] has offered evidence that in Ontario, water-borne magnesium was low enough to cause borderline magnesium deficiency. In 1975, his research team[9] measured calcium and magnesium content of human heart muscle tissue at autopsy after accidental death.

Comparing hearts from hard and soft water areas, they found no difference in calcium levels, but did find much lower magnesium levels in those from soft water areas. In 1980, Turlapaty and Altura[10] showed that heart arteries isolated from dogs and preserved in physiological solutions would constrict more in low concentrations of magnesium; and this reinforces the suspicion that low magnesium can cause fatal heart artery spasms.

People who wish to enjoy the convenience of soft water but retain the possible health advantages of hard water can use a water softener but bypass it with one pipe to the cold water tap in their kitchen.

Premenstrual Tension (PMT)

In 1973, French researchers suggested that magnesium deficiency might play a role in the symptoms that plague many women during the week before they menstruate. PMT can result in nervous tension, irritability, mood swings, headache, palpitations, fatigue, dizziness, back aches, insomnia, peripheral swellings and depression. In 1981, Drs. Guy Abraham and Michael Lubran[11] found less magnesium in the red blood cells of 26 PMT patients than in those of normal premenopausal women and speculated that magnesium therapy might relieve the symptoms of PMT. However, the noted nutrition authority, Dr. Victor Herbert[12] replied that levels of other minerals such as potassium and phosphorus fluctuate during the menstrual cycle, so why suspect magnesium as the cause of PMT without good double-blind experimental evidence of a cause-and-effect? Thus the findings of Abraham and Lubran should be considered preliminary and not a basis for dietary advice at present.

Can Megadose Magnesium Harm?

The Food and Nutrition Board[1] in 1980 stated that there is no evidence that large oral intakes of magnesium are harmful to people with normal kidney function. And Dr. Maurice Shils[7] has pointed out that: "The normal kidney is capable of excreting absorbed or injected magnesium ion so rapidly that serum levels do not rise to clinically significant levels."

What if a person has poor kidney function? Dr. Richard M. Ratzan[13] and co-workers, in a 1980 review of many research studies, notes that 5 percent of all medical prescriptions for drugs in the U.S. are for laxatives and one-third of these are for magnesium hydroxide (milk of magnesia). Just 30 ml of milk of magnesia provides 1,000 mg of magnesium which is 3 to 4 times the average dietary intake. Only 20 to 30 percent of the 1,000 mg laxative dose is absorbed but, added to the 300 mg in the diet, could result in excessive absorption. Furthermore, many of the elderly use magnesium-containing antacids frequently.

Dr. Ratzan's review cites reports of some persons, mostly elderly ones,

178

being diagnosed as suffering from magnesium "intoxication." These patients had a history of frequent use of magnesium-containing antacids or laxatives. What were the symptoms? The early ones were drowsiness, lethargy, profuse sweating, slurring of speech and unsteadiness. Patients with more serious kidney impairment, who reached higher magnesium blood levels, developed decreased tendon reflexes and abnormal heart rhythms. Sudden death occurred in a few cases, probably caused by spasmic contraction of heart arteries.

Injections of magnesium are used to control life-threatening convulsions in severe cases of eclampsia, a complication in which blood pressure rises to very high levels late in pregnancy. But infants born to mothers treated with large dosages of magnesium prior to delivery can die from magnesium poisoning.[14]

SODIUM, POTASSIUM AND CHLORIDE

No RDA is set for these minerals because all three are plentiful and widespread in foodstuffs, but the new Food and Nutrition Board[1] has issued estimated safe and adequate daily dietary intakes as noted in Appendix B of this book. Scientists call these minerals "electrolytes" because in water they completely dissociate into component ions that conduct electrical currents. Sodium and potassium ions carry positive charges while chloride ions are negatively charged.

Why are these essential? Sodium chloride, common table salt, is a neutral inorganic salt composed of 40 percent sodium and 60 percent chloride. In water, the charges on the chloride ions neutralize and balance the charges on the sodium ions. Sodium ions outside of the cell walls, together with potassium ions inside of the cells, are essential for maintaining the balance between tissue fluids inside and outside of the cells. This arrangement acts, as Ronald Deutsch[15] so aptly explains, like a tiny battery with enough electrical potential (difference) formed across the cell's outer membrane to allow the movement of nutrients into and waste products out of each cell. Chloride combines with sodium and potassium in some situations, but one of its chief roles is to form hydrochloric acid secreted by special cells in the stomach lining. Hydrochloric acid is required to activate the enzyme pepsin which performs preliminary protein digestion in the stomach.

Sodium and High Blood Pressure

Although the adult human need for sodium is only 1 to 3 grams (3 grams is the amount in two-thirds of a teaspoon of table salt), most people in the U.S. tend to consume considerably more. Healthy individuals can tolerate high amounts of sodium chloride by promptly excreting the excess in the urine. Excessive salt intake can elevate the pressure of many persons with high blood pressure (hypertension), but has not been shown to cause the disease. It appears prudent for individuals whose blood pressure is "sensitive" to sodium to avoid table salt and to restrict their intake of foods high in salt. Hypertensive individuals who wish to continue to salt their food may be better off using a 50:50 mixture of sodium and potassium chlorides, such as Morton's "Lite" salt (if advised to do so by their physician).

The Food and Nutrition Board[1] estimates that 20 percent of children are at risk of developing high blood pressure as adults and that there is a "reasonable possibility" that a low salt intake begun early in life may to some extent protect these individuals. This leaves about 80 percent of the population unlikely to be harmed by current common salt intakes of 2 to 6 teaspoons, the total from prepared foods plus the salt shaker. Thus there is no current evidence that the majority of individuals will benefit from salt restriction.

A recent study by Dr. David A. McCarron and associates[16] at Oregon Health Sciences University suggests that low intake of calcium may be a significant causative factor in the development of hypertension. The study compared the diet of 46 hypertensive individuals with those of 44 normal individuals. Their sodium and potassium intakes were similar, but the hypertensives ingested significantly lower amounts of calcium. Dr. McCarron warns that low-sodium diets which also restrict calcium may be unwise.

Use of Salt Tablets

Many people consume salt tablets during hot weather on the theory that they need to replace the salt excreted in their sweat. It is true that athletes need more salt during hot weather, but salt tablets can do more harm than good. Often they will irritate the stomach or pass through the body unabsorbed. Nationally syndicated columnist Dr. Lawrence Lamb[17] recommends that in addition to drinking plenty of water, athletes engaged in strenuous activity should drink a quart of low-fat milk or fortified skim milk a day, plus two 8-ounce glasses of orange juice. Milk has about the same salt content as the healthy human body, and orange juice contains potassium, which is also important in hot weather. Liberal use of the salt shaker during meals will usually provide sufficient extra salt for an athlete.

Potassium Deficiency

Potassium is widely distributed in foods. For this reason, deficiency usually occurs only when there is excessive loss of potassium through diarrhea, in diabetic acidosis, or in association with the use of certain diuretics and laxatives. Often patients with these conditions have a reduced intake of potassium which enhances the development of deficiency. Presumably, all persons at risk for deficiency would be under care of a physician who can advise when supplementation is needed.

Potassium supplements should never be taken without medical advice. Chapter 2 describes the case of Ryan Pitzer, a 2½-month-old infant who died after his mother administered potassium chloride for colic as suggested by an Adelle Davis book. Healthy adults would naturally be less vulnerable to toxicity, but there is simply no reason for them to use a potassium supplement.

References

1. Food and Nutrition Board: Recommended Dietary Allowances, 9th Ed., 1980.
2. Hegsted, D. M.: Chapter 6A, *in* Modern Nutrition in Health and Disease, 5th Ed. (R. S. Goodhart and M. E. Shils, Eds.) Philadelphia, Lea and Febiger, 1973.
3. Seeman, E. and Riggs, B. L.: Geriatrics 36:71, 1981.
4. Gallagher, J. C., Riggs, B. L. et al.: Journal of Clinical Investigation 64: 729, 1979.
5. Medicine (Baltimore) 44:485, 1965.
6. Burnett, C. H. et al.: New England Journal of Medicine 240:787, 1949.
7. Shils, M. E.: *In* Modern Nutrition in Health and Disease, 6th Ed., *op cit.*, 1980, p. 321.
8. Anderson, T. W.: Magnesium, Soft Water and Heart Disease, *in* The Second International Symposium on Magnesium, Montreal, 1976.
9. Anderson, T. W. et al.: Canadian Medical Association Journal 113:199, 1975.
10. Turlapaty, P. D. M. V. and Altura, B. M.: Science 208:198, 1980.
11. Abraham, G. E. and Lubran, M. M.: American Journal of Clinical Nutrition 34:2364, 1981.
12. Herbert, V.: Medical World News, Feb. 15, 1982, pp. 64-69.
13. Ratzan, R. M. et al.: Geriatrics 35:76, 1980.
14. Lipsitz, P. J.: Pediatrics 47:501, 1971.
15. Deutsch, R.: Realities of Nutrition, Palo Alto, Calif., Bull Publishing Co., 1976, p. 278.
16. McCarron, D. A. et al.: Science 217:267-269, 1982.
17. Lamb, L. W.: Personal communication to Dr. S. Barrett, 1980.

19

Zinc, Selenium and Copper

Zinc plays an incredibly versatile and vital role in human bodily functions. It is an essential part of more than 70 enzyme systems that control most of the major human metabolic reactions.[1,2] Certain zinc metalloenzymes are required for the synthesis of key tissue proteins and for the synthesis and repair of the basic genetic controllers of life, the nucleic acids, DNA and RNA. These control growth, sexual maturation, wound healing, and the maintenance of skin, hair, nails and the mucous membranes of the mouth, throat, stomach and intestines. Zinc is also required to make a special protein needed to get stored vitamin A out of the liver and transport it in the blood stream.

Zinc acts in the body as zinc ions (not metallic zinc) in salts or organic complexes.[1-4] Total body zinc is an estimated 2 to 3 grams, with about 50 percent fixed in the bones and 20 percent in the skin, hair and nails. The remaining 30 percent is in the soft tissues and fluids, with the retina of the eye and the male sex organs containing about 3 times as much as other soft tissues.

How Much Zinc Do We Need?

The RDA for zinc was set at 15 mg for adults by assuming 40 percent absorption from food, which leaves 6 mg available to meet the minimum daily requirements determined by careful balance studies. The RDA is 20 mg during pregnancy and 25 mg during breast-feeding.

The best food sources of zinc are meat, eggs, liver and seafood (especially oysters). Lesser amounts are found in milk and whole grains, though phytic acid in whole grains can bind zinc into a complex that is unabsorbable. The zinc content of most municipal water is negligible.[1]

Zinc Deficiency[1-4]

The first and perhaps most dramatic revelation concerning zinc deficiency disorders was the finding in 1963 by Dr. A. S. Prasad and co-workers[5] that zinc deficiency was the primary cause of stunted growth and underdeveloped sex organs in low-income, teenage Egyptian farm laborers. Treatment with 20 or 30 mg of zinc for a few months led most of them to grow rapidly and to mature sexually.[6,7] The researchers believed the zinc deficiency had been caused primarily by an unbalanced diet high in fiber and phytic acid, both of which bind zinc and prevent it from being absorbed.[8] Something similar has been observed in Egyptian girls but has been less extensively reported.

Deficiency of zinc can cause low sperm count, defective sperm, poor appetite, weakening of the white blood cells' ability to fight infection, impaired collagen synthesis with less healthy joints, dermatitis, diarrhea, loss of hair, and poor wound healing. Because zinc is required to mobilize vitamin A from the liver and metabolize it in the retina, lack of zinc can cause night blindness.[9] Zinc deficiency has been linked to toxemia of pregnancy, especially in teenagers,[10] and to birth defects in children born to zinc-deficient mothers.[11]

Zinc deficiency has also been reported to cause a decrease in the sense of taste and smell—especially after age 40—but not all cases of loss of taste are due to zinc deficiency. Dr. Robert Henkin and associates conducted a long series of trials at the National Institutes of Health using zinc supplements on patients with impaired sense of taste and/or smell. Their 1976 study,[12] done with double-blind design, tested 53 men and 53 women whose blood levels of zinc and copper were below those of normal volunteers. After 6 months of treatment with 100 mg of zinc per day, some individuals showed slight improvement, but there was no overall difference between the treatment and placebo groups. In 1978, J. L. Greger and A. H. Geissler[13] administered 15 mg (1 RDA) of zinc daily for 3 months to a retirement home group of 49 elderly persons and noted no significant improvement in their taste. Interpreting these two studies, the respected journal *Nutrition Reviews*[14] concluded in 1979 that no scientific basis existed for treating "ordinary taste and smell disorders" with zinc sulfate.

At a symposium on zinc in 1982, Dr. Henkin[15] reported that 16 of 63 patients he studied who had taste and smell disorders were malabsorbers of zinc. He estimated that 16 million Americans suffer with some degree of reduced sense of taste and speculated that as many as 4 million of these might be malabsorbers of zinc who have zinc deficiency. But the question remains as to why zinc supplements do little to help the diminished taste of most zinc-deficient patients.

Dr. Prasad[16] reports that some American surgeons are using 220 mg of zinc sulfate 2 or 3 times daily (100 to 150 mg of zinc) to aid wound healing. But unless the person is zinc-deficient, the evidence now shows that zinc supplements will not speed healing.

Is Zinc Deficiency Common or Rare?

Until about 1970, zinc deficiency was believed to be rare in the United States. In 1980, the Food and Nutrition Board[1] stated: "Recent evidence suggests that marginal states of zinc nutrition do exist in segments of the U.S. population." According to the studies of Dr. K. M. Hambidge and co-workers,[17] children who eat little or no meat and dairy products are at risk for borderline (mild) zinc deficiency. Vegetarians may also be at risk because of the poor absorbability of zinc in the presence of cereal grains.[7]

In 1972, Dr. Hambidge's team found that low zinc levels in hair were associated with impaired ability to taste, poor appetite and low growth rates in children from middle and upper income families in Denver, Colorado. Daily supplementation with 10 mg of zinc led to improved appetite and weight gain.[1] In 1976, these researchers[17] tested children with poor growth rates from low-income families and found that two-thirds of them had much lower zinc content in their blood and hair than did children from middle-income families.

Is It Easy to Test for Zinc Deficiency?

No, it is not! Advertisements which urge you to send a sample of your hair for zinc analysis should be ignored! Analyses of hair samples for zinc are worthless unless samples are taken of new growth near the scalp and even then, they often give unreliable results. Moreover, zinc levels in one part of the body do not necessarily tell what is going on in another part. (For example, infertile men often test as normal for zinc levels in the blood serum but low in semen zinc.) To approach a reliable figure for zinc status, one needs to obtain values for the zinc content of blood serum, red blood cells, properly sampled hair and for men, semen.

Buying Hope

An old friend, now approaching 60 years of age, gleefully told me in 1980 that he was already seeing signs of sexual resurgence as a result of taking zinc supplements. Did his doctor prescribe the zinc, and had his semen and blood serum and red cells been tested for zinc deficiency? Neither, he said, but he had read all about restoring fertility with zinc supplements in men who had low sperm counts. Furthermore, he had read that the male sex organs such as the prostate gland were richer in zinc than any other body tissue. I asked him: "Just because brain tissue has the highest cholesterol content of any body tissue (also more than egg yolk), should you take cholesterol supplements?" He shrugged and said that's different!

Unless my friend had actually been deficient in zinc (which is unlikely) any enhanced sexuality was most likely psychologically achieved. As do many vitamin E enthusiasts, he was confusing fertility with virility. Nor was he aware that unless you have a rare *medically diagnosable* abnormality, *adequate* vitamin or mineral supply is always better and safer than *excess*. The Recommended Dietary Allowance of zinc provides enough for maximum fertility and virility unless there is a *medically diagnosable* abnormality. Excess zinc is not only a waste of money, it can also be dangerous.

My friend was taking 75 mg of zinc daily. This is 5 times the RDA and might be tolerated, but what if his sexuality didn't improve enough to suit him? Would he then double his dose to 150 mg? At 150 mg—10 times the RDA—zinc can cause copper deficiency that results in anemia with impaired production of hemoglobin for the red blood cells.[16] That's what happened to Hazel.

Zinc-Induced Anemia[18]

Hazel J. was a 59-year-old woman who had celiac disease, an intestinal condition that results in poor absorption of certain key dietary essentials. Until it was discovered that she was unable to absorb adequate amounts of zinc, she had suffered a variety of troublesome symptoms and had been hospitalized several times. By 1975, zinc malabsorption was suspected of being a factor in celiac disease, so Hazel was started on 660 mg of zinc sulfate (150 mg zinc) daily, taken with meals.

After 14 months of this treatment, Hazel returned to the hospital complaining of extreme weakness and fatigue. Tests revealed that she was severely anemic and close to heart failure. Her blood level of zinc was high-normal, as would be expected, but her blood copper level was only 50 percent of normal. Concluding that Hazel's anemia was secondary to copper deficiency caused by excess zinc, the doctors stopped Hazel's zinc supplements and gave her 4 mg of copper sulfate per day for 12 days until her blood copper level returned to normal. She also received a transfusion of red blood cells. After four weeks, her anemia was gone and she was sent home. Presumably, her doctors will try much lower dosages of zinc for celiac disease patients in the future.

Will 150 mg of zinc (10 times the RDA) cause copper deficiency anemia in most people? Or was the case of Hazel J. a rarity? In 1978, Dr. A. S. Prasad[16] and co-workers reported having given this dosage daily for 4 to 24 weeks to 13 patients with sickle cell anemia. The group's average blood level of copper-protein complex (ceruloplasmin) was cut in half. Before conducting this study, the doctors had studied a 26-year-old man who had taken 150 mg of zinc daily for 26 months. He had developed anemia and low white blood cell count which returned to normal after 10 days' treatment with copper supplements—demonstrating that copper deficiency (secondary to zinc excess) was a factor in the anemia.

Zinc supplements can probably cause copper loss in normal people. A study of 11 healthy adolescent schoolgirls found that all of them excreted more copper than usual with only 15 mg of zinc administered to them daily for 30 days.[19] Dr. Harold Sandstead, a member of the research team that discovered zinc deficiency among the Egyptian teenagers in the early 1960s, warns in a 1978 editorial[7] that persons receiving more than 50 mg of zinc per day should be monitored for copper deficiency. A 1973 report by Dr. E. J. Underwood[20] describes how too much zinc can interfere with absorption of iron, copper and calcium in experimental animals.

Zinc and the Prostate

Why is there so much current interest in zinc? As far back as 1921, two French scientists reported finding very high zinc content in the prostate tissue of animals. According to Dr. William R. Fair,[21] a leader in prostate-zinc studies, medical interest in zinc was stimulated by a 1952 report that the prostate gland contains more zinc than any other organ in the body. Since that time, medical research has explored the relationships between zinc levels in sperm and prostatic tissues and a variety of abnormal conditions including benign prostate hypertrophy (enlargement), male infertility, impotence and prostate inflammations (prostatitis).

Can Zinc Therapy Prevent or Reduce Benign Prostate Enlargement?

I have found no published scientific reports of clinical trials using zinc therapy for benign prostatic hypertrophy (BPH). However, since reported assessments of zinc levels in the semen of men with this condition have been normal,[21] it seems quite unlikely that supplementary zinc would be of value.

Can Zinc Therapy Correct Male Infertility?

Some infertility cases are associated with low semen zinc, and some of these respond to zinc therapy with improvement. (Infertility can also be caused by hormonal defects or infections.) But experimental results of zinc therapy are contradictory. Dr. Joel Marmar and co-workers[22] gave 55 mg of zinc sulfate daily for 6 months to 11 infertile men with low semen zinc and low sperm counts. (These patients did not have prostatitis.) Their sperm counts and motility increased, and 3 who had been unable to father children for at least a year were then able to do so. A study by A. T. K. Cockett and associates[23] found that zinc supplements increased the sperm motility of 9 infertile men, but not their semen zinc levels. The same research team gave just an antibiotic to 20 infertile men who had prostatitis and low semen zinc levels. Sperm motility and semen zinc levels rose within two weeks but fell below normal again after the antibiotic therapy was discontinued. However, Dr. Fair has not encountered a prostatitis case in which the low prostate zinc level (semen zinc) could be raised by zinc supplements.

In 1982, Dr. Cockett's team[24] reported further studies on infertile men. Twelve of these men with normal semen zinc levels were treated with only a male sex hormone. Sixty-five infertile men with no prostatitis but initially low semen zinc levels were given 100 mg of zinc for three months. Contrary to Dr. Marmar's results, their sperm motility improved only slightly, but their average semen zinc rose significantly. Twelve other infertile men with low initial semen zinc levels were given both zinc and male sex hormone and had a significant increase in sperm motility. More work needs to be done to clarify the role of zinc in treating infertility.

Can Zinc Therapy Correct Impotence?

Yes, but only if it is due to a severe zinc deficiency, and this is very rarely the case. Impotence is most commonly caused by psychological factors, and there are many physical causes including alcohol, prescribed medications, hormonal problems, and decreased blood or nerve supply to the penis (often secondary to diabetes).

Eight cases of impotence due to zinc deficiency were reported in 1977 by L. D. Antoniou[25] and colleagues. All of these men had kidney failure which required blood purification by kidney dialysis—which causes considerable zinc loss. These patients had very low blood serum levels of zinc and male sex hormone. A controlled study found that oral zinc supplements did not help, but adding zinc to the dialysis bath led to improved potency.

Can zinc therapy aid infectious prostatitis? It is known that zinc ions present in prostatic fluid have antibacterial activity.[26,27] However, prostatitis, infectious or otherwise, is almost always associated with below-normal levels of prostatic zinc.[27] Dr. William Fair's research team recently reported that prostatic zinc levels were not raised in 27 patients with infectious prostatitis who were given from 50 to 150 mg of zinc daily for several months.[21,27] These researchers concluded that oral zinc administration is "of little value" in the treatment of prostatitis.

Zinc and Teenage Pregnancy

In 1981, a large research group[10] from Tulane University Medical Center and the Touro Infirmary Research in New Orleans together with mineral nutrition experts at the USDA Laboratories in Grand Forks, North Dakota, reported on a study of 272 teenage pregnant women whose average age was 17.6 years. Their blood zinc levels were considerably below average and were lowest during the final weeks of pregnancy. Twenty percent delivered prematurely, 20 percent had prolonged labor at birth, 11 percent had babies with low birth weights, and 19 percent suffered toxemia, a potentially dangerous condition in which blood pressure rises. The 51 mothers who had toxemia were among the lowest in zinc. Six babies in the low-zinc group had congenital defects, four with an undescended testicle and two with a clubfoot.

These young women were not representative of pregnant teenagers in general because, as the authors pointed out, they were almost all from low-income families whose dietary intakes "could have been suboptimal." Toxemia occurs considerably more often in individuals from low-income families than it does in those from middle and upper-income families.[28]

Zinc Megadose Can Harm[3,4]

A wide margin of safety exists between normal intakes of zinc from foods and the zinc intake likely to produce adverse effects in humans,[20] but high doses can be hazardous.

In 1980, Dr. Philip Hooper[29] and colleagues gave 12 healthy adult male volunteers 160 mg of zinc daily for five weeks. The zinc supplements had no effect on total blood cholesterol but did decrease by 25 percent the high-density lipoprotein (HDL) type of cholesterol complex (the "good" cholesterol discussed in Chapters 17 and 23). Dr. Hooper commented that this result, if confirmed by other researchers, may indicate that excess zinc ingestion can cause atherosclerosis and thus increase the risk of coronary heart disease. Recent reports of animal experiments[30,31] suggest that by lowering blood copper, excess zinc intake may cause blood cholesterol and triglycerides to rise.

Ingestion of single huge doses of 1,000 to 2,000 mg (1 to 2 grams) of zinc sulfate results in acute toxicity[3] with immediate vomiting, stomach cramps, nausea, diarrhea and fever. Zinc poisoning has been reported from drinking water from zinc-coated (galvanized) pipes or storage tanks, which, fortunately, are now used less frequently. A woman who took 28 grams (1 oz) of zinc sulfate (6,000 mg of zinc), mistaking it for Epsom salt, died.[3]

Stomach Irritation

Jill, a 15-year-old English schoolgirl, had a nice figure, and was witty and potentially attractive. But she had not yet attracted a boyfriend, probably because of her dreadful acne. In 1978, her family doctor prescribed "Zincomed," a brand of zinc sulfate containing 220 mg per capsule.[32] Jill took two capsules (100 mg of zinc) each day but failed to follow instructions to take them with or near the end of meals. After each capsule, Jill suffered stomach pain, but she was determined to cure her acne and kept taking them.

After one week of treatment, she suddenly fainted upon rising from a chair. During the next 24 hours she passed black "tarry" stools which frightened her parents who then took her to a hospital. Tests showed that she was anemic from loss of blood, and an endoscopic examination revealed erosion and bleeding of the lining along one curvature of Jill's stomach. Her zinc sulfate treatment was stopped and she was given 8 units of blood by transfusion. After a month of treatment with an antacid, her stomach healed completely and she remained free of anemia.

Can Zinc Supplements Help Acne?

One year after the above report, W. J. Cunliffe[33] published the results of treating 42 patients with acne of moderate severity. All were given 50 mg of zinc three times a day (150 mg total) as zinc sulfate to take immediately after meals. Twelve patients had to stop therapy after one week due to severe nausea, vomiting and/or diarrhea. Of the 30 patients who finished four months of treatment, only 3 showed any improvement in their acne, and it was slight at that. However, one of the 30 developed a perforated stomach ulcer requiring emergency surgery—a complication probably caused by the zinc sulfate.

COPPER

As early as 1935, copper was found to be essential for animals but only recently have researchers shown that it is required for humans.[1] Copper is part of several important enzymes called cuproproteins.[2] Copper absorbed from the intestinal tract is carried chiefly to the liver and bone marrow. In the liver it is incorporated into a copper-protein complex called ceruloplasmin which then circulates in the blood stream. Cuproprotein enzymes are needed for the proper utilization of iron and for the manufacture of hemoglobin and red blood cells in the bone marrow.

The best food sources of copper are liver, shellfish, nuts and dried beans. Human milk is a fair source, but cow's milk is a poor one.

Copper deficiency in humans is rare.[1] The Food and Nutrition Board's estimated safe and adequate intake of copper is 2 to 3 mg per day for adults, an amount that most Americans get in their diet. Severe copper lack in Peruvian children has resulted in anemia and bone disease. Excessive zinc supplements or megadose vitamin C can block or significantly reduce the absorption of copper.

The average copper content of human diets is about 10 parts per million (ppm). The amount of dietary copper needed to produce toxicity in humans is unknown, but many animals can tolerate diets with 200 ppm which is about 20 times human dietary supply. Toxicity from dietary copper is encountered in humans only in Wilson's disease, a hereditary metabolic disorder in which copper accumulates in body tissues. Acute poisoning has occurred with accidental ingestion of 20 grams of copper sulfate. Hot soft water can extract copper from copper tubing and from copper utensils, but according to Dr. Underwood,[20] the maximum addition to human diet from this would be about 1.4 mg daily.

SELENIUM

Selenium was for many years a controversial mineral—early reports of its benefits conflicted with reports that it might cause cancer. Today selenium is considered essential for humans[1,2] and has been suggested as protective against cancer in adequate (but not excessive) amounts. The reality seems to lie in the balance among micromineral nutrients, with neither too much nor too little of any one mineral in the long-term intake. Not long ago, selenium was discovered to be a key component in an extremely important enzyme called "glutathione peroxidase" or "the selenium glutathione-reductase system," which protects body tissues, especially the cell membranes, from oxidative damage. In this role it can substitute for vitamin E.

How Much Selenium Do We Need?

The 1980 Food and Nutrition Board's estimated safe and adequate daily dosage is 50 to 200 micrograms (μg) for people seven years of age or older. The estimated range of daily intake in the United States is 50 to 160 μg, with the average intake being 150 μg.[34] According to the Food and Nutrition Board,[34] selenium is a "paradoxical micronutrient" in that both deficiency and moderate excess in animals lead to liver failure. Supplements of selenium are potentially dangerous and should be taken only under medical supervision.

The best food sources of selenium are seafoods, liver and kidney. Whole grains are a good source and among vegetables, lesser amounts are found in tomatoes and cabbage. The selenium content of vegetables and grains depends upon the selenium content of the soil in which they are grown.[1] Since selenium content varies considerably from place to place, it is a good idea to consume foods which have been obtained from many regions of the country.

Does Selenium Deficiency Occur in Humans?

Selenium deficiency has been produced experimentally in animals,[2] causing such problems as degeneration of the heart, liver, muscle and kidney in mice; muscular dystrophy in lambs, calves and chicks; and liver damage in rats and pigs. Signs of selenium deficiency and toxicity occur naturally in animals in widely separated parts of the world as a result of wide variations of soil content of selenium.[20] In the United States, heart muscle abnormality developed in a patient fed completely by vein, but disease states attributable to dietary selenium deficiency have not been reported.[35,36] However, heart muscle abnormalities have been reported in Chinese children ingesting less than 30 μg of selenium daily.[37]

The story of a selenium deficiency "that wasn't there" began in 1970 when a researcher, D. F. L. Money,[38] suggested that sudden infant death (SID)—sometimes called "crib death"—might be caused by vitamin E and/or selenium deficiency in early infancy. He also suggested that bottle-fed babies were more likely than breast-fed babies to become victims of SID. In 1972, W. J. Rhead and G. N. Schrauzer[39] reported a preliminary finding that vitamin E and selenium levels were lower in SID infants than in other infants, but these authors emphasized that they had checked only a few babies. However, by 1975 they had accumulated enough data to show that SID is *not* caused by deficiency of either selenium or vitamin E.[40] They also concluded that the old belief that breast feeding protects against SID is not true.

Selenium Poisoning

According to Underwood[20] and Young and Richardson,[41] the level of selenium intake that produces harmful effects is 2.5 to 3.0 mg, only 10 times the likely dietary maximum. Thus, supplementation with selenium tablets is risky. Because foodstuffs nowadays usually come from many different regions, human diets even in areas with high selenium soil and water content almost never furnish more than 0.30 mg (300 micrograms), which is a safe level. It is also known that appreciable selenium is lost in processing and cooking of foods. Acute selenium poisoning in humans, which often is fatal, has occurred as a result of accident, suicide or murder.

Chronic selenium poisoning occurs in grazing animals that get a moderate daily excess of selenium at 5 to 10 parts per million (ppm) in their feed—probably equivalent to a human intake of 4 to 8 mg daily. These animals exhibit poor appetite and growth, anemia, cirrhosis (scarring) of the liver, stiffness and lameness due to erosion of the joints of long bones, and loss of hair.[20] There is no evidence that humans living in high-selenium areas develop symptoms attributable to dietary selenium.

Zinc, Selenium and Cancer

As of mid-1982, it is quite debatable whether high but safe levels of dietary selenium are needed for a protective effect against certain kinds of human cancer. Professor G. N. Schrauzer[42] published a lengthy review in 1977 covering his own group's findings as well as data from other published reports. He notes that as early as 1912, it was suggested that small amounts of selenium might have anti-cancer properties. He also states that between 1940 and 1965 there were several reports that selenium might cause cancer, but these reports later were proven invalid.

In 1969, Shamberger and Frost[43] published the results of a survey showing that in a number of U.S. cities, the higher the average selenium level in blood samples, the fewer cancer deaths; and in cities with low selenium blood content, cancer deaths were higher.

Dr. Schrauzer's group[44] then conducted an extensive survey in 28 countries to compare dietary intakes of arsenic, selenium, zinc, copper, manganese, cadmium and chromium with the incidence of cancer. They also obtained small samples of frozen blood from blood banks in different sections of 22 countries, analyzed the thawed blood for minerals and correlated blood mineral content with cancer cases. The found that the higher the selenium content in the diet or in the blood, the fewer cases of several kinds of cancer; and the more zinc in the diet or blood, the *more* cases of cancer. Schrauzer also presents evidence that zinc is an antagonist to selenium, interfering with its absorption and utilization as well as promoting excretion of selenium.

Dr. Schrauzer[42] believes that the typical American diet provides sufficient zinc for growing children but an excess amount for adults. He believes that a low-zinc, high-selenium (300 micrograms/day) diet could reduce the incidence of cancer of the colon, rectum, prostate, breast, ovary, lung, pancreas, skin, bladder as well as leukemia.

Schrauzer does not advocate selenium supplements, realizing, no doubt, the hazards of self-medication without medical supervision. He also advises against the use of zinc supplements, especially by elderly individuals. He recommends that dietary zinc intake be minimized while selenium-rich foods be increased. According to Schrauzer, excessive consumption of meat should be avoided since it is high in zinc; and whole grains are good because phytates bind some of the zinc and reduce its absorption from the gut.

High-Selenium, Low-Zinc Diet Challenged

Professor Vernon Young is a distinguished research scientist at Massachusetts Institute of Technology's Clinical Research Center and Department of Nutrition and Food Science. In 1979, he and his colleague, Dr. David Richardson, published a review article[41] in the journal *Cancer* entitled "Nutrients, Vitamins and Minerals in Cancer Prevention—Facts and Fallacies." Foremost among their criticisms was one aimed at irresponsible sections of the news media:

> It is not only premature but also unethical to suggest taking selenium tablets as a preventative measure against cancer. Despite the need to avoid sensational accounts concerning the possible protective effect of selenium, the headline, "Top doctor says simple addition to diet will cut cancer by 80-90% appeared in the April 4, 1978 issue of the *National Enquirer* . . .
>
> Newspaper statements such as these are misleading, particularly as selenium excess, as well as deficiency, can have deleterious effects on health.

Young and Richardson[41] believe that the relationship between dietary selenium intake and human cancer requires further critical investigation. They emphasize the complexities of micromineral interactions and challenge Schrauzer's advice to minimize zinc intake, because rich sources of dietary zinc include foods of animal origin that provide many other essential nutrients such as iron in a highly available form. They sum up their views by stating: "There is no evidence to suggest that manipulation or change in our usual trace element intakes would have an important impact on the incidence of human cancer." The majority of nutrition scientists who have examined the evidence seem to agree with this viewpoint.

References

1. Food and Nutrition Board: Recommended Dietary Allowances, 9th Ed. National Academy of Sciences, Washington, D.C., 1980.
2. Li, T-K. and Vallee, B. L.: *In* Modern Nutrition in Health and Disease, 6th Ed. (R. S. Goodhart and M. E. Shils, Eds.). Philadelphia, Lea and Febiger, 1980, pp. 408-441.
3. FDA Advisory Review Panel: Federal Register 44:16126-16201, March 16, 1979.
4. Solomons, N. W.: Zinc and Copper in Human Nutrition, *in* Nutrition in the 1980s: Constraints on Our Knowledge. New York, Alan R. Liss, 1981, pp. 97-127.
5. Prasad, A. S. et al.: Archives of Internal Medicine 111:407, 1963.
6. Sandstead, H. H., Prasad, A. S. et al.: American Journal of Clinical Nutrition 20:422-442, 1967.
7. Sandstead, H. H.: JAMA 246:2188, 1978.
8. Nutrition Reviews 33-18, 1975.
9. Solomons, N. and Russell, R.: American Journal of Clinical Nutrition 33:2031, 1980.
10. Cherry, F. F. et al.: *Ibid.* 34:2367, 1981.
11. Hurley, L. S.: *Ibid.* 34:2864, 1981.
12. Henkin, R. I. et al.: America Journal of Medical Science 272:285, 1976.

13. Greger, J. and Geissler, A.: American Journal of Clinical Nutrition 31: 633, 1978.

14. Nutrition Reviews: 37:283, 1979.

15. Henkin, R. I.: Presentation at a meeting of the American Chemical Society; reported in Science News, April 17, 1982, p. 262.

16. Prasad, A. S. et al.: JAMA 240-2166, 1978.

17. Hambidge, K. M. et al.: American Journal of Clinical Nutrition 29:734, 1976.

18. Lancet 2:774, Oct. 8, 1977.

19. Greger, J. L. et al.: Journal of Nutrition 108:1449, 1976.

20. Underwood, E. J.: Trace Elements, *in* Toxicants Occurring Naturally in Foods, 2nd Ed. Washington, D.C., Food and Nutrition Board, National Academy of Sciences, 1973, pp. 43-87.

21. Fair, W. R. and Parrish, R.: Antibacterial Substances in Prostatic Fluid, *in* The Prostatic Cell: Structure and Function. (G. G. Murphy, A. A. Sandberg and J. Karr, Eds.). New York, Alan R. Liss, 1981.

22. Marmar, J. L.: Fertility and Sterility 26:1057, 1975.

23. Caldamone, A. A., Dougherty, K. A. and Cockett, A. T. K.: Surgical Forum 29:644, 1978.

24. Takihara, H., Consentino, M. J. and Cockett, A. T. K.: Abstracts of the April 1982 Meeting of the American Urological Association, p. 109, Abstract No. 125.

25. Antoniou, L. D. et al.: Lancet 2:895, Oct. 29, 1977.

26. Fair, W. R. et al.: Urology 7:169, 1976.

27. Fair, W. R. et al.: Abstracts of the April 1982 Meeting of the American Urological Association, p. 149, Abstract No. 287.

28. Peake, C. (obstetrician-gynecologist, Kalamazoo, Michigan): Personal communication, Nov. 1, 1982.

29. Hooper, P. L. et al.: JAMA 244:1960, 1980.

30. Klevay, L. M.: American Journal of Clinical Nutrition 28:764, 1975.

31. Petering, H. G. et al.: Agricultural and Food Chemistry 25:1105, 1977.

32. British Medical Journal 1:754, March 25, 1978.

33. Cunliffe, W. J.: British Journal of Dermatology 101:363, 1979.

34. Food and Nutrition Board: Recommended Dietary Allowances, 8th Ed. Washington, D.C., National Academy of Sciences, 1974.

35. Johnson, R. A. et al.: New England Journal of Medicine 304:1210, 1981.

36. Young, V. R.: *Ibid.* 304:1228.

37. Keshan Disease Research Group: Chinese Medical Journal 92:471-482, 1979.

38. Money, D. F. L.: Journal of Pediatrics 77:165, 1970, cited in Rhead and Schrauzer, 1972, *loc. cit.*

39. Rhead, W. J. and Schrauzer, G. N.: Journal of Pediatrics 81:415, 1972.

40. Schrauzer, G. N. et al.: Annals of Clinical and Laboratory Science 5:31, 1975.

41. Young, V. R. and Richardson, D. P.: Nutrients, Vitamins and Minerals in Cancer Prevention—Facts and Fallacies, *in* Cancer 43:2125-2136, Supplement No. 5, May 1979.

42. Schrauzer, G. N.: Trace Elements, Nutrition and Cancer: Perspectives of Prevention, *in* Advances in Experimental Medicine and Biology 91:323-344, 1977.
43. Shamberger, R. J. and Frost, D. V.: Canadian Medical Association Journal 100:682, 1969.
44. Schrauzer, G. N. et al.: Bioinorganic Chemistry 7:36, 1977.

20

Iron, Iodine, Fluorine and Other Microminerals

Iron is a constituent of hemoglobin, the compound in red blood cells which carries oxygen to the tissues. Hemoglobin consists of an iron-organic complex called "heme" bound to a special globulin protein. Oxygen temporarily bound to hemoglobin gives arterial blood its bright red color, whereas blood returning to the heart in veins (except from the lungs) is darker because of carbon dioxide linkage to the hemoglobin. Iron is also found in myoglobin (in muscle fibers) and a number of enzymes.

Iron Requirements

Control of the proper level of iron in the human body is a complex situation.[1] Unlike its handling of other minerals, the body does not regulate iron metabolism through increased or decreased excretion. The main control of iron status is at the site of intestinal absorption. When body stores are full, absorption is minimal; when stores are reduced, more is absorbed from the food we eat.

The average loss of iron in a healthy adult man is about 1 mg per day. Women who menstruate lose an additional 0.5 mg per day (averaged over one month)—though heavy bleeders can lose up to three times this amount. Trace amounts are lost with minor bleeding and when cells are discarded from the skin and the lining of the digestive tract. The Recommended Dietary Allowances of 10 mg for men (and non-menstruating women) and 18 mg for women who menstruate are based on the assumption that about 10 percent of the iron we ingest is absorbed. Pregnant and lactating women need more (see Appendix B).

Food Sources of Iron

Organ meats (liver, kidney), other lean meats, dried legumes (beans and peas), clams, oysters, dried fruits and enriched grains are rich sources of dietary iron. Poor sources include milk, unenriched white bread, potatoes and most fruits. Whole grains contain modest amounts of iron, but often it is bound to phytic acid and unavailable. Wheat flour is currently enriched to the level of 16.5 mg of iron per pound because of concern about widespread marginal deficiency in the U.S. Efforts to increase this level or to add iron to cereals have been opposed by some nutritional scientists worried about iron "overload."

The amount of food iron available for intestinal absorption depends upon the kinds of iron compounds in the diet and the presence of certain foods. The organic "heme" iron in meat is easily absorbed, but iron in vegetables and egg yolk is not. Even iron supplements (ferrous sulfate) can have limited absorption if they encounter interference from high-dose zinc or become bound to phytic acid from whole grains. On the other hand, vitamin C enhances the absorption of iron (although it reduces the absorption of copper).

Iron Deficiency

According to Dr. Victor Herbert,[2] three groups are at risk for iron deficiency because they must make blood rapidly: children up to age five; boys and girls at the onset of puberty; and women who must replace blood lost during menstruation. Vegetarians must be particularly careful because vegetable iron is much less absorbable than is iron from animal sources. Iron deficiency is common enough in these four groups that they should be evaluated with a blood test for iron deficiency. If it is found, treatment with iron should be prescribed by a physician.

Thanks to advertisements suggesting Geritol for "tired blood," most people know that iron deficiency, fatigue and anemia are somehow related. But self-treatment with tonics is unwise. Although iron deficiency anemia can cause fatigue, it does not cause most cases of fatigue. Moreover, if you do have iron deficiency anemia, what you need is not a tonic, but a diagnosis! If a deficiency is caused by poor eating habits, they should be improved. If an anemia is caused by internal bleeding (such as a bleeding ulcer or an intestinal cancer), prompt treatment is important. If a doctor advises you to take supplementary iron, a number of generic iron preparations are available which cost much less than advertised "tonics" or multivitamin tablets with iron. If you don't have proven iron deficiency, taking iron is unwise.

Iron Overload Disease

As noted by Dr. E. J. Underwood: "Iron absorption in normal, healthy humans is regulated so efficiently in accordance with body iron needs that intakes from natural foods of sufficient magnitude to produce toxic effects are inconceivable."[3] Hemochromatosis, a disease characterized by iron deposits in many tissues, especially the liver, the pancreas and sometimes the heart, is a disorder of iron absorption in which the normal control preventing excess absorption does not work. Iron excess in such cases can lead to liver malfunction, a form of diabetes, and even to heart failure. Fortunately, hemochromatosis is a rare disorder.

Acute Iron Poisoning

Overdoses of therapeutic forms of iron are responsible for hundreds of reported poisonings each year, mostly children who take their parents' supplement pills or tonics. One such case was that of little Erin in Chapter 2. In 1974, the *Journal of the American Medical Association*[4,5] noted that iron preparations were the fourth most common cause of poisoning in children under 5 years of age; and that many such children die without prompt treatment. As few as 6 to 12 ferrous sulfate tablets have caused death in a small child.[6]

In 1975, *Medical World News*[7] described how, during an 18-month period, a Minneapolis poison control center encountered 30 children and 4 adults who had swallowed iron preparations. One was a pregnant 17-year-old girl who died of severe liver and kidney damage as a result of taking 90 ferrous sulfate capsules. The article also told of a 16-month-old boy who had swallowed 47 supplement tablets of various kinds containing a total of 325 mg ferrous sulfate. Two hours later, at a large children's hospital in St. Louis, the child was noted to be in shock with a blood serum iron level more than 50 times normal. He died despite vigorous therapy including exchange transfusions to remove and replace his blood.

IODINE

Iodine is essential for humans because it is part of the basic structure of thyroid hormones which control the body's rate of metabolism.[1] Iodine deficiency leads to diminished producton of thyroid hormones (hypothyroidism). The main symptoms of hypothyroidism are weight gain and lack of energy. It also causes low blood pressure, slow pulse and depressed muscular capability. Hypothyroidism can also occur despite adequate dietary intake in some persons with a hereditary thyroid gland of poor capability. Untreated hypothyroidism in children causes mental retardation and dwarfism.

Simple Goiter

The thyroid gland is located in the front of the neck just above the chest. In severe cases of iodine deficiency, the gland can become as large as a person's head. This condition (simple goiter) was treated, with some success, with seaweed and burnt sponge (both rich in iodides) by the ancient Chinese, Egyptians and the South American Incas.

The first modern treatment of goiter with iodine salts appears to have been done by the English physician, Dr. Prout, in 1816. This treatment soon spread throughout Europe even though no one knew why it worked. Many doctors used daily doses as high as 400 mg (over 2,500 times the RDA). This shrunk the goiters but also caused iodine poisoning. The first suggestions that iodine deficiency was the cause of simple goiter were made in 1930 and 1931 by Dr. Prevost in Switzerland and Dr. Baussingault in France.

Sources of Iodine

The Recommended Dietary Allowance of iodine for adults is 0.15 mg. Seafoods are the only consistently reliable food sources of iodide.[1] Iodine is found in water and various other foods, but in many sections of the world (including parts of the United States formerly known as the "goiter belt"), the amounts in the water and locally produced foods are too low to meet human needs.

Iodine deficiency has become rare in the United States because the federal government has encouraged the use of iodized table salt since 1924. One teaspoon of iodized salt provides 0.26 mg of iodide, nearly twice the RDA. The Ten-State Nutrition Survey of 1968-70 (see Chapter 21) found a small number of goiters, but almost none had been caused by iodine deficiency. The Food and Nutrition Board recommends use of iodized salt in all noncoastal regions of the United States. Slightly more than half of the salt used in this country is iodized.

In 1973, Dr. E .J. Underwood[3] estimated that the average dietary intake of iodide in the United States ranged from 0.27 to 0.87 mg daily (2 to 6 times the RDA). In 1975, an FDA-sponsored study[8] showed that many people who did not use iodized salt had intakes of 0.70 to 0.80. Then it was discovered that more than half of this amount came from dairy products produced on farms where products used to disinfect equipment and cows' udders contain organically bound iodine compounds that do not affect the thyroid. Dietary iodine has also increased due to use of iodine-rich dough conditioners. The Food and Nutrition Board cautions that further increase through environmental contamination or food fortification is undesirable.

Effects of Excess Iodine

The FDA Advisory Review Panel[9] stated in 1979 that acute iodine toxicity is rare since daily intakes as high as 4,000 mg for several weeks have produced no adverse effects in most people. This is probably because excess iodine is rapidly excreted by the kidneys and the thyroid has the ability to resist excess absorption. However, daily intake of 40 mg or more for many months can cause some people to develop hypothyroidism and a goiter different from that of iodide deficiency.

In rare cases, high intakes have caused iodide poisoning (iodism) with angioedema (giant hives), bleeding skin lesions, swollen salivary glands and loss of appetite. However, according to Dr. Underwood, iodism can occur in some people with intakes of only a little above 2 mg (13 times the RDA).

In recent years, kelp (dried seaweed) has been promoted as an aid to dieting—either alone or combined with lecithin, cider vinegar and vitamin B[6]. However, according to a 1975 position paper of the American Dietetic Association,[10] large amounts of kelp taken for long periods of time can cause hypothyroidism. Iodine-induced goiters are common among inhabitants of the northern Japanese island of Hokkaido who consume enough seaweed to achieve a daily iodide intake of 50 to 80 mg (300 to 500 times the RDA).[3,11]

Iodide has some usefulness as a treatment for hyperthyroidism (overactive thyroid gland), but only under strict medical supervision. Self-treatment of thyroid disease with kelp—as recommended at many health food stores—is dangerous.

FLUORINE

Fluorine is present in small but widely varying concentrations in practically all soils, water supplies, plants and animals. In water, fluorine occurs as fluoride ion, but the two terms are often used interchangeably. Fluorine has been found essential for many species of animals—with deficiency leading to stunted growth—but in humans, it is considered essential because of its beneficial effects on dental health.[1] It also plays a role in normal bone structure.

Studies conducted throughout the past 50 years have shown that the incidence of tooth decay is reduced by 60 to 70 percent when sufficient fluoride is received early in infancy and continued into adulthood. Unfortunately, this "magic" mineral is not present in sufficient amounts in foods and must therefore be obtained from another source. This can be accomplished most efficiently by adding fluoride to community water supplies so that their concentration becomes approximately one part fluoride to one million parts of water. This procedure, called fluoridation, costs only 50 to 75 cents per person per year. More than 120 million Americans in thousands of communities now drink fluoridated water.

Fluoride may strengthen the bones of the elderly. Small amounts of fluoride are known to deposit in the bones to form a stronger matrix; this may also prevent or minimize the slow loss of calcium from bones in the elderly. High dosages of fluoride are being studied for the treatment of osteoporosis (thinning of the bones).[12,13]

The Food and Nutrition Board's 1980 estimated safe and adequate intake for adults is 1.5 to 4.0 mg, a range easily obtained in communities whose water supplies contain 1 ppm of fluoride, either naturally or through water fluoridation. Mottling (spotting or staining) of the teeth of children can result from long-term consumption of water that contains 2 or more parts per million (ppm) of natural fluoride, but does not occur at a concentration of 1 ppm. Some community water supplies and deep artesian well waters contain as much as 4 to 8 ppm of fluoride, but even at 8 ppm, it would take an estimated 35 years of drinking such water to reach toxic levels of fluoride in the bones.[3]

Opposition is Unfounded

Fluoridation is a favored target for quacks and food faddists to condemn unjustly. Opponents accuse it of causing everything from warts to cancer. Thousands of scientific studies attest to fluoridation's safety and effectiveness; but given enough publicity, even a small group of persistent opponents can raise troublesome doubts in their local community. Consumers Union, publisher of *Consumer Reports*, calls the survival of the fluoridation controversy "one of the major triumphs of quackery over science in our generation."[14]

Linus Pauling, many of whose other positions are in line with those of food faddists, agrees that fluoridation is beneficial and recently reaffirmed the position statement[15] he issued in 1967:

> Over a period of more than a decade I have studied the available information about the fluoridation of drinking water. I have reached the conclusion that the presence of fluoride ion in drinking water in concentrations about equal to the average for natural water is beneficial to the health, especially because of the protection that it provides against dental caries, and that there is no evidence for detrimental effects comparable in significance to the beneficial effects. I support the actions of city, state, and national governments in ordering that public supplies of drinking water be brought to this level by the addition of fluoride, in case the water is deficient in fluoride, and by removal of some of the fluoride if there is an excess of fluoride in the water supply.

If your community water supply is fluoridated—either naturally or artificially—consider yourself lucky. If not, and you have small children, be sure to obtain a prescription for fluoride tablets or drops from your physician or dentist. Equally important, pressure your water company and/or local government officials to bring fluoridation's benefits to your community. For further information on this topic, read *The Tooth Robbers—A Pro-Fluoridation Handbook,* published by the George F. Stickley Company.

COBALT

Although cobalt is essential, no recommended dietary allowance has been established.[1] This is because the human need for cobalt is met by and limited to the availability of vitamin B_{12} (cobalamin), of which cobalt is an essential structural part. Thus it is pointless to take cobalt supplements. Humans obtain vitamin B_{12} most readily from foods of animal origin. Ruminating animals (such as sheep) have it manufactured in their intestinal tract by friendly bacteria if trace amounts of cobalt are present in the diet. Green leafy vegetables are about the only plant food source of appreciable cobalt. Vegetarians are usually borderline deficient of B_{12} unless they take supplement tablets. Those who eat no animal products should supplement with 1 RDA of B_{12} (6 micrograms) daily as prescribed by their physician.

Cobalt Poisoning

Large excesses of cobalt can be harmful but, as Underwood[3] asserts, cobalt poisoning from almost any conceivable human diet appears to be extremely unlikely. Green leafy vegetables contain 0.4 to 0.6 parts per million (ppm) of cobalt and dairy products and cereals only 0.01 ppm or less. Accidental ingestion or supplementation with excess cobalt causes polycythemia (abnormally high red blood cell counts), heart muscle damage, thyroid gland enlargement and nervous system abnormalities.[16]

CHROMIUM

Chromium[16] in tiny amounts has long been known to be essential for animals. Now it is believed that trace amounts are necessary for humans, required to maintain normal blood sugar metabolism in association with insulin. The Food and Nutrition Board's estimated safe and adequate intake is 50 to 200 micrograms daily. Food sources include meat products, cheeses, whole grains, eggs and fresh fruits. Brewer's yeast is quite rich in chromium.

Chromium deficiency produces a diabetes-like condition in animals and is associated with blood sugar abnormalities in humans. The incidence of chromium deficiency in humans is not known, but probably is low. According to Dr. Walter Mertz,[17] Director of the U.S. Department of Agriculture's Beltsville Human Nutrition Research Center:

A balanced, varied and "prudent" diet is likely to furnish the chromium requirement . . . and will obviate the need for supplementation with chromium compounds that are commercially available, but not scientifically proven to be effective. Chromium supplementation, other than by dietary means, should be used only when advised by and under the supervision of a physician.

Chromium poisoning[3] occurs in animals at levels equivalent to a human dosage of 50 mg per day, which is 1,000 times the usual dietary intake. At that level, animals suffer liver and kidney damage and stunted growth. The only danger of chromium poisoning in humans is not from diet, but from chronic industrial exposure to chromate dust or solutions or supplementation with excessive quantities.

MANGANESE

Manganese is needed for reproduction, skeletal development and functioning of the nervous system. Manganese is a key part of certain enzyme systems believed to be involved in heart muscle metabolism, though how it does this is still under study. Heart muscle contains more manganese than other tissues.

The Food and Nutrition Board's estimated safe and adequate intake of manganese is 2.5 to 5.0 mg per day for adults.[1] Most people ingest between 2.5 and 7.0 mg per day. Whole grain cereals, leafy vegetables and nuts are good food sources of manganese. Lesser amounts are present in other vegetables and fruits, and still less is present in meat, fish and dairy products. Tea is very rich in manganese, containing 0.30 to 2.3 mg per cup.

According to E. J. Underwood,[3] manganese resembles iron and zinc in having a low order of toxicity. He states that manganese poisoning from human diets seems nearly impossible because "the human body has an extremely efficient homeostatic control mechanism regulating the level of manganese in the tissues." Toxic reactions to manganese have been observed from industrial pollution and among persons who work with manganese ores. Manganese supplements are not advisable unless prescribed by a medical doctor.

MOLYBDENUM

Molybdenum is a key part of the enzyme xanthine oxidase, which is needed by animals, humans and many forms of plant life. According to the Food and Nutrition Board,[1] although deficiency can be produced in animals, molybdenum deficiency in humans has never been observed. The Food and Nutrition Board's estimated safe and adequate daily dietary intake is 0.15 to 0.50 mg for adults. The concentration of molybdenum in food varies considerably, depending on the environment in which it is grown. Most people eat between 0.1 and 0.46 mg, with the main contribution coming from meat, grains and legumes.

Excess molybdenum, like excess zinc, interferes with the proper utilization of copper. Molybdenum toxicity[3] in humans, in the form of a gout-like illness, has been reported in only one Russian province. Toxicity in cattle is a problem in many parts of the world where the grass they eat is high in molybdenum and low in copper.

What Should You Do About Trace Minerals?

A balanced diet will provide most of the trace minerals needed by humans. Fluorine, an exception to this, can be provided by fluoridated water or other supplementary forms taken throughout childhood. Iron is another possible exception, but people at risk for iron deficiency should be medically followed with blood tests. Use of iodized salts will insure an adequate supply of iodine. Supplementation with the other trace minerals discussed in this chapter is rarely if ever necessary and should never be undertaken without competent medical advice.

References

1. Food and Nutrition Board: Recommended Dietary Allowances, 9th Ed. Washington, D.C., National Academy of Sciences, 1980.
2. Herbert, V. and Barrett, S.: Vitamins and "Health" Foods: The Great American Hustle. Philadelphia, George F. Stickley Co., 1981, p. 8.
3. Underwood, E. J.: Chapter 3 *in* Toxicants Occurring Naturally in Foods. Food and Nutrition Board, National Academy of Sciences, Washington, D.C., 1973.
4. Editorial, JAMA 229:324, 1974.
5. Murphy, B.: JAMA 230:962, 1974.
6. Davis, G. K.: *In* Vitamin-Mineral Safety, Toxicity and Misuse. Chicago, American Dietetic Association, 1978, p. 27.
7. Medical World News, September 8, 1975, p. 27.
8. FDA Consumer, April 1981, p. 15.
9. FDA Advisory Review Panel for Vitamin and Mineral Products for Over-the-Counter Use. Federal Register, Vol. 44, No. 53, March 16, 1979.
10. Journal of the American Dietetic Association: 66:277, 1975.
11. Cavalieri, R.: *In* Modern Nutrition in Health and Disease, 6th Ed. (R. Goodhart and M. Shils, Eds.). Philadelphia, Lea and Febiger, 1980, pp. 395-407.
12. Riggs, B. L. et al.: New England Journal of Medicine 306:46-50, 1982.
13. Causse, J. R. et al.: American Journal of Otology 1:206-213, 1980.
14. Consumer Reports: A Report on Fluoridation, July-August, 1978.
15. Pauling, L.: The Fluoridation of Drinking Water. (Position statement of

204

November 29, 1967, reaffirmed in letter to Dr. S. Barrett, March 26, 1981.)

16. Li, T. K. and Vallee, D. L.: *In* Modern Nutrition in Health and Disease, *op. cit.*, pp. 408-441.

17. Mertz, W.: Contemporary Nutrition, March, 1982.

21

Who Is At Risk For Deficiency?

How common is nutrient deficiency in the United States? Most physicians practicing in America today have never seen a case of beriberi, pellagra, scurvy or rickets. Indeed, cases of frank deficiency are rare enough to be considered "medical curiosities." Studies indicate that some population groups have intakes below the Recommended Dietary Allowances for various nutrients, but it is important to interpret these studies carefully.

Survey Results

The largest survey covering people of all ages was the Ten-State Nutrition Survey[1] conducted during 1968-70. This included almost 30,000 families in five states classified as "low-income" and five others classified as "high-income." A large proportion of the families surveyed were living below or only slightly above the poverty level. The study included not only dietary intake but medical history, body measurements and tests for anemia, plus other biochemical tests on infants, young children and the elderly. The largest racial group covered was white. Blacks were next in number, and the smallest group were Hispanics. Here are some of the report's key findings and conclusions:

• Many persons made poor use of the money available for food and made poor food choices that led to inadequate diets. In particular, many households seldom consumed foods rich in vitamin A. Also, there was a heavy emphasis on meat in many diets, rather than use of less expensive but excellent protein sources such as fish and poultry, or legumes and nuts.

• Many diets were deficient in iron content, but this was less a reflection of poor choice of foods than of the generally low level of iron in the American diet. The dietary data also showed that there were a substantial number of children and adolescents with caloric intakes below the dietary standards.

• Some groups appeared to be *at risk* for a few nutrients because their intake was below RDA levels. In general, the lower the group's economic status, the more chance of dietary inadequacy. The two nutrients at greatest risk were vitamin A and iron. But physical evidence of deficiency disease was uncommon. The fact that someone is "at risk" (consumes amounts of nutrients below the RDA) does not mean that person must suffer adverse effects. What it means is that the individual needs to pay more attention to food selection.

In 1971-2, the U.S. Department of H.E.W. (now H.H.S.) conducted the "First Health and Nutrition Survey" or "HANES-I Survey." This study covered all age groups and included blood analyses for vitamin and hemoglobin (iron) levels. One third or more of all age groups had daily intakes below the RDA for vitamin A, vitamin C, calcium and iron. Other studies[2,3] suggest that many elderly individuals who are poor also have borderline intakes of vitamin A, thiamin, riboflavin and vitamin C.

What Do These Findings Mean?

Vitamin promoters refer to these studies as proof that nutrient deficiency is so widespread that everyone needs to take supplements. But that is untrue.[4,5] First, remember that most of the people surveyed had low incomes. Many of the individuals in these groups lacked not only the money, but the knowledge or motivation to make wise food choices. In addition, there is more to good nutrition than vitamins and minerals. If you are concerned about nutrition and health, your basic course of action should be to learn how to select a nutritious diet using the principles of the Basic Four Food Groups described in Chapter 22. You should learn which times of life, lifestyles and other situations described in this chapter are associated with increased nutrient needs or risks of deficiency. Let's examine the common situations in which the possibility of deficiency should be considered.

Premature and Full-Term Infants: Some Needs are Similar

Vitamins E and K are the only nutrients not easily passed from mother to fetus across the placental connection.[6,7] Vitamin E deficiency poses a serious risk for prematures because it causes hemolytic anemia with breakdown of red blood cells. Despite the high levels of vitamin E in the blood of most women who give birth, there is very poor transfer of vitamin E to the fetus; and all prematures have very low blood levels of vitamin E. Breast milk usually contains good amounts of vitamin E, but experts[6,7] recommend that all premature infants, whether breast-fed or not, be given 10 units daily starting not later than the 10th day of life. Blood levels of vitamin E are only slightly low in full-term infants, so breast milk will usually provide enough for them. Bottle-fed infants should be given 5 to 10 units daily if their formula does not contain this amount.

Vitamin K deficiency causes hemorrhagic (bleeding) disease of the newborn. To prevent this, it is standard practice to give all infants a one-time injection of 0.5 to 1.0 mg of vitamin K_1 at birth, although full-term babies could be given 1 to 2 mg of vitamin K_1 by mouth instead.[4,6]

Iron supplements or iron-fortified formulas are needed by all infants, but not until the end of the 2nd month for prematures and the end of the 4th month for term infants (unless solid foods such as iron-fortified cereal or red meat have been started by this time.)[4,6,8] The fetus concentrates iron from the mother and stores a supply during the last 3 months of pregnancy. Cow's milk is a very poor source of iron, and breast milk is a fair source.[6,8] Infants may need to continue on iron supplements until they are eating a good solid food source like iron-fortified cereal or red meat.

Special Needs of Premature Infants

The needs of premature infants are proportionately greater than those of term infants because of initially smaller stores, increased demands of a more rapid rate of growth, and less complete intestinal absorption. Premature infants have little ability to absorb fats, so supplements of at least the fat-soluble vitamins (A, D and E) are commonly given—even if these infants are breast-fed.[7,9] In fact, the Committee on Nutrition of the American Academy of Pediatrics[6] advised in 1980 that for the first few weeks, pre-term babies be given a liquid multivitamin supplement that provides the newborn's RDA for every vitamin except folic acid. Folic acid, which is unstable in liquid, should be given separately at a dosage of 50 micrograms a day.[6,7] Feeding of a premature infant should be supervised by a competent pediatrician.

Special Needs of Full-Term Infants

According to some authorities,[6,10] breast-fed full-term babies need no vitamin supplements provided that the mother is well nourished. However, other experts[7,9] claim that not only cow's milk, but even breast milk is not a reliable source of vitamin D and recommend supplementation for all infants. Vegetarian mothers risk having a baby with severe anemia unless they take B_{12} supplements during pregnancy and while breast-feeding or unless a B_{12} supplement is administered daily to the child soon after birth.[11]

Bottle-fed term infants are usually given supplements of approximately infant RDA amounts of vitamins A, C and D, and 5 to 10 units of vitamin

E unless these are already in the prepared formula. If the formula diet includes some *whole* cow's milk, supplementation with vitamin A is not needed. The ingredients of prepared formulas are listed on their labels.

Childhood Needs

Physicians quite properly recommend vitamins for very young children until they are eating solid foods which contain enough vitamins. After the age of two, however, it is seldom necessary to continue supplements "just to be sure." In 1980, the Committee on Nutrition of the American Academy of Pediatrics[6] addressed this issue in a lengthy statement which began as follows:

> The last 50 years have witnessed a steadily increasing understanding of the biochemistry of vitamins and trace minerals and their role in human nutrition . . .
>
> As nutritional needs became more clearly defined, essential vitamins and minerals were incorporated into processed formulas with the aim of providing an essentially complete food for infants; specific nutrients likely to be lacking in the diet of older infants and children were used to fortify certain food products, such as infant cereal. Supplemental vitamin and mineral drops or tablets continued to be used, probably to a greater extent than necessary considering the more extensive fortification of food.

Listing various groups which are at risk for deficiency, the committee advised that children with poor eating habits and those on weight-reduction diets can be given a multivitamin-mineral supplement containing nutrients at not more than RDA levels. (But of course, improving eating habits is preferable to supplementation.) Fluoride supplements should be given to infants and children in communities whose water supply is not fluoridated. Also, children on strict vegetarian diets without adequate animal protein from dairy products or eggs may need supplementation, particularly with vitamin B_{12}.

As noted in Chapter 20, iron deficiency is a risk at all ages, but especially during periods of rapid growth such as infancy. It is standard practice for doctors to check the hemoglobin level of infants at the age of 9 months to be sure that they are not anemic.

Pregnancy and Vitamins

As can be readily seen in the 1980 table of Recommended Dietary Allowances in Appendix B, the Food and Nutrition Board[4] judged pregnancy to be a time of special need for nutrients. Compared to the nonpregnant woman, the RDA is 25 percent higher for vitamins A and E, 33 percent higher for vitamins C and B_{12}, 100 percent higher for folic acid, about 25 percent higher for riboflavin and pyridoxine, about 40 percent higher for thiamin, 15 percent higher for niacin, 50 percent higher for calcium, and about 70 percent higher for iron. A good diet should provide all of these except folic acid and iron, for which supplementation is usually needed in pregnancy.

The health of the newborn depends not only on the mother's nutrition during pregnancy but also on her nutritional status at the beginning of pregnancy. Pregnant women who are well nourished before conception are very unlikely to develop serious deficiency during pregnancy, though some may become marginally deficient in folic acid and iron. In contrast, women (usually from low-income groups) in poor nutrition status at the start of pregnancy show a crucial need for both a good diet and for supplements of 500 micrograms of folic acid, 10 mg of pyridoxine and 30 to 60 mg of iron during pregnancy.

Folic acid deficiency in pregnancy has been reported to cause abnormalities in the newborn.[12] In 1975, Dr. Victor Herbert[13] and colleagues found 16 percent of low-income black and Puerto Rican pregnant women in New York City seriously deficient in folic acid and another 14 percent borderline deficient.

A nutritional cause has been suspected for the serious high blood pressure of pre-eclampsia and toxemia, conditions that afflict a small percentage of pregnant women from middle and upper income families and about 15 percent of those from low-income families.[14] A specific nutritional deficiency has not been identified,[15] but some researchers[16] speculate that deficiency of pyridoxine and possibly zinc may be involved.

Pyridoxine deficiency in the mother rarely produces a deficiency in the newborn because nature favors the fetus. Therefore it is very rare that a newborn infant is deficient enough in vitamin B_6 to suffer convulsions. Some researchers suggest supplementation during pregnancy with 10 mg daily, but the Food and Nutrition Board judges that a diet containing the RDA of 2.5 mg daily is sufficient.

Consumption of less than the RDA of vitamin A occurs in some women in all ethnic and income level groups. However, harm to the fetus seems to require a severe deficiency of vitamin A in the mother, as may well be the case in very poor families with ethnic eating patterns providing very little vitamin A. The harm to the fetus in severe vitamin A deficiency is similar to the injury caused by overdosing with vitamin A during pregnancy—defects of the skull and brain, eye cataracts, cleft palates and harelips (see Chapter 7). Pregnant women should be wary of overdosing with vitamin A as well as not getting enough. No more than 5,000 IU should be taken by those who need supplements.

Vitamin C deficiency in pregnancy is not recognized as a common problem. Most experts believe there is no need for more than the pregnancy RDA of 80 mg per day.

Vitamin E deficiency in pregnancy is rare or nonexistent. Professor William Darby and his associates[17] studied 1,572 pregnant women and found the average vitamin E daily intake from diet was constant at about 15 IU throughout pregnancy. However, the average blood levels of vitamin E rose slowly and steadily from a normal of 0.9 mg percent during the first three months to a high of 1.4 mg percent during the last two weeks of pregnancy. A small number of women had complications during pregnancy, but there were no differences in vitamin E blood levels between those who had complications and those who did not. This study, reported in 1955 when supplementation was uncommon, indicates that pregnant women get along very well without vitamin E supplements.

Niacin (nicotinic acid) deficiency in pregnancy seems to be rare. Megadose supplements of niacin or niacinamide in pregnancy can be dangerous, increasing the risk of abnormalities in the newborn.[12]

Multivitamin supplementation in pregnancy is not needed by women eating a balanced diet. Only folic acid, iron and perhaps calcium supplements may be needed. In 1978, S. O. Adams[18] and co-workers studied 227 pregnant women, all of whom had a history of delivering low-birth-weight (LBW) babies. One-third of these women received a daily multivitamin pill at the one RDA dosage level and had a normal diet during pregnancy and yet yielded the same percentage of LBW infants as the other women. Both severe vitamin deficiency and overdosage can cause abnormalities in the newborn. Therefore, it is dangerous for a pregnant woman to self-medicate with a megadose vitamin mixture without medical supervision.

Can Supplements Prevent Birth Defects in High-Risk Mothers?

Used carefully under medical supervision—and only for a short period of time, supplements have reduced the risk in women who have had one or more infants with neural tube defects (NTD). The neural tube is a structure in the developing fetus which develops into the brain at one end and the spinal cord at the other. If the tube does not close, a "frog-baby" can result with no brain and a flat top instead of a head. Failure of the neural tube to close properly can also lead to spinal bifida or other defects of the nervous system.

These defects are not rare. Dr. R. W. Smithells and associates[19,20] disclosed in 1980-1981 that their cooperative study with other medical teams in England and Ireland was able to enlist 890 of such high-risk mothers. These researchers gave mothers planning to have more children a daily supplement containing iron, calcium and 8 vitamins, most in amounts from

1 to 3 times the RDA. Supplementation was begun about a month before conception was expected and was continued for about 6 weeks afterward, well past the time at which the neural tube normally closes. This timing of the supplements is called "periconceptual," meaning just before and just after conception. Here are the results of the study:

397 supplemented high-risk mothers had 3 infants with NTD

493 unsupplemented high-risk mothers had 23 infants with NTD.

Dr. Smithells and his associates believe that many cases of NTD may be caused by inadequate or even marginal dietary deficiencies. Their findings certainly deserve clarification by further research. Meanwhile, it is important to note that the Smithell studies do not support the idea that megadoses of vitamins should be taken throughout pregnancy. As described in Chapters 7, 8 and 11, self-medication with vitamins during pregnancy can lead to abnormal infants.

Birth Control Pills and Vitamins

The first hormonal oral contraceptives (OCs) which contained both female sex hormones (a progestin and an estrogen) were marketed in the United States in 1961 under the trade name, Enovid. During the mid-1960s, two researchers presented evidence that the hormones in the OCs could interfere with pyridoxine and thus cause depression in some OC users. These researchers were cited by Dr. P. W. Adams[21] and co-workers who found that 20 percent of women taking OCs were deficient in vitamin B_6 and 80 percent had borderline deficiency. However, the Food and Nutrition Board[4] in 1980 cited recent studies indicating that pyridoxine supplements are not needed by most OC users.

Because taking oral contraceptives brings about a state that resembles pregnancy for three-fourths of each month, it is not surprising that women using OCs need extra vitamins as do pregnant women. But megadoses are not needed. Deficiencies of pyridoxine, folic acid and a few other nutrients have been found in OC users who consumed adequate diets,[22-24] but such deficiencies are not common. In 1980, Drs. L. Boots and P. Cornwell[25] of the University of Alabama analyzed hundreds of reports and concluded that only a small minority of OC users need supplements and that most experts are opposed to megadose supplements. These researchers suggest that if difficulty occurs with one type of oral contraceptive, another type should be tried or the user should switch to a different contraceptive method. For oral contraceptive users, the prudent choice seems to be to eat a balanced diet providing the RDA of all vitamins and if concerned, to take a 1-RDA potency multivitamin or have the doctor evaluate the patient's individual needs.

There seems to be no deficiency in vitamins A or E during the use of oral contraceptives by women on a good diet. In fact, vitamin A blood levels rise in OC users probably because vitamin A moves out of liver storage. Many studies have shown that OCs have no effect on vitamin E status.[26,27] However, as noted in Chapter 9, vitamin E supplements increase the risk of blood clots in OC users.

Do Smokers Need Extra Vitamins?

Vitamin promoters have advertised widely that smoking "robs" you of vitamin C, and urge all smokers to take extra vitamin C. It is true that smokers tend to have somewhat lower blood levels of vitamin C than do nonsmokers, but these levels are still mostly within the normal range. The blood level of vitamin C is about 10 times the scurvy level in most smokers and about 4 times that level even in heavy smokers.

Some vitamin promoters cite the study of Dr. O. Pelletier[28] who found that vitamin C blood levels were 50 percent lower in male smokers than in male nonsmokers, but he compared only five of each. In a much larger trial, Brook and Grimshaw,[29] studied both men (22 smokers and 32 non-smokers) and women (34 smokers and 50 nonsmokers). The vitamin C blood levels of smokers were 25 to 35 percent lower than those of non-smokers, but were still within the normal range.

The men who smoked had about 30 percent less vitamin C in their blood than did the women. Deficiency symptoms begin at blood levels in the range of 0.13 to 0.24 mg% (varying from individual to individual), and severe deficiency (scurvy) occurs in a range from 0.00 to 0.16 mg%.[30] Among the men in the Brook and Grimshaw study, moderate smokers had vitamin C blood levels of 0.51 mg%, while the heavy smokers had 0.34 mg%. (Normal is 0.4 to 1.4 mg%.) Thus, even the men who smoked heavily had about twice the blood levels of vitamin C at which the first slight symptoms of deficiency appear.

Does Aspirin Interfere with Vitamin C?

Aspirin interferes with vitamin C if you do not have a cold or severe infection, but seems not to interfere during colds and infections.

According to a series of studies by a research group led by Professor C. W. M. Wilson[31] of the University of Dublin, aspirin does not block the absorption of vitamin C from the digestive tract, but in the absence of respiratory infections, it prevents vitamin C from entering the white blood cells which are the chief storage site of "ready" reserves of vitamin C. However, the Wilson group found that during the stress of colds, when aspirin is given along with vitamin C, it no longer interferes and the vitamin C level in the leukocytes rises. After recovery from a cold, aspirin again blocks vitamin C entry into leukocytes. In their 1973 study, the Wilson group observed that treatment with 10 grains (600 mg) of aspirin every 6 hours for 7 days, without vitamin C supplements, resulted in lowering of the plasma and leukocyte content of vitamin C within 4 days to a little below the normal range. They concluded that during infections the body seems to utilize vitamin C differently and more rapidly than in full health. These findings suggest that persons who take large daily dosages of aspirin for arthritis may need extra vitamin C, perhaps 200 mg daily.

Are Vegetarians At Risk?

Some people, for nutritional, religious or philosophical reasons, choose to eliminate meat or other animal protein foods from their diet. Vegetarians tend to be leaner than meat-eaters—which can be a real boon to their overall health. A well-balanced vegetarian diet may even prove beneficial to the heart, for without meat, the diet is usually lower in total calories, fat and saturated fat. But wise vegetarians must be well educated in the facts of nutrition and aware of their dietary needs.

The three main types of vegetarians are: *strict vegetarians (vegans),* whose diet is based on plant sources only; *lacto-vegetarians,* who add dairy products (milk and cheese) to their plant food; and *lacto-ovo-vegetarians,* who expand their diet to include both dairy products and eggs. Strict vegetarianism is not desirable for children under the age of five because it is difficult for vegans to meet the high requirements for protein and some other nutrients. Nor is strict vegetarianism a good idea for pregnant or lactating women. Excellent summaries of the special problems of vegetarian eating have been published by the Food and Nutrition Board[32] and the American Academy of Pediatrics.[6]

Unless they choose a proper balance of foods, strict vegetarians are at risk from several deficiencies, especially vitamin B_{12}. The other nutrients at risk are riboflavin, calcium, iron and the essential amino acids, lysine and methionine. For vegetarian children not exposed to sunlight, vitamin D can be in critically short supply. Zinc deficiency can occur in vegans because phytic acid in whole grains binds zinc and there is little zinc in fruits and vegetables. Since B_{12} is present only in animal foods and a limited number of specially fortified foods, vegans should probably take B_{12} supplements prescribed by a physician. Here is a case report about two people who didn't.

Val and Vera: Vegetable Victims[11]

Two-month-old Val smiled for the first time and his mother, Vera, turning from preparing a vegetarian dinner, was thrilled. She took great pride in following most of the rules for healthy family living and providing her husband and herself with a wide variety of foods in their strict vegetarian (vegan) diet. But she ignored, or perhaps did not know, the cardinal rule for vegans—and this nearly spelled disaster.

At four months, young Val began to show signs of health problems. He became lethargic, listless, no longer made baby "talk" sounds, and soon frightened Vera by becoming too weak to lift his head. During the next two months, the boy became increasingly irritable, his appetite became poor, and he gradually became unresponsive to anything or anyone. Alarmed, Val's parents finally took him to a large university hospital on the advice of their family doctor who found the little boy's body temperature to be very low (94°F). Val was carried to the hospital in a warmer.

Examination by the hospital doctors revealed little Val to be very pale, unresponsive even to painful stimuli with complete loss of head control and random eye movements. They found many purplish or black-and-blue patches all over the boy's buttocks and legs (evidence of bleeding into his skin). Val's liver was slightly enlarged. His head circumference was one-third of normal size, and skull x-rays indicated that his brain was not growing normally. His electrical brain wave patterns were very abnormal. Dark spots covered the back of his hands and tops of his feet and an odd skin eruption was noted in his crotch area.

Laboratory testing revealed that Val was suffering from severe anemia caused by lack of vitamin B_{12}. Because he had been breast-fed since birth, the doctors questioned the mother about her diet and learned she was a vegan—a strict vegetarian who ate no meat, fish or fowl or any dairy products. They told Vera that plant food—vegetables, fruits, grains and nuts—contained practically no vitamin B_{12}.

On the day he entered the hospital, Val had been given a transfusion of packed red blood cells which caused him to begin to respond a little to stimuli within a few hours. As soon as the blood and urine analyses had confirmed vitamin B_{12} deficiency, Val was given an injection of 1 mg (1,000 micrograms) of vitamin B_{12} each day for four days. Within four days, Val became alert and began to smile a little. His body temperature rose to normal and the odd skin eruptions disappeared. Within a few more days, his brain wave patterns returned to normal. After two weeks, Val was no longer anemic and his blood vitamin B_{12} level was more than adequate.

After six weeks at home, baby Val was returned for a check-up. His mother had continued to breast-feed him and she stayed on her strict vegetarian diet. Although signs of deficiency were no longer present, the doctors found that Val's B_{12} blood level had dropped close to the danger zone. So they prescribed 100 micrograms of vitamin B_{12} by mouth once a week for him. By the age of 9 months, Val's head had grown to normal size and his development appeared normal in all other respects.

While treating Val, the doctors also investigated his mother's nutritional state and found that her blood B_{12} level was slowly falling and had entered the danger zone. So she was persuaded to start taking regular vitamin B_{12} supplements also.

Alcoholism

Severe alcoholics usually eat irregularly, infrequently and inadequately. As calories from alcohol replace those from food, the condition of an alcoholic resembles that of near-starvation. According to Dr. Robert Olson,[33] the most likely deficiencies are of protein, thiamin, riboflavin, niacin, pyridoxine and folic acid, magnesium, potassium and zinc. The signs of alcoholic vitamin deficiency are those to be expected from a shortage of B-vitamins: the nerve control disruption typical of thiamin and pyridoxine deficit, the anemia of lack of folic acid, and the skin and gastrointestinal problems seen in riboflavin and niacin deficiencies. According to Dr. Olson, the violent convulsions occurring as withdrawal symptoms in severe alcoholism, the so-called "rum-fits," are also linked to B-vitamin deficiency, particularly that of pyridoxine.

Treatment of alcoholism in a hospital setting is customarily done by administering a high-protein diet, with high-potency multivitamin and mineral supplements, and B-vitamins often given by injection at the start.

Elderly Individuals

A number of factors may adversely affect the food intake and nutrition status of elderly individuals. The sense of taste may be decreased, and the efficiency of absorption from the intestines may decline. Individuals not used to cooking for themselves may not feel like preparing food. Total calories are usually decreased because of a reduction in physical activity. And some elderly persons have special conditions which require supplements whether or not their diet is unbalanced.

What is known about the nutrient status of older Americans? What percentage has daily vitamin intakes below the RDAs? The San Mateo County (Calif.) Study, conducted in 1948-49, showed little evidence of vitamin deficiencies among economically secure "middle-class" Americans.[34]

However, among the elderly poor, the evidence for a poor vitamin condition is strong. Dr. Alan Whanger[3] in 1973 cited national surveys, based on dietary recall, showing 40 percent of elderly poor had below-RDA dietary intakes of vitamin A, thiamin, riboflavin and vitamin C. This does not mean that they were all deficient, however, because the RDAs are set at several times the minimum requirements.

In 1978, O'Hanlon and Kohrs[2] published an excellent review of 25 surveys and studies which included the dietary intakes of elderly Americans. They found that the most common below-RDA intake was that of total calories. About one-third of the elderly had dietary intakes below the RDA for calcium (women more so than men), iron, vitamin A, thiamin, riboflavin and/or vitamin C. However, Dr. Herman Baker[35] and colleagues reported in 1979 that among 473 elderly people, intakes of pyridoxine, niacin and vitamin B_{12} were the most common nutrients consumed at below RDA levels.

What should an elderly person do who is concerned about good nutrition? The sensible thing is to eat a balanced and varied diet based on the Basic Four Food Groups as outlined in Chapter 22. Individuals who need help with planning their diet should consult their doctor or a registered dietitian. If poor absorption due to age is suspected, a 1-RDA potency multivitamin supplement daily may be desirable.

Malnutrition in Hospitalized Patients

A number of researchers have noted that the nutritional status of many patients hospitalized two weeks or longer leaves much to be desired.[36] Protein-calorie malnutrition had been found by some researchers in 25 to 50 percent of such patients.

Other Causes of Deficiency Disease

So far we have focused on risks and deficiencies due to *inadequate intake* of nutrients. According to Dr. Victor Herbert,[37] there are five other basic causes of nutrient deficiencies in humans: inadequate absorption, inadequate utilization, increased requirement, increased excretion and increased destruction.

• *Inadequate Absorption.* Impairment of the structure or function of the digestive organs may reduce vitamin absorption from food. Examples of this are chronic vitamin A deficiency due to poor absorption of fats and fat-soluble vitamins from the digestive tract as occurs in tropical sprue and cystic fibrosis of the pancreas. Pernicious anemia is caused by the inability to absorb vitamin B_{12} from food in the digestive tract.

• *Inadequate Utilization.* This may be inborn or acquired. The acquired defects usually result from malnutrition or disease. For example, B_{12} deficiency produces inadequate utilization of folic acid, alcohol can interfere with the utilization of several nutrients, and liver disease may interfere with vitamin utilization in several ways.

Drugs used for the treatment of disease can sometimes act as chemical antagonists to vitamins. The anti-tuberculosis drug, isoniazid, acts as an anti-vitamin-B_6 agent, and patients receiving it should ingest at least 10 times the RDA of pyridoxine daily. Also the anti-cancer drug, methotrexate, blocks utilization of folic acid, so very careful medical adjustment of folic acid daily dosage to about 20 to 30 times the RDA may be required.

A group of inherited diseases known as "vitamin-dependent inborn errors of metabolism" result from lack of the enzymes needed for various metabolic reactions involving vitamins. These conditions include enzyme defects in the metabolism of thiamin, nicotinamide, pyridoxine, biotin, vitamin B_{12}, folic acid and vitamin D. For example, pyridoxine dependency in the newborn, resulting in convulsions, is caused by defective production of the protein part of an enzyme for which B_6 is needed. In one such case, an infant required 30 times the RDA daily.[38]

• *Increased Requirement.* Lack of parathyroid hormone (hypoparathyroidism) increases the requirement for vitamin D to 50 to 100 times the RDA. This results from the fact that parathyroid hormone and vitamin D normally work together to control the absorption of calcium from the digestive tract in order to maintain the proper level of calcium in the blood. Without the hormone, only huge doses of vitamin D can do the job. The required level of supplementation would be extremely dangerous to normal persons but is safe for persons with hypoparathyroidism.

Extra vitamin K_1 is needed (by doctor's prescription) during prolonged use of antibiotics, since these tend to kill the beneficial bacteria that make vitamin K_2 in the intestinal tract.

• *Increased Excretion.* Liver or kidney disease can cause rapid and uncontrolled excretion of B-vitamins. So can some drugs such as thiazide diuretics and penicillamine.

• *Increased Destruction.* "Rebound scurvy" is an example. This is due to temporary rapid destruction of RDA amounts of vitamin C caused by the sudden reduction from megadoses (above 1,000 mg daily) down to normal dietary intakes (50-100 mg).

Therapy for Deficiencies

The dosage and the length of treatment with vitamin supplements for deficiency conditions depend on the cause. If a diet is found to be substandard, vitamin and/or mineral supplementation at the 1 or 2 RDA level can be used until the diet is improved. If deficiency disease from a faulty diet is diagnosed, megadoses should be used only until deficiency symptoms are cured and proper diet is adopted. Daily dosages in the range of 5 to 10 RDA for a few weeks are usually sufficient for this purpose. The other five causes of deficiency are associated with permanent (or longtime) abnormal conditions requiring medical evaluation and special vitamin and mineral therapy, often with megadoses.

The key point to remember about deficiency disease, however, is that it

218

should always be diagnosed and treated by a physician. Most symptoms of vitamin or mineral deficiency also occur in disorders unrelated to nutrition. Some deficiency conditions present a very difficult diagnostic challenge even for experienced physicians.

References

1. Highlights from the Ten-State Nutrition Survey: 1968-1970. HEW Publication No. (HSM) 72-8134.
2. O'Hanlon, P. and Kohrs, M.: American Journal of Clinical Nutrition 31: 1257, 1978.
3. Whanger, A.: Postgraduate Medicine 53:167, 1973.
4. Food and Nutrition Board: Recommended Dietary Allowances, 9th Ed. Washington, D.C., National Academy of Sciences, 1980.
5. Herbert, V.: Nutrition Cultism. Philadelphia, George F. Stickley Co., 1981, pp. 81-82.
6. American Academy of Pediatrics Committee on Nutrition: Pediatrics 66: 1015-1020, 1980.
7. Snyderman, S.: Nutrition in Infancy and Adolescence, *in* Modern Nutrition in Health and Disease, 6th Ed. (R. Goodhart and M. Shils, Eds.) Philadelphia, Lea and Febiger, 1980, pp. 753-780.
8. Hodges, R. E.: Nutrition in Medical Practice. Philadelphia, W. B. Saunders Co., 1980, pp. 202-209.
9. AMA Drug Evaluations: Vitamins and Sources of Vitamins. *In* Chapter 14, 2nd Ed. Acton, Mass., Publishing Sciences Group, 1973.
10. Taylor, K.: Rational Drug Therapy 9:1-6, 1975.
11. New England Journal of Medicine 29:317, 1978.
12. Nelson, M. and Fofar, J.: British Medical Journal 1:523, 1971.
13. Herbert, V. et al.: American Journal of Obstetrics and Gynecology 123: 175, 1975.
14. Peake, C.: Obstetrician-Gynecologist, Kalamazoo, Michigan; personal communication, Nov. 1, 1982.
15. Gibbs, C. E. and Seitchik, J.: *In* Modern Nutrition in Health and Disease, 6th Ed., *op. cit.,* p. 749.
16. Brophy, M. H. and Sieteri, P. K.: Am. J. Ob/Gyn, 121:1075, 1975.
17. Ferguson, M. F. et al.: Journal of Nutrition 55:305, 1955.
18. Adams, S. O. et al.: Journal of the American Dietetic Association 72:144, 1978.
19. Smithells, R. W. et al.: Lancet 1:339, Feb. 16, 1980.
20. Smithells, R. W. et al.: *Ibid.* 2:1425, Dec. 19/26, 1981.
21. Adams, P. W. et al.: *Ibid.* 2:517, Aug. 31, 1974.
22. Larsson-Cohn, U.: American Journal of Obstetrics and Gynecology 121: 84, 1975.
23. Ahmed, F. et al.: American Journal of Clinical Nutrition 28:606, 1975.
24. Briggs, M. and Briggs, M. H.: Current Medical Research and Opinion 2:626, 1975.

25. Boots, L. R. and Cornwell, P. E.: Continuing Education, Aug., 1980, pp. 39-47.
26. Horwitt, M. K. et al.: American Journal of Clinical Nutrition 28:403, 1975.
27. Tangney, C. C. and Driskell, J. A.: Contraception 17:499, 1978.
28. Pelletier, O.: American Journal of Clinical Nutrition 21:1259, 1968.
29. Brook, M. and Grimshaw, J.: *Ibid.* 21:1254, 1968.
30. Hodges, R. E. et al.: *Ibid.* 24:432-443, 1971; on p. 435.
31. Loh, H. S. and Wilson, C. W. M.: Journal of Clinical Pharmacology 15:36, 1975.
32. Food and Nutrition Board, Committee on Nutritional Misinformation: Vegetarian Diets. Washington, D.C., National Academy of Sciences, 1974.
33. Olson, R.: Modern Nutrition in Health and Disease, 5th Ed. (R. Goodhart and M. Shils, Eds.) Philadelphia, Lea & Febiger, 1973, pp. 1037-1050.
34. Watkin, D. M.: *In* Vitamins in the Elderly (A. N. Exton-Smith and D. L. Scott, Eds.). Bristol, John Wright & Sons, 1968, p. 66.
35. Baker, H. et al.: Journal of the American Geriatrics Society 27:444. 1979.
36. Butterworth, C. E. and Weinsier, R. L.: *In* Modern Nutrition in Health and Disease, 6th Ed., *op. cit.,* pp. 667-684.
37. Herbert, V.: Nutrition Cultism, *op. cit.,* pp. 121-123.
38. Scriver, C. R.: Pediatrics 26:62, 1960.

22

Wise Food Selection

Eat to live, and do not live to eat.
—English proverb, ca. 1410[1]

People who live to eat are usually fanatics who abandon all reason and common sense in their behavior. Such people usually become overweight and suffer poor health, often dying 10 to 20 years earlier than need be. Much more sensible and satisfying in the long run is eating to live—eating to be fit for a full and active life in this wonderful, frightening but fascinating world! Doing this requires wise food selections guided by the advice of nutrition experts and ignoring fad diets and false claims which abound for special diets and food supplements touted by pseudoscientists.

Wise food selection does not require expert knowledge of biochemistry or even much knowledge of what the various nutrients do once they enter your body. All it requires is knowledge of a few basic principles and the willpower to follow them. As stated by Dr. Victor Herbert:

> You don't need to know the biochemical properties of specific nutrients any more than you must know how the parts of a car work in order to be a good driver. Running the human machine, from a nutritional point of view, is quite simple. You need to recognize only four basic facts:
> 1. All the nutrients you need can be obtained by eating a balanced *variety* of foods.
> 2. Body weight is a matter of *arithmetic*. If you eat more calories than you need, you will gain weight. To lose weight, you must burn off more calories than you take in.
> 3. The basic principle of healthy eating is *moderation* in all things.
> 4. No proposed remedy should be considered safe or effective until *proved* to be safe or effective.[2]

What the Experts Say

Dietary balance is easily achieved by using the Basic Four Food Groups system described below. This system, devised in 1955 by nutrition scien-

220

tists at Harvard University in cooperation with the U.S. Department of Agriculture, provides a simple, practical method to plan nutritionally adequate diets. The Basic Four Food Groups are as follows:

- Fruit and Vegetable Group (fruits, vegetables, and their juices)
- Bread and Cereal Group (enriched and whole-grain breads, cereals and pastas)
- Milk and Cheese Group (milk, cheese, yogurt, and products made from milk, except butter)
- Meat and Alternates Group (meat, poultry, fish, eggs, dried beans, peas and nuts)

The average adult individual in good health can meet the Recommended Dietary Allowances (RDAs) for essential nutrients by consuming a daily average of 4 servings from the Fruit and Vegetable Group, 4 from the Bread-Cereal Group, 2 from the Milk and Cheese Group, and 4 to 6 ounces from the Meat and Alternates Group. Foods are assigned to their groups on the basis of their "leader" nutrients. Because nutrient composition within each group does vary from food to food, it is usually best to eat a wide assortment of foods within each of the Basic Four Food Groups.

A Daily Food Guide

The following plan is adapted from the 1979 Daily Food Guide developed by the U.S. Department of Agriculture,[3] slightly modified by Dr. Herbert.[2] The Guide divides commonly eaten foods into five groups according to the nutritional contributions they make—the Basic Four Food Groups and a fifth group (Fats, Sweets and Alcohol) composed of foods which provide calories but few other nutrients.

Calories are a measure of the energy which food provides. The extra calories you get and that your body does not use up are stored as fat. The minimum recommended servings in the Basic Four Food Groups average about 1,200 calories, provide adequate protein, and supply the vitamins and minerals you need daily. Thus your day's menu should be planned around this foundation. Almost all adults eat more than 1,200 calories.

You can personalize the Guide by fitting it to your calorie needs. All foods, except water and noncaloric drinks, have calories. Nutritionally, there are no "good calories" or "bad calories." Some foods give you little *but* calories, while others give you calories *plus* nutrients. How many calories you need depends upon how much energy you use up. Generally, older people need fewer calories than younger people, women need fewer than men, and bridge players and bookkeepers need fewer than tennis players and construction workers. Special tips for vegetarians are given in Chapter 21.

If you are gaining unwanted weight, or if you want to lose weight, cut down first from the fifth group (fats-sweets-alcohol). If you are still gaining weight, cut down next on portion sizes from the other groups. Cut *down,* but don't cut *out,* and select the lower calorie foods within each group. On the other hand, if you want to gain weight, eat larger or additional portions from the first four groups and include some foods from the fifth group.

Remember, this Guide gives you only the basics. You have to choose foods which meet your special needs and tastes.

Fruit and Vegetable Group (4 Servings Daily)

Include one good vitamin C source such as a citrus fruit or juice each day. Also frequently include deep yellow or dark green vegetables (for vitamin A) and unpeeled fruits and vegetables and those with edible seeds, such as berries (for fiber). For all fruits and vegetables count either ½ cup or a typical portion. Examples: one orange, half a medium grapefruit or cantaloupe, juice of one lemon, a wedge of lettuce, a bowl of salad, or one medium potato.

This group is important for its contribution of vitamins A, C, B_1 (thiamin) and B_6 (pyridoxine) and fiber, although individual foods in this group vary widely in how much of these they provide. That's why a wide variety should be eaten from day to day. Dark green and deep yellow vegetables are good sources of vitamin A. Most dark green vegetables, if not overcooked, are also reliable sources of vitamin C and folic acid (folacin) —as are citrus fruits (oranges, grapefruits, tangerines, lemons), melons, berries and tomatoes. Dark green vegetables are valued for riboflavin (vitamin B_2), folacin, iron and magnesium as well. Certain greens—collards, kale, mustard, turnip and dandelion—provide calcium. Nearly all vegetables and fruits are low in fat, and none contains cholesterol.

Bread and Cereal Group (4 Servings Daily)

This group includes all products made with whole grains or enriched flour or meal, including bread, biscuits, muffins, waffles, pancakes, cooked or ready-to-eat cereals, cornmeal, flour, grits, macaroni and spaghetti, noodles, rice, rolled oats, barley and bulgur. Count as a serving 1 slice of bread, 1 ounce of ready-to-eat cereal, or ½ to ¾ cup of cooked cereal, cornmeal, grits, macaroni, noodles, rice or spaghetti.

Select whole-grain and enriched or fortified products. These foods are important sources of B-vitamins and iron. They also provide protein and are a major source of this nutrient in vegetarian diets. Whole-grain products also contribute magnesium, folacin and fiber.

Most breakfast cereals are fortified at nutrient levels higher than those occurring in natural whole grain. In fact, some fortification adds vitamins not normally found in cereals (vitamins A, B_{12}, C and D). These extra vitamins are unnecessary if you are eating a balanced diet. There is no nutritional reason to pay inflated prices for over-fortified breakfast cereals to obtain vitamins present in other foods in your diet.

Milk and Cheese Group (2 to 4 Servings Daily)

This group includes milk in any form: whole, skim, lowfat, evaporated, buttermilk and nonfat dry milk. Also yogurt, ice cream, ice milk and cheese, including cottage cheese. Milk used in cooked foods—such as creamed soups, sauces and puddings—can count toward filling your daily quota in this group.

The number of recommended daily servings varies as follows: children under 9, 2 to 3 servings; children 9 to 12, 3 servings; teens, 4 servings; adults, 2 servings; pregnant women, 3 servings; nursing mothers, 4 servings. Count one 8-ounce cup of milk as a serving. Common portions of some dairy products and their milk equivalents in calcium are:

1 cup plain yogurt	= 1 cup milk
1 ounce Cheddar or Swiss cheese (natural or process)	= ¾ cup milk
1-inch cube Cheddar or Swiss cheese	= ½ cup milk
1 ounce process cheese food	= ½ cup milk
½ cup ice cream or ice milk	= ⅓ cup milk
1 tablespoon or ½ ounce process cheese spread; or	
1 tablespoon Parmesan cheese	= ¼ cup milk
½ cup cottage cheese	= ¼ cup milk

Note: You'll get about the same amount of calcium in each of these portions, but various amounts of calories.

Milk and most milk products are the major source of calcium in the American diet. They contribute riboflavin, protein and vitamins A, B_6, and B_{12}, and also provide vitamin D when fortified with this vitamin. Fortified (with vitamins A and D) lowfat or skim milk products have most of the nutrients of whole milk products, but have fewer calories.

Meat and Alternates Group (2 Servings Daily)

This group includes beef, veal, lamb, pork, poultry, fish, shellfish (shrimp, oysters, crabs, etc.), organ meats (liver, kidneys, etc.), dry beans or peas, soybeans, lentils, eggs, seeds, nuts, peanuts and peanut butter. Count 2 to 3 ounces of lean cooked meat, poultry or fish without bone as a serving. One egg, ½ to ¾ cup of cooked dry beans, dry peas, soybeans or lentils, 2 tablespoons of peanut butter, and ¼ to ½ cup of nuts, sesame seeds or sunflower seeds count as 1 ounce of meat, poultry or fish.

These foods are valued for the protein, phosphorus, vitamins B_6, B_{12} and other vitamins and minerals they provide. However, only foods of animal origin contain vitamin B_{12} naturally. It's a good idea to vary your choices among these foods, since each has distinct nutritional advantages. For example, red meats and oysters are good sources of zinc. Liver and egg yolks are valuable source of vitamin A. Dry beans, dry peas, soybeans and nuts are worthwhile source of magnesium. The flesh of fish and poultry is relatively low in calories and saturated fat. Seeds (such as sunflower or sesame) contribute polyunsaturated fatty acids.

Cholesterol, like vitamin B_{12}, occurs naturally only in foods of animal origin. About 15 percent total body cholesterol comes from food; and the rest is made in our livers and other body cells. All meats contain cholesterol, which is present in both the lean and the fat. The highest concentration is found in brain, other organ meats, egg yolks. Fish and shellfish, except for shrimp, are relatively low in cholesterol. Dairy products supply moderate amounts of dietary cholesterol.

Is getting enough iron a problem? It can be, particularly for young children, teenage girls and menstruating women. Meats are reliable sources of iron absorbable by the body. Whole-grain and enriched breads and cereals, dry beans and dry peas, and various other vegetables also contain iron. But the iron in these foods is well absorbed only when they are eaten at the same time as a good source of vitamin C (such as orange juice) or along with meat.

Fats, Sweets and Alcohol Group

In general, the amount of these foods to consume depends on the number of calories you require. It's a good idea to concentrate first on the nutrient-rich foods provided in the other four groups as the basis of your daily diet.

This group includes foods like butter, margarine, mayonnaise and other salad dressings, and other fats and oils; candy, sugar, jams, jellies, syrups, sweet toppings and other sweets; soft drinks and other highly sugared beverages; and alcoholic beverages such as wine, beer and liquor. Also included are refined but unenriched breads, pastries and flour products. Some of these foods are used as ingredients in prepared foods or are added to other foods at the table. Others are just "extras." No serving sizes are defined because a basic number of servings is not suggested for this group.

These products, with some exceptions such as vegetable oils, provide mainly calories. Vegetable oils generally supply vitamin E and essential fatty acids. Carbohydrates (starches or sugars) and proteins have 4 calories per gram (113 calories per ounce). Fats and oils have 9 calories (255 calories per ounce), but keep hunger pangs away longer. Alcohol has

7 calories per gram (198 calories per ounce), but few alcoholic beverages are 100 percent alcohol. Generally, the higher the alcoholic content, the higher the calories per gram.

Unenriched, refined bakery products are included here because, like other foods and beverages in this group, they usually provide relatively low levels of vitamins and minerals compared with calories.

"Junk Foods"

Although the term "junk food" is widely used in the media, it is an unpopular one with nutrition scientists. In a recent interview, Dr. Helen Guthrie, Professor of Nutrition at Pennsylvania State University, summed up the scientific perspective on this subject very neatly:

> As a nutritionist, I contend that there is no such thing as a junk food—a *totally* worthless food—any more than there is such a thing as a perfect food—one that meets *all* our nutritional needs. Admittedly, some foods contribute more essential nutrients and dietary factors than others. But I cannot think of one food that doesn't have *some* redeeming value *under the right circumstances*. The problem arises when these so-called junk foods become so important in our diet that other foods of higher nutritional value are excluded. The result is an inadequate junk *diet*. It is equally possible to eat a poor selection of our most sacred *nutritious* foods and wind up with a diet overburdened with some nutrients, yet deficient in others—another example of a junk diet.[4]

In other words, from the scientific standpoint, there are no junk foods, only junk (nutritionally unbalanced) diets.

Food Safety

Should we be worried about pesticides, additives and the overall safety of our food supply? Most of our country's top nutrition scientists believe that our food supply is the best and safest in the world, that the amounts of pesticides in it are insignificant, and that preservatives and other additives are of minimal risk and are needed to keep our food supply safe from bacterial contamination and other types of spoilage.

Although challenges to this viewpoint occur, almost all of them come from health food industry representatives or "consumer advocates" whose scientific judgment is faulty. Dr. Fredrick J. Stare, Emeritus Professor of Nutrition, Harvard University, and his Associate, Dr. Elizabeth M. Whelan, Executive Director of the American Council on Science and Health have written a fascinating book called *Panic in the Pantry*.[5] The section called "Toward a Healthier, Better-Nourished World—Where Eating is Fun Again" states:

We have to put our faith in the potential of scientific research to separate what is acceptable from what is hazardous, and assimilate the findings in a rational, unpanicked fashion . . . Eating should be an enjoyable not an anxiety-provoking activity . . . So, in moderation, eat, drink and be wary of those who raise questions about the safety of your food.

References

1. A Dictionary of Quotations (H. L. Mencken, Ed.). New York, Alfred Knopf, 1942, p. 329.
2. Herbert, V. and Barrett, S.: Vitamins and "Health" Foods: The Great American Hustle. Philadelphia, George F. Stickley Co., 1981.
3. Food: The Hassle-Free Guide to Better Diet. Home and Garden Bulletin No. 228. Washington, DC, U.S. Dept. of Agriculture, 1979. (Out-of-print, this has recently been republished in revised form by the American Dietetic Association.)
4. Guthrie, H.: Health, June 1982, p. 42.
5. Whelan, E. and Stare, F.: Panic in the Pantry: Food Facts and Fallacies. New York, Atheneum, 1977.

23

Heart Disease, Cancer and Diet

Hardly a week goes by without some comments in the media on heart disease, cancer and diet. Unlike most of the issues discussed in this book, the possible relationships between diet and heart disease or cancer are genuinely controversial—and many of the published comments are a reflection of disagreements among experts. Let's try to place these controversies in perspective.

Risk Factors for Heart Disease

The causes of heart disease are multiple and complex. Authorities have identified 8 major factors that can help predict the likelihood of having a heart attack. Called "risk factors" for heart disease, they are: heredity, age, cigarette smoking, high blood pressure, blood lipid abnormalities, diabetes, obesity and physical inactivity. "Lipid" is the scientific term for all fatty substances. Blood lipids include triglycerides (fats), cholesterol, phospholipids and lipoproteins.

Of course, heredity and age are not subject to our control, but the other 6 factors *can* be influenced by individual behavior. Cigarette smoking is by far the most serious risk factor in that smokers have many times the incidence of heart attacks as have nonsmokers at the same age. High blood pressure, which affects about 15 percent of American adults, can usually be controlled by medication and/or dietary measures. Diabetes, particularly the type which begins during adult life, can often be controlled by dietary measures. A well-designed program of regular exercise can benefit the heart, help to control weight, and tone the muscles. It can also have positive effects upon blood pressure and blood lipid levels.[1]

Causes of Atherosclerosis

The presence of high blood lipid levels is just one of many biological events associated with the development of atherosclerosis.[2-7] Six other factors and new hopes for controlling them are outlined below:

1. *Too much "bad" LDL-cholesterol and too little "good" HDL.* LDL refers to low-density lipoproteins and HDL refers to high-density lipoproteins chemically bound to cholesterol. Men with relatively high HDL-cholesterol have less heart disease than do men with low levels.[5]

2. *Spot injury to the artery wall.* Most experts believe that this is the first event in atheromatous plaque formation. This risk can be reduced by keeping blood pressure normal and avoiding chemicals injurious to the artery wall such as carbon monoxide (found in cigarette smoke) and excessive vitamin D (as noted in Chapter 8).

3. *Clot formation at the site of artery wall injury.* Plaque formation probably starts with an unwanted clot forming at the site of artery wall injury. Arterial walls can heal themselves without forming plaque if clots can be prevented. Dr. David Kritchevsky,[7] an international authority on cholesterol and lipids related to atherosclerosis, has said that blood clotting and platelet clumping "are closer to the main event at the scene of arterial wall injury and could be more important than cholesterol."

New hopes for reducing this risk have come from the discoveries of eicosapentenoic acid ("EPA") and prostacyclin. EPA, which is a highly unsaturated fatty acid, was found by Danish scientists[8] in the fat of ocean fish and seals. Dietary EPA may be the reason that Eskimos have less heart disease than Americans or Europeans despite the fact that they eat the world's highest-fat diet. Dr. Hugh Sinclair,[9] who lived with the Eskimos of Greenland in 1979, ate their marine diet for 100 days and found that his blood cholesterol and "bad" LDL were lowered and his "good" HDL increased. However, he experienced constant diarrhea and lost weight.[10]

Prostacyclin, discovered in 1976 by an English research team led by Dr. John R. Vane,[11] belongs to a series of hormone-like substances, each with a different action. It is secreted by the artery wall and is a powerful anti-clotting agent. However, the artery wall usually does not secrete enough prostacyclin to overcome the pro-clotting type of fatty acids in the blood platelets of Americans and Europeans.

In 1978, Dyerberg and Bang[12] joined with Moncada and Vane to publish evidence that in the Eskimo, EPA in the blood platelet walls converts into prostacyclin which turns off platelet clumping and thus prevents clots. Dr. Vane believes that prostacyclin is a circulating hormone which "has a very bright future in preventing various types of cardiovascular disease" because it is thousands of times more active than aspirin-like drugs in preventing blood clots. In 1982, he shared the Nobel Prize for Medicine for his discoveries. Synthetic prostacyclin is now available for experimental use.

Future study may well lead to a legitimate recommendation to increase the proportion of ocean fish oils (such as salmon or mackerel oil) in your total fat intake. But fish *liver* oils should be avoided, except for tiny doses for children, because of dangerously high levels of vitamins A and D.

4. *Impairment of the enzyme converting cholesterol to bile acids.* Most of the cholesterol made by the body or absorbed into it is eliminated by oxidation to bile acids which are eventually removed in the feces. A liver enzyme called "7-alpha-hydroxylase" controls the first step in the oxidation of cholesterol. Vitamin C may be involved in the function of this enzyme, but amounts above the RDA do not seem to increase the conversion of cholesterol to bile acids. Any inhibitor of 7-alpha-hydroxylase could raise cholesterol levels. Dr. Mann[5] suggests that carbon monoxide is an inhibitor.

5. *Overproduction of cholesterol by the liver.* Production of cholesterol in the body is controlled by an enzyme called (in biochemical shorthand) HMG-CoA-Reductase. Influenced by this enzyme, the liver stops making cholesterol soon after a cholesterol-rich meal. A Japanese biochemist, Dr. Akira Endo recently found a substance which can inhibit the function of HMG-CoA-Reductase. Trade-named "Compactin," the substance was tested for 4 to 8 weeks in 11 patients with very high blood cholesterol levels which were lowered by as much as 37 percent.[7] A natural inhibitor of cholesterol production may be present in milk, particularly fermented milk, which has been shown to lower blood cholesterol slightly. The administration of 3 cups of yogurt daily has lowered cholesterol by 9 percent (from 252 mg% to 230 mg%) in volunteers.[13]

6. *Lack of physical exercise*: This is a major risk factor. As Professor Mann[5] informs us: "The most impressive array of epidemiological evidence suggests that fit and active people are spared the complications of atherosclerosis." He cites six references in support of this viewpoint, including long-term studies by J. N. Morris[14] and associates in England. Dr. Mann's reports on the Masai tribesmen of Kenya, described in Chapter 17, vividly illustrate the benefits of physical activity.

Diet and Blood Lipids

It is well established that abnormalities of blood lipids (especially triglycerides and lipoproteins) are a risk factor for heart disease. It is also clear that blood lipids are affected by diet. Some other points which seem well established are the following:

• High-fat diets—with more than 40 percent or so of calories in fats—pose a risk for atherosclerosis and heart disease for many people, but probably not for infants, teenagers and those doing manual labor. Diets high in fats raise blood cholesterol even more than diets high in cholesterol and also increase the "bad" LDL, with a decrease in the "good" HDL-cholesterol.

• Dietary cholesterol is only one factor involved in the blood cholesterol level. Some people on low-cholesterol diets have a high blood cholesterol level, perhaps because of impairment of the liver enzyme that converts cholesterol into bile acids; and some people on high-cholesterol diets have a low blood cholesterol level.

• Merely increasing dietary cholesterol does not usually raise the blood cholesterol level of normal individuals. In 1976, for example, Slater and associates[15] found that adding 1 or 2 eggs per day to the diet of normal men for 2 to 6 weeks had no effect upon their blood cholesterol levels.

• According to most experts, high cholesterol blood levels (above 250 mg%) can only be reduced 10 to 15 percent by reducing dietary cholesterol. Levels below 220 mg% can be reduced by dietary changes only very slightly if at all.

• Low-cholesterol, low-fat diets usually lower the incidence of coronary heart disease but not the death rate from heart attacks.[5,16]

• Coronary heart disease does not strike only people with high blood cholesterol. Many patients taken to heart surgery with atheroma-clogged arteries have "normal" (below 250 mg%) blood cholesterol—and so do Masai tribesmen (as noted in Chapter 17) whose blood cholesterol levels are 170 mg% or below.

What Should We Do?

As you can see, the subject of diet and heart disease is quite complicated. The American Council on Science and Health[17] identifies three main schools of thought held by nutrition authorities:

Group #1 believes that the evidence is sufficient to advise rather broad dietary changes for most Americans. This group appears to include the U.S. Department of Agriculture, the U.S. Department of Health and Human Services (HHS), the American Heart Association, and among the academic experts, Dr. D. M. Hegsted of Harvard.[18] Their overall view was summarized in 1980 in a 20-page booklet called *Nutrition and Your Health: Dietary Guidelines for Americans,* issued jointly by the USDA and HHS.[19] The guidelines were: 1) eat a variety of foods; 2) maintain ideal weight; 3) avoid too much fat, saturated fat and cholesterol; 4) eat foods with adequate starch and fiber; 5) avoid too much sugar; 6) avoid too much sodium; and 7) if you drink alcohol, do so in moderation. This group generally believes that everyone's total dietary fat should be reduced from the current average of 40 percent of calories to 30 percent, that total daily cholesterol should be limited to 300 mg (the amount in 1 large egg), and that the proportion of total fat which is polyunsaturated should be increased.

Group #2 believes that it is inappropriate to recommend such drastic changes in the American diet and that both epidemiological studies and diet intervention trials (comparing the heart attack rate of a large group of people put on a low-saturated-fat, low-cholesterol diet for several years, with a similar group on regular American diet) over the past 20 years have failed to prove a relationship between such diets and deaths from heart disease. Dr. George Mann[5] summarized these arguments in a 1977 article, "Diet-Heart: End of an Era." This view is supported, I believe, by D. R. Reiser[4] and also by Dr. E. H. Ahrens,[16] a previous supporter of the diet-heart "theory," who in 1976 stated: "It is not proven that dietary modification can prevent atherosclerotic heart disease in man."

Group #3 takes a more moderate view—that the diet-heart relationship does *not* apply to everyone and that recommendations for dietary change should be made on an individual basis after clinical evaluation. This is the position advocated by the Food and Nutrition Board[20] of the National Academy of Sciences (NAS) in its 1980 20-page booklet, *Toward Healthful Diets*. The Board agrees that most sedentary people should reduce total dietary fat, but that infants, adolescent boys and pregnant teenage girls, as well as adults performing heavy manual labor, probably have no need to reduce the fat level of their diet below 40 percent of calories. Dr. Alfred Harper,[21] Chairman of the NAS Food and Nutrition Board during 1980, warns that it would be tragic if the USDA/HHS recommendation in *Dietary Guidelines for Americans* to "avoid too much fat" would keep children from drinking milk.

NAS's position on dietary cholesterol is that it is a minor risk factor primarily for people with abnormally high blood levels of cholesterol—levels above 250 mg% and especially above 300 mg%. The NAS report points out that cholesterol is essential to the body which itself makes 800 to 1,500 mg of new cholesterol daily, and that when cholesterol intakes rise above 300 mg per day in normal people, the body compensates by restricting absorption from the gut and slowing cholesterol production by the liver.

Dr. Kritchevsky[10] sums up the cholesterol controversy as follows: "Nobody argues with elevated blood cholesterol as a risk factor. The bitter fight is over the relation of dietary cholesterol to blood cholesterol." My own inclination is toward the NAS position—that persons with elevated cholesterol levels plus other risk factors for heart disease may benefit from lowering their dietary intake of cholesterol under medical supervision. For the rest of us, eating a balanced diet as described in Chapter 22 appears to be both the simplest and the most reasonable course of action.

Diet and Cancer

Epidemiology is a division of medical science concerned with the relationship between environment (including diet) and diseases in population groups. Epidemiologists seek to measure and explain the differences in the incidence of diseases among population groups.

The fact that people with similar hereditary background living in different parts of the world can have different cancer patterns indicates that environmental causes play an important role. Many factors in our environment are potential causes of cancer. They include substances in the air we breathe, the food we eat, and the water we drink. Environmental factors also include exposure to radiation (including sunlight) and many other types of experiences.

It is important to understand that epidemiological evidence alone is usually not enough to establish a cause-and-effect relationship between events—and that a great deal of additional research must be done to clarify the significance of epidemiological findings.

A recent issue of the medical journal *Your Patient & Cancer*[22] observes the following:

> Nowhere are the problems of science communications more apparent than when one looks at the public's notions about the relationships of diet to cancer. To the man on the street, what to eat to avoid cancer often reduces to "everything causes cancer, so why worry," or a hypervigilance about food that runs from fad to fad, report to report, headline to headline. But neither response is appropriate. There is simply too much scientific uncertainty still surrounding the subject. What is needed, however, is a greater appreciation for the fact that when it comes to preventing cancer, there are no simple answers.

Early in 1982, the National Academy of Sciences' Committee on Diet, Nutrition and Cancer became the first major scientific group to suggest to Americans what to eat to avoid some of the risks of cancer. The committee's complete report, *Diet, Nutrition and Cancer,* was published as a thick paperback book.[23] The objectives and limitations of the NAS report are explained as follows in Chapter 1:

> The public often demands certain kinds of information before such information can be provided with complete certainty . . .
>
> It has become absolutely clear that cigarettes are the cause of approximately one-quarter of all the fatal cancers in the United States . . .
>
> The public is now asking about the causes of cancer that are not associated with smoking. What are these causes and how can they be avoided? Unfortunately, it is not yet possible to make firm scientific pronouncements about the association between diet and cancer. We are at an interim stage of knowledge similar to that for cigarettes 20 years ago. Therefore, in the judgment of the committee, it is now the time to offer some interim guidelines on diet and cancer.

The "interim guidelines" fall into four categories:

• Reduce the proportion of calories from fats—all fats, not one particular type—from the 40 percent typical of the American diet to about 30 percent. (This is based on a statistical association between fat intake and certain types of cancer. Critics of the report point out that a similar association exists between cancer and the intake of proteins and total calories —as well as between cancer and obesity.)

• Include in the daily diet plenty of whole-grain cereals, fruits and vegetables, especially the fruits and vegetables high in vitamin C and beta-carotene, the provitamin A which the body can convert into vitamin A. (Citrus fruits are rich in vitamin C, and dark green and deep yellow vegetables are rich in carotenes. The NAS committee also suggests including members of the family *Cruciferae*: cabbage, broccoli, cauliflower and Brussels sprouts.)

• Minimize consumption of salt-cured, salt-pickled, and smoked foods. Epidemiological studies have found that people in some parts of the world who frequently consume such foods have a greater incidence of cancer at certain sites, particularly the stomach and esophagus. (Critics charge that these findings should not be applied to Americans.)

• Avoid excess consumption of alcohol, especially in combination with cigarettes. While there is slight evidence that excessive alcohol intake by itself may be associated with an increase of colo-rectal cancer, there is more evidence that excessive drinking and smoking together act with greater potency than either alone to increase cancers of the mouth, larynx, esophagus and respiratory tract.

Critical Responses

Many prominent scientists have strongly criticized the NAS report's dietary recommendations as inappropriate and premature. In the newsletter of the American Council of Science and Health (ACSH), Dr. Owen Fennema,[24] Professor of Food Chemistry at the University of Wisconsin accused the NAS committee of "composing judgments and educated speculations from factual associations that may or may not be causative in nature." Dr. Elizabeth M. Whelan,[24] ACSH Executive Director, said: "It appears to me that the NAS committee looked at the very preliminary, conflicting maze of data on diet and cancer and basically came to the conclusion that, well, it wouldn't hurt for people to change their diets, and it just might help. That isn't good enough, however, Public health professionals should not make firm recommendations until they have firm evidence that the lifestyle changes they advocate will really improve health and prevent disease. In the case of diet and cancer . . . study of this subject is in its infancy."

Dr. Robert E. Olson,[25] Professor of Medicine at the University of Pittsburgh School of Medicine calls *Diet, Nutrition and Cancer* "one of the most disturbing reports to come from NAS in recent years," He states further:

It is disturbing to laymen who are told, in effect, that . . . certain quite specific and wide-reaching changes in their diet should be made in order to reduce the risk of cancer. It is disturbing to scientists because it is a superficial and uncritical review . . . followed by a series of recommendations which, in fact, do not follow logically from a critical review of the scientific literature.

Even worse was the press release . . . that inserted examples of foods to be banned or promoted that were not, in fact, discussed or even mentioned in the body of the report . . . Also, as one goes from the body of the report to the "Executive Summary" and thence to the press release, there is an increasing hardening of the conclusions of the report. The scientific uncertainties and caveats are excised, and the pronouncements and proscriptions become as thunderous as the Ten Commandments. To call these "interim guidelines" has no meaning to the public. They have been received as authoritative rules for good health.

To compare the state of knowledge regarding smoking and cancer in 1964 with that regarding the role of diet and cancer today is ludicrous. In 1964 there was clear evidence that tobacco contained carcinogens . . . Clinical observations on thousands of patients and autopsy studies of smokers and nonsmokers had shown that many kinds of damage to body function, organ cells and tissues occurred more frequently in smokers than nonsmokers.

What is particularly regrettable about this report is the emphasis put on diet, as opposed to smoking, as the major risk factor for cancer in this country . . . No rational person can escape the conclusion that cigarette smoking is the single most important health risk factor, not only for cancer, but for a variety of other diseases as well.

What Should You Do?

It seems to me that the main messages of the NAS report about your diet are to keep dietary fats below 35 percent of total calories and to avoid dietary extremes or unbalance of any type. Does this require you to do anything different from what we recommend in Chapter 22? I don't think so. The keys to good nutrition are still *moderation, balance* and *variety*. If you make it a practice to balance your diet by selecting from a wide variety of foods within each of the Basic Four Food Groups, you will automatically avoid the unbalanced and extreme forms of food intake which may be associated with a higher incidence of both heart disease and cancer.

References

1. Darden, E.: Your Guide to Physical Fitness. Philadelphia, George F. Stickley Co., 1981, p. 53.
2. Report of Task Force on the Evidence Relating to Six Dietary Factors to the Nation's Health, *in* American Journal of Clinical Nutrition 32:2619, 1979.

3. Glueck, C. and Conner, W.: *Ibid.* 31:727, 1978.
4. Reiser, R.: *Ibid.* 31:865, 1978.
5. Mann, G. V.: Diet-Heart: End of an Era, *in* New England Journal of Medicine 297:644, 1977.
6. Nutrition Today Nov./Dec. 1977, pp. 11-27.
7. Leff, D.: Medical World News, June 23, 1980, p. 47.
8. Dyerberg, J. and Bang, H.: Lancet 2:433, Sept. 1, 1979.
9. Sinclair, H.: *Ibid.* 1:414, Feb. 23, 1980.
10. Kritchevsky, D.: Personal communications, Nov./Dec. 1982.
11. Moncada, S., Gryglewski, J., Bunting, S. and Vane, J.: Nature 263:663, 1976, cited in Dyerberg and Bang, 1979, *loc. cit.*
12. Dyerberg, J., Bang, H., Stoffersen, E., Moncada, S. and Vane, J.: Lancet 2:117, 1978, cited in Dyerberg and Bang, 1979, *loc. cit.*
13. Hepner, G. et al.: American Journal of Clinical Nutrition, Jan. 1979; cited in Medical World News, March 19, 1979, p. 44.
14. Morris, J. N. et al.: Lancet 1:333, Feb. 17, 1973.
15. Slater, G. et al.: Nutrition Reports International 14:249, 1976.
16. Ahrens, E. H., Jr.: Annals of Internal Medicine 85:87, 1976.
17. ACSH: Diet Modification: Can It Reduce the Risk of Heart Disease? New York, American Council on Science and Health, 1982, pp. 12-13.
18. Hegsted, D. M.: American Journal of Clinical Nutrition 31:1504, 1978.
19. Nutrition and Your Health: Dietary Guidelines for Americans. Washington, D.C., U.S. Departments of Agriculture and Health and Human Services, 1980.
20. Food and Nutrition Board: Toward Healthful Diets. Washington, DC, National Academy of Sciences, 1980.
21. Harper, A. E.: *In* Nutrition Today, March/April, 1980, p. 19.
22. Mazola's Nutrition/Health Information Service: Diet and cancer—what do we know, so far? Your Patient & Cancer, June 1982, pp. 49-59.
23. NAS Committee on Diet, Nutrition and Cancer: Diet, Nutrition and Cancer. Washington, DC, National Academy of Sciences, 1982.
24. ACSH News and Views, Nov./Dec. 1982.
25. Olson, R.: Diet, nutrition and cancer—a critical review. *In* Diet, Nutrition and Cancer: A Critique, Special Publication No. 13, Council for Agricultural Science and Technology (CAST), Oct. 1982, pp. 55-61.

24

Should You Take Supplements?

A poor diet plus vitamins is still a poor diet.
—Art Ulene, M.D.

Three issues should be involved in deciding whether to take supplements: need, safety and cost. Most people who take supplements take a daily multivitamin or multivitamin/mineral pill for "insurance"—to be sure they get enough. I believe that most healthy individuals can get all of the nutrients they need by eating a balanced variety of foods as described in Chapter 22. Promoters of "nutrition insurance" claim that everyone needs to take supplements. This is certainly *not* true. As described in Chapter 21, some groups have special nutrient needs or are "at risk" for deficiency for other reasons—but the decision to supplement or not to do so should be based on logic and made on an individual basis.

How to Get Expert Advice

Supplement promoters also make it a point *not* to tell you that vitamins and minerals are needed only in tiny amounts that are readily available from foods. Rather than falling for scare propaganda, if you are worried about whether your diet contains enough nutrients, why not have it analyzed by an expert? Simply write down everything you eat over a 1-week period and ask your doctor or a registered dietitian what they think of your food choices. The name of a suitable dietitian can be obtained from your doctor or by calling your local dietetic society or a local hospital dietary department. Be wary of people who call themselves "nutrition consultants." While some people using this title are highly trained professionals who have studied at reputable universities, others are "graduates" of unaccredited schools or other types of diploma mills.

If you learn that your diet is deficient in any respect, the wisest course of action is to improve your food choices to achieve dietary balance. Dr.

Victor Herbert expresses this point very elegantly by calling foods "the rational packages of nature."

Don't Go Overboard!

Whatever the reason, if you decide to take a supplement for "insurance," you should look at the labels of multivitamin or multivitamin/mineral products and select one which contains no more than 100 percent of the U.S. RDA for any ingredient. Dosages over the RDA do not give extra protection but increase your chances of toxic effects. Despite suggestions to the contrary, there are no significant differences in quality from brand to brand, so buy the least expensive one you can find. You probably won't need to spend more than a penny or two a day.

If you have a health problem, I suggest that you seek medical care and don't try to out-think your doctor by attempting to "cure" yourself with high doses of vitamins or minerals. If you are inclined to take them, share this information with your doctor. Remember that the number of medical conditions which large dosages might help is quite small and that all such conditions require medical supervision. Remember, too, that you are more likely to have troublesome side effects than to benefit from large amounts of self-prescribed supplements.

Appendix A: Glossary

"a": As a prefix to a word, meaning "without" or "absence of."

Abort (from Latin *abortere,* to miscarry): 1) To cause expulsion of the fetus before time of survival ability (viability); 2) to slow or stop the progress of disease; 3) to slow or stop growth or development.

Acetylcholine: An ester derivative of choline, widespread in the body, that plays an important role in the transmission of nerve impulses.

ADA: American Dietetic Association, an organization of professional dietitians, most of whom are "Registered Dietitians" (R.D.s).

Additives: Chemical compounds added to foods to improve flavor, appearance, shelf life and/or nutritive value.

AMA: American Medical Association.

Amino acids: Some 22 basic chemical compounds which are the building blocks of proteins. The 8 which cannot be made by the body are called "essential" and must be obtained from food.

Amygdalin: A bitter tasting substance in bitter almonds and apricot kernels, recently promoted as the quack cancer cure, laetrile.

Anemia: A group of disorders characterized by deficient oxygen-carrying capacity of the blood caused by a defect in the number and/or quality of the red blood cells.

Angina pectoris: Pain and oppression (feeling of heavy pressure) about the heart. A paroxysmal attack caused by insufficient supply of blood to the heart and characterized by severe pain usually radiating from the heart to the shoulder and down the left arm.

Antibiotic: Any of a variety of substances both natural and synthetic that inhibit the growth of microorganisms or destroy them.

Antioxidant: A substance that protects sensitive compounds from being oxidized, usually by letting itself be oxidized. Vitamins C and E are antioxidants.

Apoenzyme: The protein portion of an enzyme system. (See holoenzyme and coenzyme.)

Arteriosclerosis: "Hardening of the arteries," a condition characterized by

239

thickening and hardening of artery walls which become narrower and less elastic.

Ascorbic Acid: The chemical name for vitamin C.

Atheroma: Fatty degeneration or thickening of the wall of the large arteries, usually in the form of a bulge or plaque. (See plaque.)

Atherosclerosis: A type of arteriosclerosis characterized by cholesterol-filled fatty deposits which develop inside artery walls.

ATP: Adenosine triphosphate, a compound which contains three phosphoric acid groups linked in high-energy bonding which, when split by an enzyme within tissue cells, releases much energy.

Biopsy: Excision (cutting out) of a small piece of tissue for microscopic examination.

Biotin: One of the B-vitamins.

Calorie: A unit of measure that expresses the energy value of foods. Physicists use the word "calorie" to mean the amount of energy needed to raise one gram of water one degree centigrade. When nutrition scientists refer to the number of calories in food, they use the unit "kilocalorie" or "Calorie" (spelled with a capital C) which is actually 1,000 little calories. In common usage, however, the term "calorie," although spelled with a small c, means kilocalorie.

Carbohydrate: A ready source of food energy commonly found as starches and sugars and made up of carbon, hydrogen and oxygen.

Carcinogen: A cancer-causing substance.

Cholecalciferol: Vitamin D_3, formed by the action of sunlight on human skin and present in a few animal products.

Cholesterol: A waxy, fat-like substance essential to life and present in every animal and human cell. Cholesterol is manufactured by several body tissues (particularly the liver). It is found only in foods of animal origin.

Claudication: As an "intermittent claudication," a severe pain in the calf muscles during walking which subsides with rest, and caused by inadequate blood supply to the leg.

Cobalamin: Vitamin B_{12}. Found in foods of animal origin, it is bound in a stable complex until freed in the stomach where it unites with Intrinsic Factor—without which it is unabsorbable.

Coenzyme: This is the "missing" non-protein part that combines with the protein part (the apoenzyme) to form a complete enzyme. A good way to visualize this is to think of the enzyme's protein part as a key which cannot turn a lock or a power switch because one of its teeth (the co-enzyme) is missing. Most coenzymes are vitamins or minerals.

Coronary: Meaning "encircling," the word is used to describe the cluster of blood vessels that supply the heart muscle (coronary arteries).

Cortisone: One of the powerful anti-inflammatory hormones secreted by the cortex of the adrenal gland.

Creatine: A compound, synthesized by the liver, which forms the high-energy-releasing creatine phosphate needed for optimum muscle function.

Cyanocobalamin: A stabilized form of vitamin B_{12}.

Cyst: A closed sac or pouch with a definite wall which contains fluid, semi-fluid or solid material. A cyst is usually an abnormal structure.

Dietitian: Registered Dietitians (R.D.s) are nutrition professionals, usually bachelor or master level nutrition graduates, who have additional clinical experience, pass a comprehensive written examination, and participate regularly in continuing education programs approved by the American Dietetic Association.

DNA: Deoxyribonucleic acid, one of the two types of nucleic acids (the other is RNA) found in the cells of almost all living organisms. Each DNA strand carries a specific set of genes that determine hereditary traits.

Double-blind technique: A method of investigation in which about half the subjects are given the actual test substance (a drug or vitamin) and the rest receive a placebo (dummy pill) which looks and tastes the same as the test substance. Neither the subjects nor the investigators know who is receiving the test substance.

ECG (EKG): Electrocardiogram, a method of recording patterns of electrical activity of the heart.

Embolism: Obstruction of a blood vessel by a mass (usually a blood clot) carried through the blood stream.

Encephalomalacia: Abnormal softening of the brain tissues.

Enrichment: The addition of nutrients to foods to return their nutrient value to pre-processing levels.

Enzymes: Protein substances, usually needing a non-protein coenzyme (a vitamin or mineral), which trigger and speed up chemical changes within the body.

Ergocalciferol: Vitamin D_2, made synthetically by irradiating ergosterol with ultraviolet light. It is as potent as natural vitamin D_3, but has a minor difference in molecular structure.

Essential nutrients: Specific nutrients which cannot be synthesized by the body and must therefore be obtained from foods.

Estrogens: One class of female sex hormones, the other class being the progestins. The naturally occurring estrogen is estradiol.

Et al.: An abbreviation of the Latin *et alii,* meaning "and others."

Extrinsic Factor (EF): An old term for vitamin B_{12}, it refers to the fact that B_{12} must be obtained from the diet (outside of the body—extrinsic) and must combine with an internal (intrinsic) factor secreted by the stomach before it can be absorbed.

Faddist: In nutrition, one who attributes non-existent health-promoting properties to foods or food substances.

Fat: A chemical compound composed of three fatty acids plus glycerol. Fats may be animal or vegetable in origin, man-made or synthesized in the laboratory, solid or liquid at room temperature.

Fatty acids: Components of fat which are structurally classified as "saturated" or "unsaturated."

FDA: Food and Drug Administration, the branch of the U.S. government's Department of Health and Human Services charged with monitoring food safety and controlling the permits for marketing new drugs.

Fibrocyst: A fibrous tumor, usually benign, which has undergone cystic degeneration or has accumulated fluid.

FNB: Food and Nutrition Board, an advisory panel of experts which is a subdivision of the National Research Council (NRC) of the National Academy of Sciences (NAS).

Fluoridation: A valuable public health procedure by which the concentration of the mineral nutrient *fluoride* in water supplies is adjusted to one part fluoride to one million parts water. Use of fluoridated water throughout childhood reduces the incidence of tooth decay by 60 to 70 percent.

Folacin: A generic term covering several complex micronutrients that intestinal bacteria split to form folic acid, one of the essential B-vitamins.

Folic acid: One of the B-vitamins essential to the production and maintenance of red blood cells.

g: Abbreviation for "gram."

Gastrointestinal ("G.I."): Pertaining to the stomach and intestines.

Gram: A metric measure of weight, equal to 1000 milligrams, 1/1,000 of a kilogram and 1/28 of an ounce.

HDL: High-density lipoprotein, one of three main types of lipoproteins in circulating blood which carry cholesterol. The others are LDL and VLDL. (See *Lipoprotein.*)

HEW: Former name of the current U.S. Government Department of Health and Human Services; HEW meant Health, Education and Welfare.

Hepatic: Pertaining to the liver.

Holoenzyme: The complete enzyme including the apoenzyme (protein part) and the coenzyme (usually a vitamin or mineral).

Homeostasis: The body's complex control mechanism for maintaining equilibrium and constancy of character of the body fluids (including blood).

Hydrocortisone: One of the powerful anti-inflammatory hormones secreted by the adrenal cortex.

Hyper-: A prefix meaning above, excessive or beyond. It commonly refers to abnormally high levels.

Hypo-: A prefix indicating less than, below or under. One synonym is *Sub-:* A synonym for *hypo-.* It commonly refers to a lack of or deficiency in.

Hypochromic: Having less color. Hypochromic anemia is a condition of the blood in which the red blood cells have a reduced hemoglobin content, as is found in iron deficiency anemia.

Idiopathic: Pertaining to a disease or condition for which no cause has yet been determined.

Intrinsic Factor (IF): A specialized protein secreted by the stomach wall with which dietary vitamin B_{12} must unite before it can be absorbed. Without IF, pernicious anemia develops despite adequate B_{12} in the diet.

Infarction: Formation of an infarct, an area of tissue which is injured or dies following cessation of blood supply. A myocardial infarction is one type of heart attack.

Intravenous: The introduction of substances directly into a vein by injection or slow infusion.

Isomers: Chemical compounds that have the same chemical structure except for variation in the spatial arrangements of their atoms. They can be limited to one pair or comprise several.

IU: International Unit, a standard of potency used by the FDA for vitamins A, D and E.

Laetrile: A quack cancer remedy derived from apricot pits. Consisting mainly of amygdalin, laetrile is capable of releasing cyanide within the body. It is also called "vitamin B_{17}," although it is not a vitamin.

LDL: Low-density lipoprotein, one of three main types of lipoproteins circulating in the blood. (See *Lipoprotein.*)

Leukocytes: The white blood cells of circulating blood.

Lipid: A general term for fat and other substances with chemical and physical properties similar to those of fat.

Megadose: A very large dose. For vitamins it is usually 10 or more times the RDA—except for vitamin D for which it is 5 times the RDA.

Megavitamin: A high-dosage vitamin.

Metabolism: A term used to describe the chemical processes which occur in the body.

Microgram (μg): A unit of weight equal to 1/1000 of a milligram or one-millionth of a gram.

Milligram (mg): A unit of measure of weight, equal to 1/1000 of a gram or about 1/28,000 of an ounce.

Monounsaturated fats: Liquid at room temperature, these fats are believed neither to raise nor lower blood cholesterol levels. They are found primarily in olive and peanut oils.

Myocardial: Pertaining to the heart muscle.

Nanogram: A unit of measure of weight equal to one-billionth of a gram, or one-millionth of a milligram.

National Academy of Sciences (NAS): An independent select group of scientists within which operates the National Research Council (NRC), the U.S. government's primary source of advice on science-related matters. The Committee on Dietary Allowances is part of the Food and Nutrition Board, a division of the NRC.

Neurological: Pertaining to the nervous system.

NHF: National Health Federation. An organization that promotes unproven methods.

Niacin: A term commonly used for nicotinic acid, one of the B-vitamins (formerly called vitamin B_3). However, the niacin content of a food usually includes not only its preformed nicotinic acid food, but also the smaller amounts of niacin the body can make from the amino acid, tryptophan.

Niacinamide: The amide derivative of nicotinic acid—the form that is biologically active in the body.

Nicotinic acid: One of the B-vitamins, commonly called niacin, which converts in the body to an active form, nicotinamide (niacinamide).

Nicotinamide: Niacinamide.

NRC: National Research Council, one of the main subdivisions of the National Academy of Sciences.

Nutrients: Some 50 known food substances—including protein, fat, carbohydrate, vitamins, minerals and water—which are required to nourish the body.

Nutrition: The science of foods, their components, and their relationship to health and disease.

Obesity: Excessive body weight due to the presence of surplus fat.

Osteoporosis: Loss of bone density, with increased porosity and subsequent brittleness.

Oxidant: A chemical readily capable of oxidizing (withdrawing electrons from) adjacent molecules. In the human body, oxygen is essential, but small amounts can sometimes form peroxides which are powerful and destructive. The body needs antioxidants to destroy these peroxides.

Oxidation: The action of an oxidant which, in oxidizing a substance, undergoes "reduction" itself.

Placebo: An inactive substance given to satisfy the patient's demand for medicine. Placebos are also used in controlled studies of drugs, wherein one group of subjects is given a placebo and a similar group is given the drug being tested.

Plaque: An arterial plaque is a fatty deposit in the inner artery wall that accumulates calcium and fibrin and results in a bulge (see atherosclerosis). Dental plaque is the bacterial film on the surface of the teeth.

Platelets: Small, colorless bodies in circulating blood. They aid blood clotting in wounds by releasing an enzyme which, together with calcium, converts prothrombin into thrombin, an enzyme which causes the final phase of clotting. Platelets also help clotting by clumping together in an open wound.

Polyunsaturated fats: These fats abound in plant seed oils (safflower, sunflower, cottonseed, soybean, sesame and walnut) and are liquid at room temperature. They may be effective in lowering blood cholesterol when used to replace some of the saturated fat in the diet.

Progestin: One of the two types of female sex hormones, the other type being the estrogens. The naturally occurring progestin is called *progesterone*.

Proteins: Very large compounds of many kinds of amino acids linked together in very long chains. Proteins are essential to tissue synthesis and the regulation of body function.

Prothrombin: A chemical substance in blood, which, when activated by a certain enzyme, interacts with calcium to produce thrombin.

Prothrombin time: A test of clotting time. Too short a clotting time indicates an abnormal tendency toward clotting; too long a time means a tendency toward internal bleeding.

Pyridoxal: A natural form of vitamin B_6 which occurs in foods of plant origin and is biologically active in the body.

Pyridoxamine: Another natural form of vitamin B_6 which occurs in foods of plant origin and is biologically active in the body.

Pyridoxine: A third naturally occurring form of vitamin B_6, which is obtained only from animal products and is converted in the body to the active forms, mainly to pyridoxal.

Pulmonary: Pertaining to the lungs or structures serving the lungs.

RDAs: Recommended Dietary Allowances. As defined by the Food and Nutrition Board of the National Research Council/National Academy of Sciences, they are: "the levels of intake of essential nutrients considered

. . . on the basis of available scientific knowledge to be adequate to meet the known nutritional needs of practically all healthy persons."

Reduction: The opposite of oxidation in chemical and biological systems.

Renal: Pertaining to the kidney.

Retina: The structure at the back of the eye that receives the visual image from the eye's lens and converts it into nerve signals so that the brain can visualize.

Retinal: An active form of vitamin A (retinol), essential for the formation of the "visual pigments" in the retina of the eye.

Retinoids: Derivatives of vitamin A (retinol), usually the acids formed by vitamin A oxidation, such as retinoic acid.

Retinol: Scientific name for vitamin A.

Riboflavin: Vitamin B_2.

Rickets: A vitamin D-deficiency disease in children characterized by poor and defective bone growth, with permanent crippling in some cases.

RNA: Ribonucleic acid, one of the two genetic controllers present in the nucleus of all cells of living things.

Saturated fats: These fats are found primarily in animal products (meat, eggs, lard, butter, cream, whole milk and whole milk cheese) and are usually solid at room temperature. They are also found in coconut and palm oils.

Schizophrenia: A group of mental disorders characterized by disturbances of thinking, mood and behavior.

Scorbutic: The condition of scurvy, a vitamin C-deficiency disease.

TE: Tocopherol Equivalent, a new unit of potency for vitamin E.

Thiamin: Vitamin B_1.

Thrombophlebitis: Blood clot and inflammation of the blood vessel, usually in a leg vein.

Thrombosis: The development of a blood clot.

Thrombus: A blood clot that obstructs a blood vessel or a cavity of the heart.

Tocopherols: The various forms of vitamin E.

Triglycerides: The primary form of lipid in the diet and the blood, and the usual storage form of fats in the body. Triglycerides are synthesized in the body from carbohydrates, protein and alcohol. They are also absorbed from food.

Unsaturated fats: Fats which contain less hydrogen than saturated fats. They are liquid or semi-solid at room temperature.

Vitamin: An organic (carbon-containing) substance required in tiny amounts to promote one or more specific and essential biochemical changes within the living cell. Its lack for a prolonged period of time must cause a specific deficiency disease which is quickly cured when the substance is resupplied.

Warfarin: An anticoagulant drug to prevent blood clotting in patients at risk of forming blood clots. Brand names are Coumadin and Panwarfin.

Xerophthalmia: A severe dryness and hardening of the structures of the eye, usually caused by severe vitamin A deficiency.

Xerosis: An abnormal dryness of skin, mucous membranes, or conjunctiva (membranes of the eye).

APPENDIX B
Recommended Dietary Allowances

FOOD AND NUTRITION BOARD, NATIONAL ACADEMY OF SCIENCES–NATIONAL RESEARCH COUNCIL
RECOMMENDED DAILY DIETARY ALLOWANCES,[a] Revised 1980

Designed for the maintenance of good nutrition of practically all healthy people in the U.S.A.

	Age (years)	Weight (kg)	Weight (lb)	Height (cm)	Height (in)	Protein (g)	Vitamin A (μg RE)[b]	Vitamin D (μg)[c]	Vitamin E (mg α-TE)[d]	Vitamin C (mg)	Thiamin (mg)	Riboflavin (mg)	Niacin (mg NE)[e]	Vitamin B-6 (mg)	Folacin[f] (μg)	Vitamin B-12 (μg)	Calcium (mg)	Phosphorus (mg)	Magnesium (mg)	Iron (mg)	Zinc (mg)	Iodine (μg)
Infants	0.0–0.5	6	13	60	24	kg × 2.2	420	10	3	35	0.3	0.4	6	0.3	30	0.5[g]	360	240	50	10	3	40
	0.5–1.0	9	20	71	28	kg × 2.0	400	10	4	35	0.5	0.6	8	0.6	45	1.5	540	360	70	15	5	50
Children	1–3	13	29	90	35	23	400	10	5	45	0.7	0.8	9	0.9	100	2.0	800	800	150	15	10	70
	4–6	20	44	112	44	30	500	10	6	45	0.9	1.0	11	1.3	200	2.5	800	800	200	10	10	90
	7–10	28	62	132	52	34	700	10	7	45	1.2	1.4	16	1.6	300	3.0	800	800	250	10	10	120
Males	11–14	45	99	157	62	45	1000	10	8	50	1.4	1.6	18	1.8	400	3.0	1200	1200	350	18	15	150
	15–18	66	145	176	69	56	1000	10	10	60	1.4	1.7	18	2.0	400	3.0	1200	1200	400	18	15	150
	19–22	70	154	177	70	56	1000	7.5	10	60	1.5	1.7	19	2.2	400	3.0	800	800	350	10	15	150
	23–50	70	154	178	70	56	1000	5	10	60	1.4	1.6	18	2.2	400	3.0	800	800	350	10	15	150
	51+	70	154	178	70	56	1000	5	10	60	1.2	1.4	16	2.2	400	3.0	800	800	350	10	15	150
Females	11–14	46	101	157	62	46	800	10	8	50	1.1	1.3	15	1.8	400	3.0	1200	1200	300	18	15	150
	15–18	55	120	163	64	46	800	10	8	60	1.1	1.3	14	2.0	400	3.0	1200	1200	300	18	15	150
	19–22	55	120	163	64	44	800	7.5	8	60	1.1	1.3	14	2.0	400	3.0	800	800	300	18	15	150
	23–50	55	120	163	64	44	800	5	8	60	1.0	1.2	13	2.0	400	3.0	800	800	300	18	15	150
	51+	55	120	163	64	44	800	5	8	60	1.0	1.2	13	2.0	400	3.0	800	800	300	10	15	150
Pregnant						+30	+200	+5	+2	+20	+0.4	+0.3	+2	+0.6	+400	+1.0	+400	+400	+150	h	+5	+25
Lactating						+20	+400	+5	+3	+40	+0.5	+0.5	+5	+0.5	+100	+1.0	+400	+400	+150	h	+10	+50

[a] The allowances are intended to provide for individual variations among most normal persons as they live in the United States under usual environmental stresses. Diets should be based on a variety of common foods in order to provide other nutrients for which human requirements have been less well defined. See text for detailed discussion of allowances and of nutrients not tabulated. See Table 1 (p. 20) for weights and heights by individual year of age. See Table 3 (p. 23) for suggested average energy intakes.

[b] Retinol equivalents. 1 retinol equivalent = 1 μg retinol or 6 μg β carotene. See text for calculation of vitamin A activity of diets as retinol equivalents.

[c] As cholecalciferol. 10 μg cholecalciferol = 400 IU of vitamin D.

[d] α-tocopherol equivalents. 1 mg d-α tocopherol = 1 α-TE. See text for variation in allowances and calculation of vitamin E activity of the diet as α-tocopherol equivalents.

[e] 1 NE (niacin equivalent) is equal to 1 mg of niacin or 60 mg of dietary tryptophan.

[f] The folacin allowances refer to dietary sources as determined by *Lactobacillus casei* assay after treatment with enzymes (conjugases) to make polyglutamyl forms of the vitamin available to the test organism.

[g] The recommended dietary allowance for vitamin B-12 in infants is based on average concentration of the vitamin in human milk. The allowances after weaning are based on energy intake (as recommended by the American Academy of Pediatrics) and consideration of other factors, such as intestinal absorption; see text.

[h] The increased requirement during pregnancy cannot be met by the iron content of habitual American diets nor by the existing iron stores of many women; therefore the use of 30–60 mg of supplemental iron is recommended. Iron needs during lactation are not substantially different from those of nonpregnant women, but continued supplementation of the mother for 2–3 months after parturition is advisable in order to replenish stores depleted by pregnancy.

U.S. Recommended Daily Allowances (U.S. RDA)

Vitamins, Minerals and Protein	Unit of Measurement	Infants	Adults and Children 4 or More Years of Age	Children Under 4 Years of Age	Pregnant or Lactating Women
Vitamin A	International Units	1,500	5,000	2,500	8,000
Vitamin D	"	400	400[a]	400	400
Vitamin E	"	5.0	30	10	30
Vitamin C	Milligrams	35	60	40	60
Folic Acid	"	0.1	0.4	0.2	0.8
Thiamine	"	0.5	1.5	0.7	1.7
Riboflavin	"	0.6	1.7	0.8	2.0
Niacin	"	8.0	20	9.0	20
Vitamin B_6	"	0.4	2.0	0.7	2.5
Vitamin B_{12}	Micrograms	2.0	6.0	3.0	8.0
Biotin	Milligrams	0.5	0.3	0.15	0.3
Pantothenic Acid	"	3.0	10	5.0	10
Calcium	Grams	0.6	1.0	0.8	1.3
Phosphorus	"	0.5	1.0	0.8	1.3
Iodine	Micrograms	45	150	70	150
Iron	Milligrams	15	18	10	18
Magnesium	"	70	400	200	450
Copper	"	0.6	2.0	1.0	2.0
Zinc	"	5.0	15	8.0	15
Protein	Grams	18[b]	45[b]	20[b]	15

[a] Presence optional for adults and children 4 or more years of age in vitamin and mineral supplements.
[b] If protein efficiency ratio of protein is equal to or better than that of casein, U.S. RDA is 45 g. for adults, 18 g. for infants, and 20 g. for children under 4.

U.S. DEPARTMENT OF HEALTH AND HUMAN SERVICES   Public Health Service   Food and Drug Administration
Office of Public Affairs   5600 Fishers Lane   Rockville, Maryland 20857   HHS Publication No. (FDA) 81-2146
Revised March 1981

Appendix C:
Recommended Reading

Nutrition Advice

A Diet for Living (1975), by Jean Mayer, Ph.D. David McKay, New York.

Dear Dr. Stare: What Should I Eat?: A Guide to Sensible Nutrition (1982), by Fredrick J. Stare, M.D., and Virginia Aronson, R.D. A practical guidebook based upon Dr. Stare's correspondence. Written in humorous but serious style. George F. Stickley Co., Philadelphia.

Family Guide to Better Food and Better Health, by Ronald Deutsch, Meredith Corporation, Des Moines, Iowa.

Food, Nutrition and You (1977), by F. M. Clydesdale, Ph.D., and F. J. Francis. Prentice-Hall, Inc., Englewood Cliffs, N.J.

Your Basic Guide to Nutrition (1983), by Frederick J. Stare, M.D., and Virginia Aronson, R.D. George F. Stickley Co., Philadelphia.

Rating the Diets (1979), by Theodore Bergland and the editors of Consumer Guide Magazine. Analysis of popular weight-reduction diets, both recommended and non-recommended. Beekman House, New York.

Realities of Nutrition (1976), by Ronald Deutsch. An easy-to-read explanation of food biochemistry and nutrition advice. Bull Publishing Co., Palo Alto, Calif.

Books Exposing Quackery

The Health Robbers: How to Protect Your Money and Your Life (1980), edited by Stephen Barrett, M.D. A comprehensive analysis of quackery written by a nationwide team of experts. George F. Stickley Co., Philadelphia.

Health Quackery (1980), by the editors of Consumer Reports. Consumers Union, Mount Vernon, N.Y.

The Medicine Show (1980), by the editors of Consumer Reports. Deals primarily with nonprescription drugs used to treat common ailments. Consumers Union, Mount Vernon, N.Y.

The New Nuts Among the Berries: How Nutrition Nonsense Captured America (1977), by Ronald Deutsch. Bull Publishing Co., Palo Alto, Calif.

Nutrition Cultism (1981), by Victor Herbert, M.D., J.D. Analysis of nutrition facts and fictions, including a devastating indictment of laetrile, "B-15" and their promoters. George F. Stickley Co., Philadelphia.

The One-Hundred-Percent Natural, Purely Organic, Cholesterol-Free, Megavitamin, Low-Carbohydrate Nutrition Hoax (1983), by Elizabeth M. Whelan, Sc.D., and Fredrick J. Stare, M.D. Atheneum, New York.

The Vitamin Conspiracy (1975), by John J. Fried. An in-depth look at megavitamin therapy and its promoters. Out-of-print, but a new edition will be published in 1984 by Prometheus Books, Buffalo, N.Y.

Vitamins and "Health" Foods: The Great American Hustle (1981), by Victor Herbert, M.D., J.D., and Stephen Barrett, M.D. How the "health food" industry is organized to mislead you. George F. Stickley Co., Philadelphia.

Other Publications

Environmental Nutrition, a reliable monthly newsletter written by dietitians for the general public, available for $36 from Environmental Nutrition, Inc., 52 Riverside Drive, Suite 15-A, New York, NY 10024.

Nutrition and Your Health: Dietary Guidelines for Americans (1980), a 20-page booklet by the U.S. Dept. of Agriculture and the U.S. Dept. of Health and Human Services. U.S. Govt. Printing Office, Washington, D.C.

Nutrition Labeling—How It Can Work for You (1975). National Nutrition Consortium, 9650 Rockville Pike, Bethesda, MD 20014.

Nutritive Value of Foods (1978), U.S. Dept. of Agriculture Home and Garden Bulletin No. 72. Lists the vitamin and mineral content of many foods by ounce or serving. U.S. Govt. Printing Office, Washington, DC.

Toward Healthful Diets (1980), a 20-page booklet by the Food and Nutrition Board, National Academy of Sciences, 2101 Constitution Ave., N.W. Washington, DC 20418.

Index